Maurice Ravel

Maurice Ravel

By

VICTOR I. SEROFF

ILLUSTRATED WITH PHOTOGRAPHS

HENRY HOLT AND COMPANY

NEW YORK

To my Amore

Contents

vii

CONTENTS

Maurice Ravel

∾∾∾∾∾∾∾∾∾∾∾∾∾∾∾∾∾∾∾∾∾∾∾∾∾∾∾∾

Chapter One

Background

"I am Basque," Maurice Ravel used to say. Was he?

Certainly not a pure-blooded Basque. "He is a Swiss watchmaker," Igor Stravinsky said, obviously referring to Ravel's music, but his remark also echoed the claim that Maurice Ravel was of Swiss origin, since his father Pierre Joseph Ravel was a French Swiss.

The roots of the composer's family have been found in Collonges-sous-Salève, a small village in the Haute Savoie, where the composer's great-grandfather François Ravez was born in 1769. The last letter in the family's name underwent several changes: thus, for instance, the last name of François was spelled with an "x" in his son Aimé's baptismal certificate, while four years later, when François died in 1804, his last name, written into the Register of the Deceased, was spelled with the letter "t." It has since been explained that the present spelling of the name occurred because someone misread letter "t" for "l," and the last name of Maurice Ravel's father and uncle Edouard were finally spelled with an "l" in the official papers in Geneva.

It is known that the composer's grandfather Aimé, who was also sometimes called Ami, Amy, or Aimy, had become an orphan at the age of four, when he was taken by his relatives to Geneva, that in his youth he had to shift for himself and that at the age of twenty, in 1820, he had gone to Versoix,[1] a small suburb of Leman, to work as a farmhand and later as a butler on the estate of a certain M. Girod-Megard, a wealthy landowner. In 1827 he acquired a small piece of land of his own—a vegetable garden—and either in 1828 or 1829 (there is no record of the date) he married Anne Caroline Grosfort, a young woman from Versoix, who brought him as her dowry a little store which originally had sold supplies of salt.

By 1834 Aimé must have obtained sufficient stature as a bourgeois to have been granted Swiss naturalization—he had a capital of 18,000 florins, was a Catholic and well thought of in the community. His store was "doing well," it had become a "general" store—that is, Aimé was selling a little of everything. He had settled down to a happy family life, and in the first eighteen years of their marriage Aimé and Anne Caroline had five children, all born in Versoix: Marie Françoise in 1830; Pierre Joseph, Maurice Ravel's father, in 1832; Louise Antoinette in 1838; Philomène Alexandrine in 1834; and Edouard John in 1847.

---

[1] By the terms of the Act of the Congress of Vienna in 1815, Versoix was returned to the canton of Geneva, Switzerland.

It was not until 1843 or 1845 that Aimé bought a house, No. 64, at Versoix and set up shop as a baker, the profession by which he was remembered in the family stories. But Maurice Ravel did not know his grandparents, since Anne Caroline died in Geneva in 1865 and Aimé in Plain-Palais in 1872.

Of Maurice Ravel's three aunts it is only known that the eldest, Marie Françoise, was a good pianist and worked at making rolls for music boxes. Both Aimé's sons showed talent, although in different fields; Edouard John, the youngest, became a painter of note. As a boy, according to the family stories, he helped keep the customers happy by painting their portraits *à la fresque* on the walls of the family store. Later on he studied painting under Barthelemy Menn and Alfred van Muyden and eventually settled down in Geneva where he married Marie Lancats, also a painter.

Edouard John often showed his pictures in Paris and his canvases can be seen in the museums in Geneva and Lausanne, in Neuchâtel and Lugano, as well as in France in Marseille and Lille, and it was his portrait of Maurice Ravel's mother which hung on the wall next to the piano in the composer's study. He died in Geneva on March 8, 1920.

As for Pierre Joseph, Maurice Ravel's father, who was fifteen years Edouard's senior, he was supposed to have been a child prodigy. He, like his brother Edouard, exhibited his talent in his parents' store. When his mother asked him to make some paper sacks for their wares, Joseph (as he was usually called), then twelve years old, invented a machine to make them *en series* in order to have more time to play with the village children. Joseph also was interested in the arts, studied the piano, and, according to Maurice Ravel, had more knowledge of music than the average amateur. But he chose mechanical engineering as his profession and in 1857 went to France.

That Joseph Ravel was more than a merely competent mechanical engineer can be seen from the patent registered under No. 82,263 J.R., which he received in Paris on September 2, 1866—a patent for "a steam generator heated by oil and applicable to locomotion on regular roads." If Joseph Ravel was not the inventor of the motor car, he certainly was one of the pioneers in that industry. His invention consisted of a two-cylinder reciprocating steam engine, similar to the present automobile gasoline engine. In the three-steam-horsepower engine, which weighed about two hundred kilograms, the coil containing the water was heated by a burner. Dry, slightly superheated steam was thus obtained and fed into the two reciprocating cylinders, which activated the rear axle of the car.

According to the records of *Histoire de l'Automobile*, in January, 1869, this vehicle, driven by the inventor himself, made the distance of three miles from La Revolte to Saint-Denis and back in two hours' time. However, there were some who insisted, probably out of pure malice, that the vehicle never left the working shack at Saint-Ouen and that the inventor at that time either was still working on the last fine points of its construction or may even have destroyed it. Be that as it may, Joseph Ravel's further progress was stopped short by the outbreak of the Franco-Prussian war in 1870. Three years later he was called to Spain, this time as a civil engineer, to take a railroad construction job in the province of New Castille, and it was there, according to the family stories, that he met and married the future mother of Maurice Ravel, Marie Delouart.

The meager information on the background of Maurice Ravel's ancestry which is accepted as authentic reaches its zero point when one inquires about his mother's origin. Yet it was through his mother's blood that Ravel claimed to belong to the Basque nation. There is not a single document available which proves this assumption. In no book nor article published up to the present time is there anything said except for the passing statement that "Marie Delouart was a Basque."

Where she came from, where she was born and brought up, who her parents or relatives were, and whether she was an only child or had brothers and sisters—all this is shrouded in mystery. Probably because Marie Delouart gave birth to Maurice in Ciboure near St. Jean-de-Luz in the French Basque country and because the family enjoyed returning there for their summers it was presumed that Marie Delouart was born there. But when I talked in Ciboure to the few people who still remember Marie Delouart, although they assumed she was Basque, they did not think she had been born in Ciboure and they did not know where she came from.

"My mother," Maurice Ravel wrote in his short autobiography,[2] "belonged to an old aristocratic Basque family." Maurice Ravel was romanticizing. Knowing the Basques

---

[2] Autobiographical sketch (*Esquisse biographique*) which Ravel dictated on October 15, 1928, at the request of a firm that manufactured mechanical pianos.

well, as presumably he did, he should have known that they are a truly democratic people. They have neither patricians nor plebeians for the simple reason that feudalism never took root in the Basque country. No Basque ever had a title and all Basques are noblemen outside of their own country. Nobility for the Basques is not individual, it is collective; nobility is obligatory, but titles are forbidden (laws of the fifteenth and sixteenth centuries).

In this ingenuous way the Basques coped with the situation they had to face in neighboring countries, and particularly in Spain, where only the sons of noblemen could attend the select military schools, become officers in the army, be appointed to high government posts or gain other privileges and benefits denied to plebeians. Thus those cunning measures were defensive rather than decorative privileges.

And had Ravel meant that his mother came from an old, wealthy, and influential family in the Basque country, he was mistaken. The name Delouart (or the Basque name Deluhartea from which the name Delouart could have been Gallicized) was not among them. But noble or commoner, Marie Delouart must at least have been brought up in the Basque country for it was she who taught her children Basque—a language so complex that it can be given only with one's mother's milk, as the Basques say. "Seven times did the devil try to learn it, but had to give up." Maurice Ravel spoke Basque but, according to the Basques who knew him, not too well.

Judging by her photographs Marie Delouart was definitely a southern type, but she was not Spanish, for Manuel de Falla, the Spanish composer, remarked on her ability to speak Spanish with great ease. He would hardly have referred to it had she been his compatriot. Inquiries into Marie Delouart's personal history are further complicated by the fact that she seems to have retained a youthful freshness to a remarkable degree. Those who remembered her as a young woman were mistaken by some fifteen to seventeen years when speaking of her age. According to the traditional story she was "a very young girl" when she married Joseph Ravel. The Basques marry early, and at the age of sixteen the girls are not considered too young for matrimony. Actually, Marie Delouart was thirty-four years old when she married Joseph Ravel, a year before she gave birth to Maurice in 1875.[3] I was told in Ciboure by an old friend of Maurice Ravel that on one occasion a woman who wanted to hurt the composer told him his mother's true age. Ravel was so horrified that for a long time he could not get over it.

Thus, during the thirty-four years before she met Joseph Ravel, Marie Delouart may have been single, but she also could have been married, divorced, or widowed—in short she could have lived a whole life of her own. She may have led the pious, nunlike life or she may have been anything from a gypsy to a smuggler—a popular profession among the people who live on the borders of France and Spain.

The true story of Ravel's mother's origin has been carefully concealed. I have had several talks with Ravel's brother

---

[3] According to the inscription on her tombstone, Marie Delouart was born in 1840.

Edouard in Paris and in St. Jean-de-Luz, and although he was ready to discuss the artistic career of his brother in general terms, he promised "to look up" and send me the dates and places of his mother's birth and marriage. On my return to New York I wrote him about these questions. Four months later he answered, saying that he saw no reason why I should talk about their mother in a book about his brother. "Roland-Manuel[4] did not," he said.

Here is what Roland-Manuel wrote about the origin of Mme Ravel and her marriage to Joseph Ravel—information which has since been repeated by the French authors.

> At New Castille, in 1873, he met the girl he was to marry. Maurice Ravel places the first meeting of his parents in the leafy shades of Aranjuez. It would be pleasant if truth could join hands with fantasy at this point; if some overwhelming destiny had chosen the garden of the 'Ile,' there to link the lives of these two who were to be the parents of the composer of *Jeux d'eau*, the *Miroirs*, *L'Heure espagnole*, and *Le Tombeau de Couperin*. For this park in the French style, set like a fairy oasis in the center of the Castilian desert, forms the most Ravelian landscape in the world, with its *alamedas* [public walks shaded with trees] and a palace still dreaming of Marie-Louise of Savoy and Domenico Scarlatti; from the fountains the water of the Tagus gushes into the pools where the birds come to drink, close by a porcelain room whose ornamentation is rich in representations of an altogether fantastic Cathay.
>
> To judge by her old portraits as well as by the gentle, refined features which were still hers under the lovely white hair of the last years of her life, Marie Delouart must have

---

[4] Ravel's first biographer. Roland-Manuel, *Maurice Ravel* (*Nouvelle revue critique*, 1938); trans. by Cynthia Jolly (Dennis Dobson, Ltd., 1947).

been a charming fiancée. She was a Basque from the lower Pyrénées, and her name, though originally Deluarte or Eluarte, was Gallicized on the French side of the mountains, and serves to make her nationality quite obvious.

Joseph Ravel and Marie Delouart were married in 1874, and lived for some time at Ciboure.

This information, if I may say so, is the most peculiar bit of twaddle I have ever read in a book which claims to be an authentic biography. I grant that the author, out of a rather touching tribal loyalty to his chieftain (Roland-Manuel belonged to a circle of Ravel's closest friends and was one of the few Ravel pupils) often prefers writing insipidly to casting a single shadow on the character of his deceased friend. This is understandable, but unpardonable for a critic and a biographer. Still, what can he be insinuating by "it would be pleasant if truth would join hands with fantasy at this point . . . ," if not that the marriage never did take place? Does he give the year of 1874 for the marriage as the last respectable date available, since Maurice Ravel was born in 1875?

In a letter to me Edouard Ravel gave the place of his parents' marriage as the Mairie in the 9th Arrondissement in Paris. Actually, two men named Ravel were married there in a three-year period when Ravel's parents could have been married, but neither was Joseph Ravel.

One reason for concealing the place of their marriage might be that, according to French law the marriage register must contain the names, birth places, and dates of both parents as well as of the bride and groom. This information must also be given in the death register.

The complete information is in the files at the Mairie in Levallois in Paris where all the burials in the Levallois cemetery are registered. The customary procedure is to release this freely, but in the Ravels' case the clerk in charge will not give it without Edouard Ravel's authorization. So far M. Ravel has refused every request. In Ciboure, however, after a long search for relatives of the Delouart family, I was taken to see an old Basque woman (older than eighty-four, I was told), Marie-Sabine Delouart, the last survivor of the Delouart family. She said she knew Mme Ravel well and remembered the two boys. She said Mme Ravel may not have been Basque by birth although she spoke Basque, since she was a Delouart only by adoption. She said that Marie Delouart came from the *assistance publique*, which means that she was either a foundling or an illegitimate child and was brought up by the state. In France, even at the present time, this is considered a disgrace by the people of the middle class. But a century ago it was a never-to-be-acknowledged brand, so shameful that one may easily understand great pains being taken to conceal it.

And no one seems to know how Marie Delouart happened to be in Spain when she met Joseph Ravel, except perhaps for Mlle Marie Gaudin, an old friend of Maurice Ravel, at whose home in St. Jean-de-Luz he spent many summer months. I offer her story though there is no way of checking it.

"My mother was a great friend of Maurice's mother and I remember her telling us how at that time, when they were young, large covered wagons carrying clothes, silks, and perfume from Paris used to travel through St. Jean-de-Luz on their way to Madrid." Mlle Gaudin pointed at an old painting of just such a caravan on the wall of her sitting room. "Madame Fels—I guess that was her name—who was in the business, was looking for a young woman who would take the job of traveling to Spain and selling the goods there. It had to be a young, good-looking, and enterprising woman and Marie Delouart was just the type. It was on one of these trips that she met Joseph Ravel." Marie Gaudin also told me that she thought Marie Delouart was then in her early twenties.

This is all that is known about Ravel's parents up to the time when on March 7, 1875, Maurice Ravel was born.

There are no records left, either official or in the recollections of the few who remember Maurice Ravel's parents, as to when the Ravels left Spain for good and moved to France, what happened to Joseph Ravel's job on the construction of the railroad, what the reasons were for their leaving Spain and going to Ciboure, a little fishing village, and whether Joseph Ravel was present at his son's birth or joined his wife later.

According to the present curé at Ciboure among others the place of Maurice Ravel's birth was purely accidental— Marie was on her way to Spain and stopped to visit in Ciboure. This is also evident from the wording of the first official record concerning Maurice Ravel, which I read in the birth register at the town hall in Ciboure, where it is stated that at noon on March 8, 1875, Gracieuse Billac, a fifty-year-old fishmonger, declared that Marie Delouart, the twenty-eight-year-old wife of Pierre Joseph Ravel, *presently*[5] living in Ciboure, had given birth to a child of male sex on the previous day at ten o'clock in the evening,

[5] Italics mine, V. S.

whom she wished to name Joseph Maurice. This document was signed by two witnesses: Renaud Haramboure, a constable, forty-three years old, and Michel Harrispuru, a teacher, thirty-six years old, both domiciled in Ciboure. Gracieuse Billac did not sign the declaration because she did not know how to write.

The fact that the same Gracieuse Billac (this time spelled with one "l") was also the witness at the christening of the child on March 13 (Joseph Ravel was *represented*[6] by Simon Goyenague, a sea captain and Marie Delouart's next-door neighbor) led some people to believe that Marie Delouart was a fishmonger, while according to Roland-Manuel, Gracieuse Billac was Maurice Ravel's aunt on his mother's side. Whether she was Marie's elder sister or her sister-in-law remains unexplained, for there is no indication anywhere whether she was single, married, or a widow.

The supposition that Marie Delouart was a fishmonger was not extraordinary since the Basques either are fishermen or take care of the cattle in the mountains, and those who live in Ciboure were almost all in the fish business.

Ciboure, or Cibouri as it is called in Basque, is derived from Subi-buru, a bridgehead (the Basques spell names phonetically). It lies in the district of Urrugue or Ur-onia—good waters—and is a small village separated from St. Jean-de-Luz by a bridge across the river Nivelle. Today it has a population of twelve hundred but in 1875 there were hardly seven hundred inhabitants, living in small houses with slanted roofs resembling Swiss chalets. Then, as it does today, Ciboure differed distinctly from its neighbor St. Jean-de-Luz, a smart summer resort with large

[6] Italics mine, V. S.

hotels, a casino, and a beach. Ciboure remains a picturesque but primitive little place. The Quai de Maurice Ravel (renamed in honor of the composer in 1930), which leads from the bridge along the bay up to the hills where large new villas form the residential district, was then Rue de Quai, two or three blocks long. The house numbered 12 now carries a plate with the inscription, "In this house Maurice Ravel was born on March 7, 1875," and it is the largest in the row of houses on the quai, three stories high with balconies on the second and third floors. The house, originally built by wealthy shipowners, is Dutch in style.

"It has been all modernized," the concierge tells the visitor. But the entrance hall is so dark that one wonders what was modernized. The concierge has been there for over twenty years but she does not know for sure whether Ravel was born on the second or the third floor. A lawyer from Tours, who has listed on his visiting card all the associations to which he belongs, occupies the second floor during the summer months and is obviously annoyed by the very idea of anyone inquiring about someone who lived there before he modernized the apartment, while a painter occupies the third floor. Not many in Ciboure know who Maurice Ravel was, and the few who remember the family can not decide in which apartment he was born. A few insist that he was born in a "wretched dark room" in the back of the house facing the old church across the crooked, cobblestoned Rue Pocalette. But true or false, the established tradition has it that Maurice Ravel was born in the apartment of three rooms on the second floor with a balcony and three large windows facing the bay and St. Jean-de-Luz.

Three months after the child was born, in June, 1875,

the Ravels moved to Paris—the city that was to become Ravel's home. Only those who could question whether Caesar was a Roman could consider Maurice Ravel anything but a Parisian and French. Yet when in August of 1932 Ravel was contemplating going to San Sebastian in Spain for a small celebration in his honor he felt, for obvious political reasons, the need to explain such a phenomenon. "Oh, yes! . . . I am not French . . . and they are not Spanish!" he said. He meant that *he* and *they* in San Sebastian were Basques. But just because a kitten is born in an oven it does not make it a biscuit. Or does it?

How much of a Basque, then, was Maurice Ravel?

The Basques are one of the old nations whose origin has never been definitively established by historians. Had the Basques sprung into being as the result of some dramatic event like war or revolution, their history would have been recorded. As it is, Basques proudly claim they were "conceived in liberty" and compare themselves to Americans, the only difference being, they say, that they would have to add several zeros to the first words in Lincoln's Gettysburg address for, they explain, they can describe many battles they fought in defense of their freedom, but can not tell which was the first. Their main spiritual characteristic —the democratic conception of an organized society—they owe, they say, to their traditions. These traditions were their supreme laws even when they had kings, who themselves had to bow to the rules handed down from generation to generation. Where written laws and customs conflicted, it was the latter which had to be observed. Habeas corpus written as a law in the British Magna Charta, may, they say, precede their *Fuero*, but they have no doubt that it was in practice in Euzkadi (the Basque country) long before the writing of the Magna Charta.

Various theories trace the ancestors of the Basques as far north as Ireland and as far east as Georgia in the Caucasus. Hannibal was supposed to have used them in his cohorts because of their bravery and particularly for their thirst for revenge; and the Romans, when they occupied Caucasian Georgia in the first century, called the Georgians the Iberians. All the historians agree at least on this one point: the ancient Basques were the last survivors of the Iberians who at one time owned not only the Iberian Peninsula but all the land north of the present Spain up to what today forms the south of Belgium.

There are just as many problems in defining, if not the origin of the Basque language, at least the relationship with other known languages on the European continent. Some philologists claim that Basque as it is spoken today is a mixture of Spanish and Latin as the Roman soldiers spoke it; others find a relationship with Hungarian and Finnish. I, myself, who was born and raised in Caucasian Georgia, heard a definite similarity, if not always in the words, then in the pure sound of the language, to that spoken by the Georgians in the Caucasian Mountains. This similarity is even more evident in Basque songs; not those which are performed at festivals for tourists but those which are sung by the Basques in the taverns where men relax drinking their red wine. The four-part singing of these songs, strongly colored with Oriental elements, stands apart from any folk singing that can be heard in continental Western

Europe, and to anyone acquainted with the singing of the
Caucasian Georgians it points to a relationship with it.

A similar harmonic treatment has characterized Irish and
Scottish songs since the fifteenth and sixteenth centuries,
one fact leading to the supposition that present-day Basques
have Irish blood. Those who claim this base their theory
also on the old legend, still alive in the Basque country,
which speaks of their ancestors as blond men with blue eyes
who lived in caves. Others say that the Basques are a mixture of the Iberian, the Irish, and the Jews who fled Spain
during the Inquisition. They point to the Basques' own
assertion that they do not know where their people came
from, but that they do know that theirs is an old nation, that
they came from very far, and that they once were ruled
by the richest and the wisest of kings. The advocates of this
theory call attention to the general look of a Basque: a
slender man with a hooked nose and black hair and black
eyes. And finally there are those who prefer to think of
them as the last remnants of the people of Atlantis.

But no matter what mixture of blood may flow in their
veins, no matter whom they resemble, whether tall or small,
thin or stocky, dark- or blue-eyed, no matter that they have
no cultural accomplishments to speak of in comparison with
their neighbors, the Basques have lived for centuries a most
civilized life, like one family, like a tree with its roots,
trunk, and branches fed by the soil where "nothing belongs
to anyone and everything belongs to everybody." One thing
is certain—no nation living on the European continent has
had so mysterious and romantic a past and still holds such
untold fascination.

Today the Basques live on the slopes of the Pyrénées which stretch across the south of France and north of Spain. Their main occupations are agriculture and fishing. They are hardy, diligent, proud, sober, and religious. They consider themselves as a nation apart, neither Spanish nor French. Their traditions are patriarchal and they scorn intermarriage. The hardships of their land led to a large immigration to Argentina and Chile, but in spite of the course of world history and civilization the Basques remain—no matter where they are—what they always have been: farmhands and fishermen.

What then had Ravel in common with the Basques, what could he claim as his inheritance?

Ravel was a most sophisticated Frenchman—and who in the world is more sophisticated than a sophisticated Frenchman? No one could picture his tilling the soil behind the plow or fishing for sardines and tuna, drinking wine from a leather *gurda* or playing *pelota*, the Basque national game. There was nothing rural about him. On the contrary, Ravel was known as an immaculately dressed gentleman rather given to dandyism, who could spend night after night sitting on a high chair at the bar in a fashionable night club and sipping the latest concoctions of which he was very fond, a man whose manners were those of a prince but who was not a snob, a democrat but not of the slapping-on-the-back variety, who never would *tutoyer* anyone, a freethinker of high principles and artistic integrity.

It is a matter of conjecture whether all these characteristics come from his background or were the result of Ravel's own make-up, but one of them, namely the lack of

religious belief which differentiated him conspicuously from
the Basques, Maurice Ravel must have acquired from his
mother. In Ciboure a Basque told me that his mother once
had asked Mme Ravel, then already an elderly lady, to go
to church with her. "Why should I?" Mme Ravel replied,
"I do not believe in any of it. I would much rather go to
hell where I will join my husband than go to heaven."

Maurice Ravel was not easily given to explaining much
either in his music or in his relationship with people. But
the unusual secrecy about the usual vital statistics of his
parents' lives leaves no doubt that there was some rebellious
feeling in the family against the established moral code.

Romantic Ravel, who lived in a world of his own make-
believe, who was as fond of imitations as he was of the
originals, once remarked to his friend Dmitri Calvocoressi,
the music critic, "And how do they know—perhaps I myself am artificial."

Chapter Two

Musical Studies and Influences

BUT HAD MAURICE RAVEL said that he was a natural son of art and chance, as so many less illustrious men have declared, it would have been closer to the truth, for when three months after his birth he had taken his first look at the world in which he was going to live, he looked right at the very center of its artistic activities: Montmartre, a district in Paris where his father had brought the family to 40, Rue des Martyres.

Cézanne, Monet, Sisley, Renoir, Pissarro—all had their studios in the little streets on the slopes of Montmartre. This was where they worked and could be seen sitting in cafés with their friends, violently discussing the future of Art, and where in 1874, a year before the Ravels arrived at their new home, they launched the exhibition which labeled them as the Impressionists after Monet's picture "L'Impression"—thus introducing a school in art against the background of which Maurice Ravel grew.

It seems reasonable to presume that it was because Joseph Ravel was interested in the arts and had a great many friends among the artists, that he chose that part of Paris for his home, yet it may be that he did so guided by purely financial reasons—one lived cheaper there, and a touch of bohemianism substituted for what would have been considered the necessities in other Paris quarters. Or it may have been both. At any rate, this is where the Ravels stayed for many years and where on June 13, 1878, their second son, Edouard, was born.

In the history of many composers' lives, it was the mothers who influenced them at the beginning of their careers, but in Ravel's case it was his father who wanted at least one of his sons to become a musician. Both children showed an interest in music, and only after long deliberation did Joseph Ravel make his choice. Henri Ghys, a musician known for compositions in the form of popular waltzes and particularly for his *Air Louis XIII (Amaryllis)*, a favorite piece in the drawing rooms of that time, was engaged for the sum of 50 centimes per half hour to teach the elder of the two boys—Maurice. The piano lessons began on May 31, 1881, and Henri Ghys wrote on that day in his diary, "I am starting a little pupil, Maurice Ravel, who seems to me intelligent."

But Maurice Ravel was not a child prodigy. Five years passed during which the "little pupil" was docile but not particularly enthusiastic about practicing on the piano. His father had to pay him 10 centimes for a half hour of "actual presence at the piano," a rather considerable sum at that time for a little boy's pocket money, but Maurice felt that he was earning it with his blood. It was only at the age of twelve, when he joined the class of his new professor, Charles-René, who taught him the first rudiments of harmony, that he showed any real interest in his studies.

Charles-René was Léo Delibes' pupil, and one of the characteristics of his teaching was his demand that, besides regular homework on the harmony problems, his pupils were to bring him their own short compositions. Accordingly Maurice Ravel brought him one: *Variations on a Chorale by Schumann*. It made such an impression on his teacher that twenty-five years later he still remembered it and declared that Maurice Ravel's *Variations* were "really an interesting essay which already showed his aspirations toward that refined, elevated, and ultra-polished art which today is his noble and constant preoccupation. There has been a real unity in his artistic development; his conception of music is natural to him and not—as in the case of so many others—the result of effort."

Two years later, in 1889, at the age of fourteen Maurice Ravel successfully passed the examination at the Conservatory in Paris. He remained a student there for almost sixteen years. But although by the end of another two years in Eugène Anthiome's preparatory piano classes he had won the first prize and was advanced into the superior class of Charles de Bériot, it eventually became evident that Maurice Ravel was not predestined to become a professional performer.

"Instead of being the last in the class, you could have

been the first," de Bériot was supposed to have said to Ravel, but those who knew Maurice Ravel did not agree with his professor and did not blame his failure entirely on his lack of interest in practicing. In their opinion Maurice Ravel's small, bony hand was not a hand easily adaptable to piano virtuosity. He could hardly stretch an octave; later, when Maurice Ravel had to play his own works, he used to leave out the lower notes of the octaves. Also, his thumb was curved to such a degree that he could navigate from black to white keys like a duck in a pond, but otherwise this abnormality of his thumb did not prove to be of any particular advantage.

Maurice Ravel himself had no illusions about his capacity as a pianist. Many years later when, after a triumphant success of his orchestral works at a concert in Brussels, he had to play the piano, he whispered to the conductor, "Now, it's all going to be spoiled."

But while he was in Charles de Bériot's class he was more preoccupied with learning the works of Schumann, Chopin, and Liszt than with learning how to perform them. However, two events which belong to this early period of his life had far more significance in Maurice Ravel's development than the formal music classes. The first of these was his friendship with Ricardo Viñes, a boy of his own age and one of the most promising talents in de Bériot's piano class. Ricardo Viñes later became a prominent pianist in France. His chief contribution to the history of music was his outstanding record as a champion of everything new and worthy in the musical literature, be it the works of the young French, or heretofore unknown Spanish, Italian, or

Russian composers. Besides, he was among the best-informed men of his time in all branches of the arts. They used to say in Paris that one could see Viñes anywhere and everywhere. As a matter of course he went to concerts, but also he never missed an art exhibit, a new play, a lecture, or an informal gathering of the literati, where he would astonish them with his encyclopedic knowledge, or by hour-long recitations of poems by Verlaine, Baudelaire, and Mallarmé.

In his youth he developed a prodigious memory, when he was, as if possessed, eager for everything new. And this interest in everything new in art was shared by Maurice Ravel. But there was still another reason for their close friendship. The Viñeses were Spanish and Mme Ravel enjoyed talking to Ricardo's mother in a language which, since she had come to Paris, she had had little occasion to use. The traditional family stories paint a rather sentimental picture of the two mothers gossiping over their needlework while the two boys play, four hands, "all the symphonic music they could lay their hands on."

This friendship proved very beneficial to Ravel. Ricardo was a far better pianist than he and Maurice had to practice more in order to keep up with Ricardo at their duet sessions. Until then he worked "taxi-wise," as he later said himself, while Ricardo had already undergone several years of serious training. Born in Lerida in Spain on February 5, 1875, at the age of twelve he won the first prize at the Conservatory of Barcelona and received a scholarship from his native town for three years of study at the Paris Conservatory.

Judging by his early photographs Maurice Ravel must have been a charming little boy with bangs and flowing long black hair, and Ricardo Viñes' reminiscences of their first meeting confirm this impression. "He looked like a Florentine page," Viñes said, "Slender, but unusually small for his age, he carried himself stiffly and cautiously, with a serious expression in his deep-set brown eyes, which occasionally lit up with an ironic smile."

However, one should not presume from the favorite family stories about the two happy mothers that the two boys were glued to the piano. The only record left of these early years of their friendship is Ricardo Viñes' journal,[1] which he kept up to the time of World War I. In it one finds a page where Ricardo describes spending an evening at the Ravels' playing with Maurice and his brother Edouard and enjoying a game of their own invention: each boy would draw the head or torso or limbs of a figure separately from the body, and then they were much amused by the grotesque results when they constructed the figures by putting the separate parts together.

Other stories show that they were growing up like so many Parisian boys, roaming through the long avenues in Montmartre crowded with the annual fairs, merry-go-rounds, exhibitions of the world's strongest man, fakirs who swallowed snakes or fire, and magicians who sold their magic. Both boys were very fond of the country fairs and the circus as they were of all sorts of toys—a feeling which remained with them throughout their lives.

And of course, there was another aspect of the life in Montmartre that could not escape the boys' curiosity: the

---

[1] Ricardo Viñes' Journal, written in Spanish. Property of José Viñes, his brother. St. Jean-de-Luz.

life of the cafés with their awnings extending over the little round tables and chairs on the sidewalks, crowded with workmen, artists and their models, clerks, and sometimes whole bourgeois families with their children and nurses, giving place, as the day wore on to those who sought pleasure and amusement in Parisian night life. For Montmartre was its heart—with its small smoky night clubs and dance halls where respectable visitors shared the floor with *midinettes*, vaudeville stars, prostitutes, and apaches. These last were petty thieves and pimps who danced with forced impassiveness to shield their self-esteem, unanimously exhibiting their utter disdain for the world by their caps worn at a rakish angle on their pomaded heads and cigarettes drooping from their disgusted lips.

Nor could the boys miss the almost periodical passion murders which would strike the pastoral Montmartian life like a thunderbolt. Then police squads would invade the crooked, winding little streets where night clubs, brothels, and dancing halls nestled against old dilapidated houses inhabited by the honest middle-class families, searching for culprits, breaking up couples' embraces to examine the young women's papers, and starting the old concierges on their long round of visits to gossip with their tenants or neighbors, to "oh-and-ah" and to mourn about "what the world is coming to."

It is hardly possible that the boys could have grown up in the shadow of all this without being both fascinated and repulsed by its sardonic glamour. Yet some of Ravel's biographers prefer to speak of "the sound of the ocean's waves," which incidentally can not be heard in Ciboure "and the shadows of Pyrénées" as the inspiring background against which he grew up, rather than the life in Montmartre vibrating with passion, crime, and pleasure. It is almost as if they thought Ravel's childhood and adolescence were spent in one of the fashionable Paris Faubourgs where children were shielded from life by their foreign governesses, who dressed them and taught them manners according to ancient etiquette.

Be this as it may, it is certainly true that the boys spent most of their time in intellectual pursuits, discussing literature and paintings together, reading Baudelaire, Edgar Allan Poe, and Stéphane Mallarmé, and rejoicing in the discovery of J. K. Huysmans. It was one of those friendships that should have lasted a lifetime. When Maurice began to compose he dedicated his first work to Ricardo Viñes, and Viñes gave the first performances of Maurice Ravel's works and would no doubt have been the first to play his piano concertos had their friendship lasted. But in the last years of Maurice Ravel's life there was a definite "cooling off" in their relationship. Curiously enough, it was not on artistic but purely political grounds: Viñes was a Spanish royalist; Ravel did not share his views and appeared a revolutionary to Ricardo Viñes.

But at the time of their studies at the Conservatory no such problems troubled them. In the spring of 1889 there was great excitement in Paris. *La Grande Exposition Universelle* commemorating the centennial of the French Revolution for which the famous Eiffel Tower was built opened its gates on April 2, and the two boys found in it a new and stimulating world. White stucco palaces with marble-floored patios and mosaic fountains, mosques with their minarets, Cambodian temples, and Chinese pagodas surrounded by Tahitian palm-roofed huts and Tunisian bazaars, all teeming with crowds of merchants and artisans from the Orient in their national dress, brocaded saris, tigerskins, loincloths, and kimonos, singing, yelling, and dancing to attract the visitors' attention to Congo chieftains and voodoo priests from Martinique, to Annamese snake-charmers, Timbuktu rug-weavers, prancing Arabian thoroughbreds, proud camels, and bored elephants . . . these rose out of the barren Champs de Mars like a dream from *A Thousand and One Nights* come true.

The boys explored the street where natives from far lands bivouacked as if they were at home. They spent hours browsing in the Oriental shops and country theaters, and listening to the groups of popular musicians whose free renditions of their national music seemed to flow from inspiration. Here Ravel and Viñes were introduced to music unrestricted by the laws of harmony taught at the Conservatory, they heard music composed of sounds of unrelated chords and scales that enchanted them like a tantalizing perfume. It was there, in those Oriental bazaars, that Ravel tasted for the first time the exotic. To the last days of his life this intoxication never left him.

Maurice and Ricardo easily found their way to the Javanese village, transplanted from the Indian ocean to the Esplanade des Invalides right in the heart of Paris. There the *gamelang*, a weird orchestra, accompanied the performances of the Bedayas, the native dancers, "now swaying to their voluptuous undulations, now emphasizing their stiff, hieratical gestures." The orchestra was made up of percussion instruments, drums, clappers, and gongs which supported the only string instrument, a kind of a two-stringed viola on which the lonely player improvised.

The *gamelang* was one of the principle attractions for the musicians who visited the Exhibition, and who knows if the two boys did not rub shoulders there with Debussy and Rimsky-Korsakov, two composers so impressed by the Javanese orchestra that it showed its influence in their later works. But that was not all. The boys' greatest treat came on June 22 and 29, when at the Trocadéro they heard two concerts of Russian music under Rimsky-Korsakov's direction. At a time when Russian music was almost unknown in France, with the exception of Anton Rubinstein and Tchaikovsky, these two concerts were sensational. Besides the works of Glinka and Dargomijsky, Rimsky presented for the first time the works of The Mighty Five—Borodin's Polovetskian Dances from *Prince Igor*, Balakirev's *Thamar*, his own *Antar* and *Caprice espagnole*, and Mussorgsky's *Night on the Bare Mountain*—revealing all their Oriental sumptuousness and the untold riches of their brilliant orchestral coloring—pure magic to the boys' ears.

At these concerts at the Trocadéro one more unforgettable impression was in store for them—*España*, the work of a Frenchman, Alexis Emmanuel Chabrier.

Emmanuel Chabrier, then forty-eight years old, was one of the first French composers to bring forth in his music the characteristic traits of his nation: emotional vitality, ironic humor, lyrical tenderness, and sentimental poetry. It must be remembered that at this time French musicians were just getting over the hang-over they had suffered from the Wagnerian intoxication. Chabrier had been no exception; he also had made pilgrimages to Munich and Bayreuth, and had composed an opera *Gwendoline* in such pure Wagnerian style that it was produced in Paris only after its success in Germany.

Chabrier's first triumph, however, his orchestral rhapsody, *España*, written in 1883, may be considered historically important as a sort of manifesto of a new spirit of national independence and a blow to reactionary eclecticism. He did not adhere to the established forms in musical composition: sonata, symphony, or fugue. Form and style were of secondary importance where subjective expression was involved, and music to him was only a medium with which he expressed himself.

Fat and exuberant, of powerful physique and compelling personality, always jesting but a deep-feeling man, Chabrier wrote music either bursting with energy and passion, or tender and at times sentimental, as well as some that was so boisterous and frank that it reached the borderline of vulgarity, although it never crossed it. "I am virtually self-taught," he used to say. "There are many things which one must learn in his youth which I shall never reach."

For Chabrier spent fifteen years working in the Ministry of the Interior to the delight of his colleagues and the utter misery of his superiors. He earned a modest living there as a minor clerk until he became the assistant director of the famous Lamoureux Orchestra. "But I live and breathe music," Chabrier said. "I write as I feel, with more temperament than technique—I think I am an honest and sincere artist." This was particularly evident when Chabrier played his own compositions on the piano.

"He played the piano as no one had before him and as it will never be played again," said Alfred Bruneau, a French composer who had witnessed many a Chabrier performance. "To see Chabrier advancing toward the frail instrument from the back of a salon ornamented with women of elegance and performing his *España* in fireworks of torn strings, hammers in pieces, and broken keys was a sight unspeakably droll, but a sight which also attained epic grandeur."

Some of Chabrier's musical subjects were ascribed to his sympathy with the new movement in poetry and painting and to his belief in the correlation of all the arts. He was a close friend of the Impressionists Monet, Renoir, Sisley, and Manet, and their canvases hung in his apartment.

In the history of French music Chabrier has remained a man hard to classify—so complex was his nature. A Wagnerite, he was one of the most ardent members of the National Society of Music which fought for the preservation of the French tradition, a hard worker who was taken seriously by some as a professional musician while others, suspicious of his jesting, regarded him merely as an amateur, and still others thought of him as the personification of an art not known in France since the days of Rabelais. But all had to consent to the general opinion that whatever his failings, he had a great influence on the French "modern" school of music, then in its cradle.

Maurice Ravel and Ricardo Viñes shared their enthusiasm for Chabrier and after learning his *Trois Valses roman-*

tiques the two boys decided to play them for the composer. Chabrier received them—so the story goes—with his usual exuberant cordiality, but he treated their performance with so much encouragement as well as criticism and constantly interrupted them with so many contradictory remarks that they left his home completely bewildered.

However, there is some doubt that this meeting ever took place, for it could have happened only in the years 1891 or 1892 and by that time Chabrier had been stricken with cerebral paralysis, did not see anyone, and had moved from Paris to La Membrole. But whether Maurice Ravel met him or not is less important than the fact that he remained a great Chabrier enthusiast. He considered him as vital in the development of French music as Manet in painting. Speaking of this many years later, Ravel remarked that the works of both Chabrier and Manet had evoked in him similar beautiful emotions during his adolescence, and that looking at Manet's "Olympia" he could find in it all the melancholy of Chabrier, transplanted and expressed in a different medium.

Ravel's admiration for Chabrier can be compared only to that he held for Erik Satie, the second composer who had a great influence on him. It was Joseph Ravel who arranged a meeting with Satie for his son—a meeting which Maurice Ravel believed to have been decisive in his development as a composer.

Although a quarter of a century has passed since Erik Satie's death, no final word has been said, either in France or abroad, as to the place his name should occupy in the history of French music. He was born in 1866, and his life spanned the most important period in the development of French "modern" music, the era of Fauré, Debussy, and Ravel, and later on that of The Six: Milhaud, Honegger, Auric, Tailleferre, Poulenc, and Durey. Opinion is equally divided between those who hail Satie as the forerunner of all the innovations and a musical personality whose influence is deeply felt in the works of his contemporaries, and those who scoff at the very idea of considering his work as anything but the trivialities of an amateur and buffoon. Not only as a boy of fourteen, when his father introduced him to Satie, then in his twenties, but also as a mature composer, Ravel was among those who held Satie in great esteem.

On January 16, 1911, when Ravel was already a well-known composer, he arranged a concert of Satie's works, for he sincerely believed in their importance. "Even though some of them are clumsy," he said, "they are nevertheless the works of a genius."

In contrast to his relationship with Chabrier, whom Ravel may or may not have met but whom he did not know except through his works and what he heard about him, Ravel's relationship with Satie was that of a devoted friend. When he said that he owed a great deal to Satie he meant not only to Satie's work but to Satie the man. Satie was unassuming and quiet in manner, with a bald head fringed by longish hair, rosy cheeks, a long, pointed fair beard and eyes slyly twinkling behind his glasses. He remained poor all his life but carried his lot with dignity, never asking anyone for help. His saucy remarks, witticisms, and practical jokes were often quoted in the musicians' community, which during a period of more than thirty years somehow never failed to hear Satie's voice coming either from his apartment at 6 Rue Cortot on the top of Montmartre, a room the size of a wall closet, or (since the autumn of 1898) from a room over a bistro at 22 Rue Gauchy in Arcueil.

"We want our own music, and if possible—without the sauerkraut," Satie declared right at the start of his career, thus clearly stating his position among those who still vacillated between the German influence and the old French tradition. Not aspiring to be grandiose, his work was modest, but off the beaten path. In his music Satie succeeded in raising his humoristic fancies above the style of the music hall, and imparted to his compositions a quality which was a manifestation of the happy union between this fantastic bantering spirit and music.

It was Satie's personality, his wit, and the manner in which he applied it in his music that without doubt accounted for the attention first paid to his work. He gave fancy titles to his compositions and the most improbable indications as to their interpretation. For example, it is reported that Satie himself explained that he was prompted to call some of his compositions *Morceaux en forme de poire* *(Pieces in the Shape of a Pear)* because Debussy had declared them shapeless. This confession led some critics to presume that many of Satie's titles were intended as veiled but malicious thrusts at Debussy. The truth of the matter was that Satie ridiculed program music, and his arrows did not spare either Debussy with whom he later quarreled, or Richard Strauss who was too far away, or Ravel who—it must be said—remained his loyal friend.

Satie burlesqued program music by driving it to "logically illogical extremes," making the program ludicrous through the meaninglessness of the music. In his work one finds such directions as "counsel yourself meticulously," "arm yourself with clairvoyance," "a little bloodily," "without blushing a finger," "in the manner of a nightingale with a toothache," "dry as a cuckoo," as well as advice to play "superstitiously, with deference, very sincerely silent, without pride, and obligingly."

But in the final analysis one must admit that either the titles or the directions for interpretation alone would hardly have sustained the musical value of his work. Satie worked slowly and diligently, often composing three versions of each work with only slight variations in nuance. *"Les deux manches et la belle"* (two hands and then the decisive one), he would explain with a sly smile. But his musical output was not large, probably for want of publishers. It ranged from dances in a slow tempo to *Socrate*, a symphonic drama which surprised those who saw in Satie a clown, rather than a tragedian, in music.

· Satie's name came to the attention of musical Paris in the nineties, when he composed incidental music for Joseph Peladan's play, *Les Fils des Étoiles*, subtitled *Wagnerie chaldeenne* and subsequently with his encounters, both verbal and pugilistic, with Colette's first husband, Gautier-Villard (Willy), the only critic who at that time mentioned his name in print. Later he gained notoriety by challenging M. Eugène Bertrand, the manager of the Opéra, to a duel, because the latter failed to acknowledge the receipt of the ballet, *Uspude*, Satie had offered for production. In those days a challenge to a duel was a serious matter since it involved one's honor. Fortunately the duel did not take place. When Satie received an official communication from the Opéra house stating that his ballet had been "duly examined and found unsuitable" he decided he had received "satisfaction."

The ballet's libretto concluded with the following announcement:

> In preparation: Ballets with and without characters.
> *Onotrotance*, ballet in two acts.
> *Irnebizolle*, ballet in three acts.
> *Corcleru*, ballet in four acts.

Although the announcement was received at the Opéra with raised eyebrows, Satie was serious about these ballets and insisted that he had even written down some of the music, and the rest was in his head.

> Let me see [he would say to his friends]. *Onotrotance* . . . I haven't done much to that one yet, but it will be good, quite good. *Irnebizolle* . . . oh! There is quite a lot of that done. It's a ballet in which no single person appears on the stage. As for *Corcleru*, it exists. . . . Oh yes, it exists all right. There are people on the stage in it. It's difficult to explain, though. In the third act there is a miraculous apparition. I am rather pleased with *Corcleru*. . . .

But, when Ravel first met Satie, Satie was almost unknown as a composer, and it is not surprising that it created quite a commotion in the class at the Conservatory when Ravel played Satie's *Gymnopédies and Sarabandes* for the first time. The suggestion that Satie's title *Gymnopédies* was a Satie-ized word derived from the Greek γυμνοπκιδικι[2]

---

[2] A yearly festival, mentioned in Herodotus and other authors, in honor of those who fell at Thyrea, at which naked boys danced and went through gymnastic exercises.

and that his composition was intended to picture some graceful arabesques by naked boys dancing under an early-morning Grecian sky only added to the common suspicion about Satie's choice in bedfellows and prejudiced the Conservatory teachers against it.

Ravel's admiration for Chabrier and Satie was not destroyed by his teacher's criticism of their work. Émile Pessard, who methodically taught Maurice Ravel the laws of harmony, considered Ravel's interest in Satie's work merely a manifestation of Ravel's desire to shock, or at least to astonish—the trait so many later believed to be the basis of Ravel's work.

At the Conservatory Ravel's first attempt at composition was a *Sérénade*. Goustave Mouchet, Ravel's classmate, relates that when Ravel submitted this piece in manuscript, their teacher, Émile Pessard, started playing it, but, after reading the first page, suggested that Ravel play it himself. "Ravel obeyed and performed it admirably." Pessard's reaction was that although the piece made a curious effect, Ravel seemed to have been "riding fantasies," and he advised him to control his ideas and to take fewer liberties.

There is no evidence that Maurice Ravel heeded his teacher's admonitions. Four compositions for voice and piano belong to this experimental period, but all remain in manuscript form and none were ever performed: "Rouet" (without a date); "Ballade de la reine morte d'aimer" (1894), influenced by Satie and based on a poem of the young Belgian Roland de Marès; "Un grand sommeil noir" (August 6, 1895), written on a text of Verlaine, a curious piece which in its deliberate monotony foreshadows the

Prélude to *L'Heure espagnole* as well as the sound of the bell in *Gibet*, composed twelve years later; and finally "Si morne" (1899), inspired by Émile Verhaeren, the well-known Belgian Impressionist poet.

Thus, after having composed five pieces, Ravel, at twenty, finally wrote his Opus 1, *Menuet antique,* and *Habanera,* for two pianos. Later on Ravel said that these two compositions contained in embryonic form many elements which predominate in his later works, and Ravel connoisseurs like Vuillermoz, Roland-Manuel, and others assert that no other composer in the history of music reveals himself so completely from the first published page of his work.

But this did not mean that Ravel had achieved at last the zenith of his knowledge and was henceforth going to compose from a wealth of impressions and experience accumulated in all these years. Far from it. Following Massenet's precept, which was taught at the Conservatory, "to know one's art one must learn the art of others," Ravel continued to examine and re-examine the works of Schumann, Chopin, Liszt, and the Russians, and he advanced into the classes in counterpoint and fugue under André Gédalge, and under Gabriel Fauré in composition.

Gabriel Fauré was Ravel's last official guide in the study of composition and the third of the three composers who had a decisive influence on him. The name Gabriel Fauré has a different connotation in France than in the rest of the world. The French unanimously consider him one of the great composers, placing him along with the German classics. One can agree only to part of this assumption: Fauré may be compared to Brahms, Schubert, and Hugo

Wolf as a lyricist, as a writer of songs, but certainly not as a symphonist or composer for piano. He wrote close to one hundred songs, a great number of piano compositions, thirteen *Barcarolles*, thirteen *Nocturnes*, nine *Préludes*, a *Fantasie*, and a *Ballade* as well as several works for the stage, *Shylock*, *Caligula*, *Pelléas et Mélisande*, and the two masterpieces, his *Messe basse* and the *Messe de Requieme*, the latter considered as unique in the history of religious art.

But Fauré's music seems never to have crossed the borders of his country, as I have said, except for his songs which reveal a sensitive man who felt deeply and had good taste and a good sense of proportion. The Germans ignored him, the Russians found him boring, and the English thought his music "bloodless" or just "negatively delicate." No satisfactory explanation has been found for this phenomenon and one has to accept it as one does certain German stories— "*es geht nur auf Deutsch.*" Apparently one must be French fully to appreciate Fauré.

Like Chabrier, Gabriel Fauré made his pilgrimage to Bayreuth, but the current Wagnerian mania did not affect him. He returned to his modest work as though it had been laid out for him. His music is not compelling, but instead insinuates itself into the listener's heart and then gently leads into its own field of poetry.

One might say that one of Fauré's principles, "to make little noise, but say much," had worked against him, yet Fauré's influence on French music was of paramount importance. In his own quiet, unobtrusive way Fauré was as subversive, if not as revolutionary, as Debussy and, later, Ravel, his pupil; but the guardians of the *status quo ante* failed to notice his credentials or to examine carefully his dossier, which was a record of the methodical, rational, and irrevocable imprint of Fauré's style on French music. "Say it gently," was Fauré's maxim, "but say it at any cost." His music did not prompt heated discussion or explosive comment. It was taken for granted as great music, and, what was even more remarkable, accepted as such by all parties: the old-school guard as well as d'Indy and Debussy and later such extremists as the Six.

As a musician Fauré exerted a steadying influence on Ravel. Shy of publicity, not to say notoriety, Fauré lived within his means a quiet bourgeois life, seeking neither wealth nor fame nor power, but respected by the officials who offered him every available honorable and important position. Where the anecdotes about Satie could fill a volume, nothing much was said about Fauré—so discreet was the record of his private life. From this, however, one should not conclude that he lived the life of a hermit. On the contrary, Fauré, a good-looking man with the face of an inspired poet, also had a personal charm so irresistible that the doors of Parisian society were open to him; while at the Conservatory all the female students were in love with him. But in France the consequences of such relationships are taken for granted and do not furnish sufficient material for gossip.

Fauré's method of teaching was that of a senior artist discussing and solving problems with his younger colleagues in an informal atmosphere, so that his class has been often compared to the meetings at the home of Mallarmé, where the literati spent evenings in stimulating discussion. Al-

though he often criticized his students' works severely—
according to a popular story about Fauré's relationship with
Ravel—he would readily admit that he may have been
wrong in his judgment and would ask to see the work again.
He never imposed his own personality on his pupils' work,
but guided them in the development of their own characteristics. This no doubt accounts for the impressive list of
composers who came from his class, all as different in their
work as their names: Georges Enesco, Florent Schmitt,
Roger-Ducasse, Charles Koechlin, Nadia Boulanger, Louis
Aubert, and, of course, Maurice Ravel.

Fauré's students, on the other hand, did not try to imitate him; although their admiration for the perfection of
Fauré's compositions was so strong that when Ravel was
asked to orchestrate one of Fauré's piano pieces he refused,
saying that no change of tone coloring would add to the
persuasive force of Fauré's original work.

In reviewing the first part of Maurice Ravel's life, that
is, up to his early twenties, one finds that four musicians
played cardinal roles in his development from adolescence
into manhood: Chabrier as a composer, Fauré as a teacher—
a senior fellow artist—Satie more as close friend than merely
as composer, and Ricardo Viñes as best friend and comrade.

No other names have been mentioned, either by Ravel
himself or those who knew him at that time. Ravel's lack of
wider friendships among boys of his own age and of acquaintances outside the musical field can partly be explained
by the fact that Ravel, contrary to custom, was not gradu-
ated from any public school and may even never have gone
to one. This fact has never been explained. Nor was a reason

ever given for the extraordinarily long period of his studies at the Conservatory—sixteen years—when he did not seem to have been occupied by anything else.

Sixteen years of apprenticeship in a music school is a very long time, no matter how thorough the schooling may have been; and one short composition accomplished during one or sometimes two years is hardly a credit to a productive artist even as a beginner. Even taking into consideration that Ravel, contrary to the stories told about the rapidity with which he worked, composed with a great deal of difficulty, making numerous sketches before he started on a composition and polishing every detail after the composition seemed to have been achieved, "squeezing it drop by drop" out of himself, as he said, his attitude toward life was certainly never that of a mature and responsible adult.

Since the Ravels were far from well-to-do it is particularly baffling that young Maurice made no effort to become independent and if not to help his family at least to partially relieve them of an extra financial burden. Instead he seemed to have been content to live in a dream—a composer by profession—a luxury for a son of parents in straitened circumstances, rather than to earn as much as he could by practicing one of a number of professions open to a musician with the knowledge he had already acquired.

Ravel's devotion and love for his parents did not go any further than that of a helpless puppy who was protected and pampered and who apparently paid no heed to the years that were passing. On the contrary he developed that "artistic" disregard for time for which later in his life he often paid the penalty and a rather unusual preoccupation with himself which must have been the basis for his privileged position in his family.

To this rather extraordinary record of Ravel as a young man one has to add still another peculiar aspect: Ravel seems to have completely ignored the feminine sex. Not even an innocent adolescent infatuation has ever been disclosed by those who knew him or ever mentioned by Ravel himself. And finally, as if his "mama's boy" status needed an official stamp, he was rejected for the military service to which every young Frenchman is called, presumably because of his slight build.

But if, at this age, Ravel lacked the initiative to achieve the most elementary kind of responsibility he certainly showed no apathy toward visiting many people, most of whom seemed to have been not even friends but mere acquaintances. This indulgence, however, would have been a complete waste of his time and energy had he not collected for himself an impressive number of young people who were interested in him—stanch Ravelites before he had created anything to warrant such a following.

Perhaps one of the most enlightening remarks about his adjustment to life was made by Ravel himself when he said shortly before he died, "It's lucky I've managed to write music, because I know perfectly well I should never have been able to do anything else."

On March 5, 1898, Maurice Ravel, then twenty-three years old, made his official début as a composer at a concert organized by the National Society of Music in Paris. The first of its kind in France, this society was founded by Saint-Saëns on November 17, 1871, the day following the end of the Franco-Prussian war, for the defense of French music "to aid in the production and the popularization of all serious works, whether published or unpublished, of French musicians." The composition with which Ravel made his bow before the Parisian audience was a suite for two pianos with the rather far-fetched title, *Les Sites auriculaires (Landscapes for the Ear)*, made up of *Habanera* and *Entre Cloches*.

Ravel's first public appearance turned out to be a complete failure. In advance of the concert, the title *Les Sites auriculaires* provoked astonishment. Was it a symbolic poem? Was it in any way related to Henri de Régnier's small, thinly bound book of sonnets, *Sites*, published in 1887? Or was not the title reminiscent of the famous title of Verhaeren's *Les Villes tentaculaires?* The literary part of the audience amused itself with these speculations while the musicians suspected the influence and suggestions of Erik Satie. In any case, neither of *Les Sites auriculaires* was intended to be facetious.

The suite was performed by the capable pianists Ricardo Viñes and Mlle Marthe Dron, but the performance turned into a catastrophe when the *Entre Cloches* was "massacred" by the performers, who struck chords simultaneously instead of alternatively (as indicated), thereby producing a series of meaningless discords. This mishap was blamed on the fact that the two pianists were playing a new Pleyel instrument, a sort of a duo-piano in which the two keyboards faced each other. Since Viñes and Dron were playing from the music they could not see or signal to each other. The deplorable result evoked laughter and catcalls from the audience.

As for the *Habanera*, it passed without particular notice,

except from one man—Claude Debussy—and this also was unfortunate. It seems that Debussy was in the hall and later on borrowed the manuscript of *Habanera* from Ravel. Debussy said he mislaid the piece before he had a chance to examine it carefully. But when five years later in 1903 Ricardo Viñes played Debussy's group of piano pieces called *Estampes: Pagodes, Soirée dans Grenade,* and *Jardins sous la pluie* which won immediate recognition, many were surprised by the close resemblance of the *Soirée dans Grenade* to Ravel's *Habanera* in harmonic effect, pedal treatment, and rhythm. Later, the same characteristics were found in Debussy's piece *Lindaraja,* which he composed in 1901 but which remained forgotten among the pages of his other manuscripts and was not published until 1926. Still another piece, also resembling *Habanera,* was composed by Debussy in 1904. Although not as good as *Lindaraja,* this piece was first published in March, 1904, in the album *Paris Illustrée* under the title *Esquisse* and later in the same year was brought out by the Edition Schott Brothers of Brussels under the title *D'un Cahier d'esquisses.* The incident of *Habanera* stirred up the inner musical circles in Paris.

The Debussyites argued with the Ravelites who accused Debussy of the "well-known" trait of "borrowing" from other musicians; and while the matter never got into open public discussion, it was thought to have been one of the reasons for the cooling-off of the relationship between the two composers. Manuel de Falla's comments in his article in the *Revue musicale* of December, 1902, on the authenticity of the Spanish atmosphere in *La Soirée dans Grenade* only added fuel to the fire. "The descriptive skill which is condensed into the few pages of the *Soirée dans Grenade* seems nothing short of miraculous when one considers that this music was written by a foreigner, guided almost entirely by his own insight and genius . . . ," said de Falla. "This is indeed Andalusia that he depicts for us: unauthentic truth, we might call it, seeing that not one single bar has been directly borrowed from Spanish folk music and that, notwithstanding, the entire piece down to its smallest details is characteristically Spanish."

A curious sequence to the whole affair was that it was Ravel who in 1910 gave the first performance of the *D'un Cahier d'esquisses* at the then new *Société Musicale Indépendante*—unless it was Ravel's way of proving his point, for two years before that, in 1908, his own *Habanera* received favorable appreciation when it appeared as the *Rapsodie espagnole*, its value being much increased by the splendor of the orchestral dress. But in 1898 the dreamy poetry did not correspond to either the sarcasm or the parody expected by the audience, and the budding composer's début was received with no particular welcome.

Nevertheless, the National Society of Music gave Ravel another chance. This was due to Ernest Chausson who, approached by Vincent d'Indy, generously withdrew one of his own compositions from a program to make place for Ravel's *Shéhérazade*, an overture to an opera which Ravel planned to write inspired by *A Thousand and One Nights*. Although special program notes, giving in detail the whole structure of the overture, were distributed to the public, the playing of the orchestra failed to arouse enthusiasm.

Vincent d'Indy was scheduled to conduct. At the last moment, however, he was unable to come to the performance and the baton was given to the composer. Those who, after World War I, heard Maurice Ravel perform his *La Valse, Boléro,* or *Concerto* know that he was a very poor conductor. Ravel himself knew his limitations in leading an orchestra. After laying down the baton at the end of a concert he is quoted as saying with a deep sigh, "Oh my Lord! I had no idea what was going on."

Ravel's incompetence in conducting showed itself even more at the time of his début. Because of his inexperience and a natural lack of authority as a performer, he did not succeed in bringing out in the proper perspective either the grand lines of his piece as a whole or the details, so that the public which could not recognize in the music all the clear indications of the program notes became impatient. Ravel's victory seemed to hesitate. Some faithful young friends tried to force it by their cries of bravo, but succeeded only in unleashing loud protestations and catcalls.

The critics mauled it.

On May 29, 1899, M. Willy denounced *Les Sites auriculaires* as a clumsy and uncouth debasement of the Russian school. "A bit of Rimsky *tripatouillé* by a Debussyite who aspires to be Erik Satie's equal," wrote Willy. "The author who made his début is endowed with a mediocre talent, that is true, and could perhaps in the course of ten years become something—if not somebody—provided he worked very hard."

And Pierre Lalo, the eminent critic of *Le Temps,* summed up Ravel's work on June 13, 1899, with the following comments: ". . . M. Maurice Ravel is a young pupil at the Conservatory over whom his comrades and his professors make a great fuss." Speaking of the *Shéhérazade* overture he said:

> . . . It is composed of very short fragments without any natural relation between them and attached one to the other by extremely loose links. One hears ten measures, or fifteen or thirty, which seem to present an idea, then suddenly one passes on to another idea and then again to another. One does not know where one comes from or where one is going and if this is what M. Ravel believes to be an overture 'constructed on the classical form,' one must admit that M. Ravel has a great deal of imagination. His style makes one think of the structure or lack of structure of M. Grieg and still more of that of Rimsky-Korsakov or M. Balakirev. There is the same incoherence in the plan of the orchestration and the tonal relationships, but these characteristics, already striking enough in the models, are carried to excess by the pupil who lacks first of all the spontaneity of the semi-popular Norwegian as well as the magnificence and colorful glitter of the Russians. However, one should not think that *Shéhérazade* is a score without merit. The harmonization is undoubtedly new. M. Ravel here suffers plainly from the dangerous influence of a musician whom one should know how to love without imitating—Claude Debussy. . . . From all this still may come an artist. One should advise M. Ravel to think more often of Beethoven.

Neither *Les Sites auriculaires* nor the overture to *Shéhérazade* were ever published in the form in which they were then presented and Ravel himself many years later said that the overture was "badly made" and that indeed it had been influenced by the Russians (Balakirev's *Thamar*,

Rimsky's *Antar,* and Glinka's *Russlan and Ludmila*—all introduced to the French public at the Exposition of 1889).

However, one piece written at this time (1899), about which Ravel later said, "I no longer see in it any virtues but, alas, I do see its faults—the influence of Chabrier, very flagrant, and its poor form," won Ravel an immediate popularity—a popularity comparable only to that caused by his *Boléro* at a much later date. "The remarkable interpretation of this incomplete and unaudacious piece contributed greatly, I think, to its success," was Ravel's own verdict.

This piece, *La Pavane pour une Infante défunte* became a favorite with the ladies, young and old, who gave the composition all sorts of romantic backgrounds. Those who wished it to be of Spanish origin attributed its inspiration to Ravel's mother, who was supposed to have told him about the ritual dances at the cathedral in Seville. Others pointed at the pictures of Velasquez and finally, a decade later, some wove into it Raymond Schwab's fable *L'Infante Porqué-porqué,* written and dedicated to Ravel in 1910. As a matter of fact, none of these had anything to do with the title of the piece which, as Ravel himself said, he chose solely because of the alliteration.

In 1925, when Ravel visited the interpretation course at L'École Normale in Paris, he is quoted to have said, "Do not attach to the title any more importance than it has. Do not dramatize it. It is not a funeral lament for a dead child but rather an evocation of the pavane which could have been danced by such a little princess as painted by Velasquez at the Spanish court." And to a young pianist whom he heard play the composition Ravel said, "The next time remember that I have written a 'Pavane for a deceased princess' and not a 'Deceased pavane for a princess'. . . ."

Thus, at the age of twenty-five, with a dozen pieces composed and either already discarded as the products of his youth or used as sources for his later compositions, Maurice Ravel met the twentieth century rather poorly armed except for a small group of followers who believed in him, and his own assertion that he had found what he wanted to say and that he was sure he would say it, a century in which—if he did not entirely change the course of French music—he certainly left a definite imprint of his own.

Chapter Three

"Les Apaches"

THE FIRST YEARS of the twentieth century saw many changes in the Ravels' fortune. Because of Joseph Ravel's business they moved to 19, Boulevard Pereire near Levallois —the industrial part of Paris where the machine shops were located—and for a while the family's interest focused on Maurice's younger brother Edouard, who worked with his father as a mechanical engineer.

With Joseph Ravel's help Edouard had constructed a car, which, after a dash down an inclined track, made a somersault and then continued on its way. Edouard spent most of his days and evenings at the *Casino de Paris* supervising the exhibition of the "Whirlwind of the Death," as the experiment was called. The newspapers were full of detailed descriptions of this acrobatic stunt and the Ravels received invitations from all over the country as well as from abroad for the exhibition of the new model. Finally they accepted an offer from the United States.

"Here is, perhaps, the beginning of a fortune!" Maurice Ravel wrote to a friend in St. Jean-de-Luz. "I have to admit, it is high time as far as my father is concerned."

This acrobatic stunt was actually performed at the Barnum and Bailey circus during the two seasons of 1906 and 1907 and was called "The Dip of Death." A young Frenchman, Maurice Ancilotti, dressed in a duster and a cap, would face the tense audience from a platform on a specially erected scaffold fifty feet above the ground. Then the driver would get into his topless touring car, dramatically race the engine with colorful backfiring, and dash down the 40-degree incline. He would make a vertical circle, straighten out at the bottom, leap a ten-foot gap, and come up bowing.

Bailey paid twenty-four hundred dollars a week for this act, a fortune at the time, and "The Dip of Death" was a sensation since the automobile was itself still a curiosity.

But the Ravels' good fortune was of short duration. On September 1, 1907, a giant tornado hit the circus at Iowa City and destroyed the framework for "The Dip of Death." The act was never performed again either because of this catastrophe or, according to the French story, because the driver was killed in an unfortunate accident during a performance. This put an end to the Ravels' dreams of a fortune and they continued to live together making ends meet as best as they could.

Once again Maurice was the center of attention in whose brilliant future they implicitly believed—the only source of diversion in their rather monotonous life in Levallois. For Maurice was now convinced that he had found the key to the composer's problems.

"Inspiration is nothing but a reward for daily work," Ravel quoted out of his Baudelairian catechism. Perhaps he did believe in what he used to say to his friends and later on to the few pupils he had: "Everybody is gifted. I am not any more gifted than any one else. With a little effort every one of you can do what I am doing." And in his advice to imitate the old masters, to work always from a model, he disclosed the procedure of his own work: "If you have nothing to say, you had better keep quiet, rather than repeat what has already been said well. If, on the other hand, you have something to say, this 'something' will never appear as clearly as in your subconscious infidelity to the model."

For his own models Ravel's choice fell on works by Couperin, Liszt, Schumann, and Scarlatti's piano sonatas, as well as some works by Rimsky-Korsakov, Borodin, Saint-Saëns, and Meyerbeer, depending on the subject of his composition.

However hard he worked at music, Ravel must have worked just as hard on his image of himself—in the same way, imitating his chosen models—and this is how he has been remembered: a deliberately sarcastic and proud young man who read Mallarmé and visited Erik Satie.

Although very sociable, at a first meeting, Ravel held himself aloof. He spoke in a rather hollow voice without any particular accent. A characteristic mannerism, whenever he made a caustic remark, was to slide his right hand behind his back and standing as though he was about to pirouette, to lower his eyelashes, covering the malicious gleam in his eyes, and to drop his voice in the last part of the sentence. Ravel listened attentively, always letting a few minutes pass in silence as though he were turning over in his mind the phrase he had just heard before he finally answered, thus giving the impression of being obstinately argumentative.

He seems to have suffered particularly because of the abnormally small size of his body: Ravel was just about five feet tall. Fear of not being noticed or, worse still, of being criticized was part of the reason why Ravel paid so much attention to his physical appearance. He periodically changed the way he wore his hair and his abundant whiskers. At one time he displayed a long pointed beard, later he wore it with two whiskers à la Franz Joseph, before he finally, in 1911, shaved his face clean and had his hair cut the way it appears in the familiar photographs.

Despite the meager means of his family (Maurice was not earning any money himself), Ravel paid minute attention to the choice of his wardrobe: his suits, hats, shoes, waistcoats, socks, ties, and an assortment of little handkerchiefs for his breastpocket, all had to match and none were of conventional taste. At the age of twenty-five as well as at the age of fifty Ravel would consult his friends about the materials from which his shirts and suits were to be made, carefully examining the samples which he carried in his pockets, and making the final decision only after long and serious deliberation. It seems that later in his life Ravel claimed with great pride to have introduced the fashion of wearing fancy waistcoats and that when someone remarked on his dandyism he said, "I would at any time rather have been Beau Brummel than Maurice Ravel."

Was Ravel in love with anyone at that time? This question which puzzled many did not have an answer, for if his heart did beat particularly for someone, the fanciful waistcoats kept it well hidden.

"Music is my mistress," Ravel has been quoted to have said. This phrase has been attributed to so many musicians that it is no longer original, but in Ravel's case music was his main interest. He had joined a group of young men who met together once a week on Saturdays at 39, Rue Dulong on the top of Montmartre. There, in the fourth-floor apartment of Paul Sordes, the painter, an amateur musician but above all a great enthusiast and a connoisseur of everything that was going on in the arts, they sat in a semicircle around either an upright piano or a table listening to a new composition, a story, or a new poem, or were involved in long discussions of this or that theory in art that lasted almost all night.

The group, originally started by Florent Schmitt, the composer; Léon-Paul Fargue, the writer; Émile Seguy, the designer; and Tristan Klingsor, the poet; grew in its membership. Ricardo Viñes, the pianist, and Dmitri Calvocoressi, the music critic, took an active part in it and eventually it became even larger with many newcomers among whom were Émile Vuillermoz, the music critic; Inghelbrecht, the conductor; and Maurice Delage, who became Ravel's first pupil.

They all presumably had about the same taste in painting and literature as well as in music. Maurice Ravel shared with them their mania for Chinese art and their enthusiasm for Mallarmé and Verlaine, Cézanne and van Gogh, their love for Chopin and Couperin, Whistler and Valéry, and their admiration for the Russians—The Mighty Five—and Debussy. Basically they all agreed in their opinions for, as one of them said, you can not discuss a subject except with those who agree with you, and then you actually dispute only the details.

It was a group of young men whose art was their religion. They were ready to sacrifice everything to it. None of them, except for Maurice Delage, who inherited a fortune, had much money. In fact, they had an utter contempt for money and claimed to have lost their respect for an artist when his work brought him some—they were that foolish. They sincerely believed that it was sufficient to sing, figuratively speaking. That is the way it was with them. And if they could buy enough tobacco, dark and strong, which was weighed and sold in large paper sacks, usually accompanied by a package of "Job" cigarette paper, to last them through the night, it was all they needed. Despite their poverty they were happy and managed to go *en masse* to the theater, concerts, and art exhibits. They lived in such close harmony that they claimed that each one knew what every other one of them was doing, what he was thinking, and where he would be on the following day.

The audiences of those days were different from ours. There were not so many snobs, who sit looking bored while examining their fingernails, reading the programs on their neighbors' laps, or yawning and watching their wrist watches out of the corners of their eyes. The Paris audiences of that time listened intensely, passionately, jumped to their feet, and cheered or booed their approval or disgust and then, red in the face with jaws upthrust as if to demonstrate their spontaneous infallibility, they stormed into the corridors of the hall for the cigarette *liberatrice*, to exchange their views with their friends and to deliver the last *coup de grâce* to those who dared to disagree.

Often the serene premises of a concert or theater hall were turned into a battleground for the *gilets-rouges*, some fifty to one hundred young poets, painters, University and Conservatory students, and art lovers, who were always present in the top galleries, keyed up like fighting cocks to charge at anyone who would disturb the high pitch of enthusiasm for the performance they chose to favor. Many a work owed its existence to these generous crusaders who took it under their protection and would battle for it again and again at every repeated performance until the work was well launched and could survive on its own.

In France everything becomes a subject for a discussion and every discussion serves as a reason for forming a group. A quarrel is in a Frenchman's blood. There were always those who preferred the old to the modern; in the eighteenth century they battled to decide whether they preferred French taste in music to Italian; then came the Romantics and later the Wagnerites, the Parnassians, the Naturalists, the Symbolists, and then the Impressionists—they all formed groups, sacred battalions ready to stand fast against public opinion or to go to battle like fanatics for what they believed to be true.

Ravel's comrades differed from these *cameratas* since

they did not work together for any particular purpose. On the contrary, the group pursued its aims, each member in his own way, each developing his art so differently from the rest that the group as a whole did not have any particular face, as it were, any identity except—and this was their binding link—that they all were eager for everything new and that they negated dogma, banality, doctrine.

But, with all the cohorts with banners and slogans around them, they too had to have a name, and mere chance offered them one. On a Sunday, after a concert, walking up the street Rue de Rome *en masse* as was their custom, and taking up the whole of the sidewalk, arguing and gesticulating, they bumped into a newspaper vendor. "*Attention, les Apaches!*" the newspaper boy shouted at Viñes who was leading the procession, and Viñes picked up the epithet and with it christened their group. It seemed so romantic to them. They were delighted with it. And now all they needed was to have a code of their own, some mysterious signs by which they, and they only, could communicate with each other, to make them sound like the members of some kind of secret society. This also they did not fail to find very soon. They were enchanted with the first theme from Borodin's Second Symphony and adopted it as their rally call. It served them to find each other in the concert hall or theater when the ushers, tired of waiting for the end of their discussions in the corridors, would shut off the lights, or if they were in a crowd on the street.

And finally, Maurice Ravel, or Rara as they called him, had invented "Gomez le Riquet," a fictional character, who was supposed to be their friend, waiting for them either for a glass of *porto* or a cup of tea, depending on the hour. This name they used for a graceful exit whenever they found themselves in a company of "bores" or "pedants," and all pedants were bores, because they did not think the way the Apaches did.

There was, however, one exception to their strict ruling against receiving strangers into their midst, even if only as visitors. These were the Godebskis: Cyprien or Cipa, a music critic, and his sister Marie or Misia. The unusual position of the Godebskis and particularly of Misia in Parisian artistic circles must have been responsible for this privilege with the Apaches.

The Godebskis, although of Polish nationality, came from a wealthy family which, apparently, because of their father's fear of loneliness, sprawled across the European continent from Tsarskoye Syelo near St. Petersburg in Russia to Hall near Brussels in Belgium and Paris and Valvin near Fontainebleau in France. Père Godebski was a sculptor so successful in his art and with women that before Misia was seven years old she had a second stepmother, half a dozen brothers, half-brothers, half-sisters, uncles, and aunts, some of them half Belgian or half German, others Russian, German, or French, and learned that she was a granddaughter, on her mother's side, of François Servais, the famous "cellist to the King of the Belgians." In the memories of her childhood the years spent at her grandmother's luxurious home at Hall (Misia's grandfather died before she was born) were the most fascinating. She remembered well the hospitality of her grandmother, who continued in her husband's tradition to keep open house for artists and particularly for musicians. The eight pianos in the house never stood silent and Misia learned to read music before she knew the alphabet. Misia's feet could not reach the pedals when she played Beethoven's *Bagatelles* sitting on Franz Liszt's knees. It was in the same sitting room in her grandmother's home that two or three years later Jules Zarembsky, whom Liszt called the chief of the "*jeunes matadors du piano*," was brought downstairs from his sickbed dressed in a black velvet jacket and white silk shirt, à la Danton, to play Chopin's *Funeral March*, as a final romantic gesture a few minutes before he died of consumption at the age of thirty. Misia also remembered how frightened she was of her uncle Franz, a pianist and composer, who used to press his ear to the case containing a Stradivarius, a ritual lasting about five minutes every night before he went up to his room. Misia never knew what he was listening to, nor did Misia know that Franz Servais was not her uncle but Franz Liszt's and Princess Wittgenstein's illegitimate son, whom her grand-father had adopted.

Cipa was Misia's half-brother by her first stepmother, Mme Natanson, who also had a mansion on the Rue de Prony in Paris frequented by artists and the literati, where Misia stayed when she was not at the Sacré-Coeur convent, at her grandmother's in Hall, or at the home on the Rue de la Pompe in Paris of the Marquise de Gauville, her second stepmother. In this large family Misia and Cipa were the closest of friends, linked together by a common love for music, since Cipa, a sickly child, crippled by infantile paral-ysis, was never sent to a regular school and music was his chief interest in life. At the age of fourteen Misia ran away from the old family home at Hall first to London and later to Paris, rented an apartment in Montmartre on the Rue Saint-Jean off Avenue Clichy, studied piano with Gabriel Fauré, and supported herself giving piano lessons at eight francs an hour. A year later she married Thadée Natanson, her first stepmother's nephew, and after her husband founded the *Revue blanche* on which the most brilliant men of letters of that time collaborated, Misia became the muse of the literati and painters. Their apartment on the Rue Saint-Florentine was a "second home" to Mallarmé, Paul Valéry, Toulouse-Lautrec, Vuillard, Bonnard, Jules Renard, Henri de Régnier, Colette and Willy, and Pierre Louys who invited Misia one day to join a small circle of friends for whom Debussy sang his *Pelléas et Mélisande*, accompanying himself on an upright piano, long before its first performance at the Opéra-Comique. The Godebskis' credentials were more than satisfactory to open the doors of the *Apachie*.

Since at that time concerts were not numerous and music was being made "at home," in salons, where there was always the danger of encountering the "bores," the Apaches' own gatherings were musicales with performers, programs, and audiences of their own choice; these served them as a sympathetic sounding board, the try-out field for which a creative talent naturally feels a need. Not all of the Apaches reached the top of their aspirations, but all were alive, eager, and responsive to the questions with which Ravel used to greet them: who is doing what, who is talked about, who said what, when and where, and, of course, who is wearing what, what is it made of, etc.

The eldest in the group was Florent Schmitt, who became one of the foremost composers in France. Born in
1870 in Lorraine on the border of Germany, he was more
influenced by the German composers than by the new
French school which was then in the making. He combined
in his music the French refinement and taste for the intellectual with the German appetite for musical obsessions.
Among the works which include the quartets of Fauré,
Chausson, Debussy, Dukas, d'Indy, and Ravel, Florent
Schmitt's Quintet is a contribution of no small value, and
his *Tragédie de Salomé* is probably the most vivid example
of the complexity of his art: the attraction to violence and
ruggedness and the refinement and rich color with which
he dressed his ideas—the latter showing the influence of the
Russians and of Chabrier.

Florent Schmitt introduced Dmitri Calvocoressi to the
group when Calvocoressi was beginning his career as a professional music critic particularly interested in the Russians
—The Mighty Five. Later Calvocoressi became known for
his works on Mussorgsky and Glinka, but at that time he
served the Apaches as a link with the St. Petersburg musicians since he was in correspondence with Mili Balakirev,
the former leader of the group. Fortunately for the Apaches,
Balakirev, a man with whom it was very difficult to deal,
was particularly amiable and cooperative with Calvocoressi.
He had learned that the latter was of Greek origin and of
the Greek Orthodox faith—thus making them brethren.
Balakirev in the later period of his life suffered from a
religious obsession which, combined with other personal
peculiarities of his unruly character, incidentally wrecked

his musical career. Balakirev used both Calvocoressi and Ricardo Viñes, with whom he also was in correspondence, as his agents to foster the music which was being written in Russia, and the Apaches profited by being the first to have been introduced to it. Thus Ravel, in this direct way, learned much which influenced his early compositions and which otherwise was almost unknown in France.

But, curiously enough, it was not the musicians among the Apaches who had a paramount influence on Ravel, but Paul Sordes, a man of endless enthusiasm, an inspired dreamer, and a delicate sensualist, and Léon-Paul Fargue, to whom Ravel was indebted for his guidance in literature. In those days it was not Ravel who enlivened a party. On the contrary, he sat, listened, and absorbed. The floor belonged to Léon-Paul Fargue whose least important remarks were regarded as authoritative statements, whose few descriptive words created images, rich and fascinating as magic, and who offered the whole treasure of his "friendly irony," "affectionate maliciousness," and "lyric reprobation" in a language which dazzled them. He was Ravel's mentor in taste. Small wonder that Léon-Paul Fargue's eccentricities were just as contagious. It was an era in the history of artists when eccentricities in dress and behavior were considered an integral part of unconventional thought and being misunderstood was accepted as the fate of every genius.

Ravel's was not a rare type in the years between 1895 and 1910. One could easily find it among those who tried their prowess in the arts of literature and music. These young people still had vivid memories of Baudelaire, they watched their mannerisms carefully and even the way they spoke—they wanted to be equal to their master who had been dead more than thirty years. The difference between Ravel and these young men was that not all of Ravel's traits were the product of affectation. The serious and rather meditative air with which he carried himself and a sentiment of disappointment and even distress had been present in him ever since his adolescence and were not something he culti- vated under the influence of the vogue.

But, according to Ricardo Viñes, who certainly knew him longer and better than any other of his friends, Ravel went out of his way to appear mysterious and misunder- stood. Ravel worked on himself just as assiduously as he did on his compositions.

The final product was full of complexities. A man to whom order per se was alpha and omega in his compositions, who in his relations with his fellow men developed almost an ancient court etiquette, in his daily life disregarded the conventional regulation of time even when such neglect led to disrespect of others. Finally, his childish naïveté, which served him more as an excuse than as the reason for some of his concepts as well as actions, was another element he nourished throughout his life, to complete that image of an "artist" which apparently he had set for himself.

Léon-Paul Fargue to whom Ravel looked up with ad- miration was no doubt his model. The stories about Ravel always being late to appointments, concerts, dinner engage- ments, or trains could have been the stories told about Léon- Paul Fargue, so similar were these two in this respect. Except that Léon Fargue on arriving late for dinner would join his hosts for dessert saying that he had already eaten, rather than admit that he was a couple of hours late, and then proceed to eat the whole dinner in reverse order. Fargue used the same form of childish naïveté as an excuse for his lack of ability to cope with the simple matters of everyday life. To illustrate how really difficult it was for him to make any decision he would blame his mother for making him several hours late to a very important appointment. "She knows me well enough," he would relate to the Apaches with glee in his eyes, "yet what does she do but put out two pairs of shoes for me to choose from!" This could have been a typical Ravel story, true to the last detail.

Léon-Paul Fargue walked for months on the streets of Paris carrying a large camera slung across his shoulder. The camera was not loaded and, as far as anyone knew, he had never in his life taken a picture, but he carried the camera purely to give him an air of importance. Ravel at that time used a more conventional device—he wore a monocle for the same purpose. But, taken as a whole, Léon-Paul Fargue's influence was rather beneficial than detrimental, and the happy atmosphere of their circle can not be emphasized strongly enough for, while among those devoted friends, Ravel wrote his most spontaneous works.

Their sessions on Saturdays continued in Sordes' apartment until the noise proved to be too much for the patient neighbors. Léon-Paul Fargue was blamed for his late arrivals —usually at one or two in the morning—when everything had to be performed all over again to keep him informed of their progress. Paul Sordes was warned about their night meetings and the Apaches had to look elsewhere for a residence. Fortunately, just at that time Maurice Delage had rented a little bungalow, a wigwam, as the Apaches called it, on 3, Rue de Civry in Auteuil—a part of Paris near the Bois de Boulogne which was then still semirural.

Delage's new studio at the back of an old neglected garden was a perfect place for their reunions. The large room was barely furnished: a few chairs, a few benches, at first one grand piano and later two, a large stove which never kept them warm, and Delage's bed hidden in the closet until the last Apache said good-by—such were the accommodations to which their circle moved like a Congress to hold its sessions. Austere surroundings, but there were no neighbors to complain. It was there that in the tight silence of conspiracy Ravel played for the first time his *Jeux d'eau*.

Jeux d'eau was Ravel's first major piano work. Inspired by the Henri de Régnier poem and taking its first sentence "a river god laughs at the waters as they caress him" as his starting point, Ravel created an enchanting picture of a waterfall illumined by rainbow light. Its originality lies in its harmonic texture and its fairy-like qualities, sprinkled with sonorous dust, as it were; and in purely pianistic technique it surpasses that of Chopin and Liszt.

When asked how to interpret *Jeux d'eau*, Ravel said, "With even more simplicity than the *Pavane*. It should be played in the way you play Liszt," and Ravel meant Liszt, whose influence he acknowledged and not Debussy, of whose direct imitation he was accused. Each Ravel composition was still first appraised in its relation to Debussy, and never failed to start a discussion of whether Ravel was not merely an ingenious imitator of Debussy.

However, the virtues of the piece, particularly as a first step in the further development of piano technique, were unanimously recognized, even though Ravel himself saw its importance only much later and at the time told his publisher not to bother with taking out the world copyright—so little importance did he attach to this work. It was performed by Ricardo Viñes on April 5, 1902, at Salle Pleyel. It was not booed, but neither did it create a sensation.

In order not to remain a composer of the *Pavane* and *Jeux d'eau* only, Ravel completed his *Quartet* for strings in the following year. He dedicated the piece to his teacher Fauré and contrary to his custom let his friends see the score before the composition was publicly performed. Although today Ravel's *Quartet* is considered as one of his most spontaneous works, his friends' opinions varied. "It is a piece worthy of any composer's work at the end of a long career," Vincent d'Indy said, despite Fauré's verdict that the last (fourth) movement was a failure, too short and unbalanced. "In the name of the gods of music, and in mine, do not touch a single note of what you have written in your *Quartet*," Debussy wrote to Ravel, and this message decided Ravel's own attitude toward the manuscript. He never did "touch a single note" in the score and the first performance, given by the Heymann Quartet on March 5, 1904, at the National Musical Society, won applause from even the most critical. For the first time fortune seemed to be in Ravel's favor.

One more composition was the immediate result of the happy atmosphere of the meetings on the Rue de Civry—Ravel's *Shéhérazade*. This composition was neither a varia-

tion nor a development of his early work by the same name
—the overture to an opera, the plans for which he had abandoned for good. The new *Shéhérazade* was a selection of
three poems from Tristan Klingsor's work with the same
title.

Tristan Klingsor, despite his doubly Wagnerian name,
was not a Wagnerite, but one of the most ardent members
of the Apaches. Better known as a poet, he was also a
musician. He studied music because he considered it essential for a poet, particularly a writer of free verse, to have a
knowledge of rhythm, accents, and syncopes. Klingsor had
no explanation for Ravel's interest in his *Shéhérazade*, except
perhaps the popularity of Rimsky-Korsakov's piece by the
same name, the then recent translation of *A Thousand and
One Nights* by Mardrus, and the particular fascination the
Orient had for all of them. To Klingsor's great surprise
Ravel selected the three poems which in the poet's opinion
were the least adaptable to singing: *Flûte enchantée, L'Indifférent, Asie.* Then Ravel made him read them aloud to
him but, contrary to Klingsor's expectations, Ravel set the
text to music almost diametrically opposite to that of
Klingsor's own declamation.

Among these three, *L'Indifférent* caused most of the
comment because it was considered as the first and, as it
became later evident, the last manifestation of Ravel's most
secret inner self. Ravel kept this so well hidden that even
to the Apaches, his closest friends, it remained an enigma.
However, when Calvocoressi asked Ravel whether he took
particular care to exclude from his music anything that
might resemble a direct expression of his emotions, Ravel

pointed to *L'Indifférent* as one composition in which the direct expression of emotion, far from being excluded, was deliberately attempted. During Ravel's life this was never openly discussed by music critics, but after his death Émile M. Vuillermoz, music critic and Apache, wrote the following:

> *L'Indifférent* is a real feat of elegance and delicacy. The poem is charming but the music increases its sparkling power. Within a few bars Ravel has been able to introduce in his description a warmth and an intensity that one would look for vainly in most of his other works, realized with a more intent composure and a more watchful authority. In it Ravel expresses a rare ambiguity. This young stranger whose eyes are "gentle as a girl's" and who goes his way "slightly swaying in his feminine and weary gait" disdains the call—of whom? We do not know. Does this youth reject the invitation of a courtesan or that of a Greek philosopher?
>
> When one has heard of what has been called the sexual enigma of Ravel, who was also an *indifférent*, one is left perplexed by all the delicate mystery which hovers over this small text, and one becomes aware that this page is one in which the musician has revealed one of the most hidden and best aspects of his sensitivity. He abandons his usual timidity to give way to a kind of discreet but impressive and lyrical effusiveness which makes it, more than any other of his works, a confession.

On this evidence alone rests the discreet insinuation of Ravel's homosexuality.

Chapter Four

The First "Affaire Ravel"

THERE WAS MORE than one reason why Maurice Ravel ardently and persistently desired to win the Prix de Rome. His friendship and success with his fellow artists, with the Apaches, were gratifying, but they were far from official recognition of his talent. Besides the Apaches Ravel, as I have said, saw a great many people. He went into "society" to see and to be seen in the salons of Prince and Princess Edmond de Polignac, on Sundays to Cipa and Ida Godebski, to Misia and her second husband Alfred Edwards, the owner and publisher of the daily, *Le Matin*, and on Wednesday evenings after dinner to Mme de Saint-Marceau—just to name a few.

The elite of the Parisian society appreciated the fine arts; they had beautiful collections of pictures on their walls, first editions on their library shelves, and an impressive list of names of poets, painters, and musicians who moved about in their salons as though they were at home. Maurice Ravel was a welcome guest, but his desire was to be among those about whom society talked. This desire for outside admiration is logically in sheer contradiction to a deep scorn for the judgment of other people, but logically incompatible beliefs have been known to coexist without difficulty in human beings even stronger than Ravel. No one can deny that Ravel sought recognition, wanted fame. The Prix de Rome would not necessarily make him famous, but it would be the first step toward official recognition and besides, it would open to him the road to financial independence from his family—high time, since Ravel was approaching thirty.

The Academy of France in Rome, known for its Prix de Rome, is an old institution, established in 1666 by the French government with the intention of giving young French artists a chance and enabling them by means of a financial grant to devote themselves for seven years entirely to their art while living at the Medici Palace in Rome. Since the number of well-known French composers (as well as painters and writers) who failed in obtaining the Prix de Rome almost equals that of those who won the prize, it was not entirely the prestige but rather this financial independence that the aspirants were coveting when joining the competition.

As early as 1901 Ravel put up his bid after successfully passing the preliminary examination. With four other contestants he stayed at the Palais de Compiègne where in "solitary confinement" each man was to write a fugue and a four-part cantata on a subject chosen by the jury. Fernand

Bessier's poem, written in uninspired and uninspiring language, describing Sardanapale, who is joined by his slave Myrrha ready to mount the scaffold, was the subject of that year's cantata.

Ravel probably would have received the first prize had he not let his sense of humor interfere with such a solemn task as a cantata on a religious subject. Annoyed by the insipid text of the poem Ravel set it to music in a slow and languishing waltztime, which provoked the wrath of the jury. "M. Ravel should not imagine that he can ridicule us. M. Ravel may well consider us flatfooted pedants, but he will not go unpunished for taking us for imbeciles," it was reported that one member of the jury remarked.

The professors of the Conservatory were not particularly predisposed toward Ravel—to put it mildly. He was considered an *enfant terrible*, a revolutionist, and his interest in Satie was not forgotten. He was quoted to have said that "Beethoven could not score for beans," when all Ravel actually had said was that "Beethoven's orchestration, as regards the brass section, was not always free from imperfections."

Ravel's treatment of the cantata was judged to have been written with tongue in cheek. A young aspirant may be forgiven anything except irony, and in Ravel's case they thought it downright mockery. Ravel was given the second prize, a gold medal, and no financial reward, but he found some consolation in a remark of another member of the jury who said that "melody flows from Ravel like water from a tap."

Ravel competed again in the following years 1902 and

1903, but although the second prize usually assured the contestant of eventually winning the first prize, Ravel this time not only was not awarded any prize at all but, when in 1905 he again wanted to join the competition, he was not admitted to even the preliminary examination. This decision, based on the fact that Ravel had passed the age limit of thirty, was considered as a flagrant example of personal prejudice.

The indignation which had been accumulating during the four years since Ravel joined the competition in 1901 for the first time now reached its boiling point. It ceased to be a subject for discussion among only the Apaches on Rue de Civry. The news, swelled with gossip, rumors, and the latest authentic reports, reached into the homes of everyone who was interested in music or had ever heard of Ravel, and then into every artist's studio and every writer's home, since it was a subject which was under the jurisdiction of the Academy of Fine Arts and every kind of artist could therefore be affected by a similar decision. Finally, supported by sympathizers from all walks of life, it broke into the open, creating a scandal, a national scandal, *l'affaire Ravel*.

The two principal newspapers of France, *Le Temps* and *Le Matin*, made space for articles written by outraged music critics, who must have been waiting for just such an occasion to speak their piece. Since the members of the Prix jury do not enjoy the immunity and the anonymity of regular court juries, the critics gave their names in full (Charles Lenepveu, Théodore Dubois, Paladilhe, Massenet, and Reyer) and then analyzed the accomplishments of every one of them to show clearly in whose hands so vital a decision was entrusted. These reports were followed by even more detailed articles in the monthly magazines, so that public indignation was kept alive until something had to be done about it.

Far from being aloof from what was going on, as was later reported, Ravel himself at first signed his name to the protest which was written by his comrade contestants. Later, however, he withdrew his name, not wanting to embarrass those of his friends who won the favors of the jury. But Ravel did try to solicit an interview with M. Bienvenue Martin, the Minister of Education, during which he was going to present him with a letter of protest against the unjust decision of the jury.

Meanwhile on May 21, 1905, *Le Temps* published an interview with Ravel, "since it is the policy of the paper," so said the editorial note, "to give both sides in the dispute the chance to be heard."

I am not going to Rome [Ravel said]. This was decided by the institute, which is the only one with the power to open to young composers the road to the Villa Medici. This misfortune upsets me. The award of the second prize, my diligent work, encouraged and appreciated by my professor M. Gabriel Fauré, my works, published and favorably received by the public, allowed me to hope, without any ridiculous presumption of writing a perfect cantata, or one superior to that of my comrades, that I would be permitted to join the competition at Compiègne. The opportunity seemed particularly favorable to me since M. Pech, because of his desire to marry,[1] had renounced his right to the first prize—thus making room for two first prizes.

[1] M. Pech won the first prize in the previous year, 1904, but according to the rules of the competition, a Prix de Rome winner had to remain single for the duration of his fellowship.

Ravel expressed further his conviction that the cause of all the trouble was M. Charles Lenepveu, one of the three members of the jury, who taught composition at the Conservatory, had six pupils of his own admitted to the competition, and would also have had the seventh admitted had there been a place for one more (Ravel said that he was quoting newspaper reports). He added that it reflected very badly on the other two professors, Gabriel Fauré and Charles Maria Widor, making it look as if they could not teach the rudiments of composition, and that, summarizing the whole affair, he—Ravel—did not regret the "illusory" prestige of the Prix de Rome as much as he did the financial grant which assured seven years in a young composer's life, a sojourn in Rome, traveling as an artist whenever it was necessary and finally providing him with material which could lead to important developments in the artist's life.

Ravel confessed, and this should be mentioned in parentheses, not in this interview but privately to Calvocoressi, that the whole Prix de Rome business called for a great financial sacrifice on his part each time he entered the competition. The contestants, who had to spend a whole month living in the Palais de Compiègne, were given only a room and a grant-in-aid of 100 francs (about 20 dollars) toward their upkeep, while it actually cost them five or six times that amount.

Some newspapers tried to hush up the whole affair. But five days after the *Le Temps* interview, on May 26, 1905, Romain Rolland, whose authority was respected by every one, wrote the following letter to Paul Léon, director of *Beaux-Arts:*

Dear Sir:

I read in the papers that there is no *affaire Ravel*. I believe it my duty to tell you (just between ourselves) that this case exists and can not be evaded. In this *affaire* I am personally entirely disinterested. I am not a friend of Ravel. I may even say that I have no personal sympathy with his subtle and refined art. But justice compels me to say that Ravel is not only a student of promise—he is already one of the young masters, the most apparent in our school, which does not have many. I do not doubt for an instant the good faith of the judges: I do not challenge it. But this is rather a condemnation for all time of these juries; I can not comprehend why one should persist in keeping a school in Rome if it is to close its doors to those rare artists who have some originality—to a man like Ravel, who has established himself at the concerts of the National Society through works far more important than those required for an examination. Such a musician did honor to the competition; and even if by some unhappy chance, which I should find it difficult to explain, his compositions were or seemed to have been inferior to those of the other contestants, he should nevertheless have been granted the Prix de Rome. It is a case rather similar to that of Berlioz. Ravel comes to the competition for the Prix de Rome not as a pupil, but as a composer who has already proved himself. I admire the composers who dared to judge him. Who shall judge them in their turn?

Forgive me for mixing into an affair that does not concern me. It is everyone's duty to protest against a decision which, even though technically just, harms real justice and art, and since I have the pleasure of knowing you, I feel I should give you—I repeat, entirely between ourselves—the opinion of an impartial musician.

After signing the letter Romain Rolland added the following postscript: "N.B. Isn't there any way for the State (without going against its decision) at least to prove its interest in Ravel?"

But the state did nothing. At least not at that time, and Ravel remembered this well. Many years went by: five, ten, fifteen years passed before Ravel received his satisfaction. But meanwhile the music critics did not let the Ravel case rest and their articles were not as dignified as Romain Rolland's letter. If the members of the jury suspected that perhaps Ravel mocked them and considered them imbeciles, the critics were forthright in condemning the whole shameful business as the party politics of one professor trying to outdo another to get the nomination to the post of a director at the Conservatory. The critics demanded that the whole organization should be thoroughly investigated and swept clean immediately.

A great scandal has occurred in connection with the Prix de Rome [Jean Marnold, an eminent music critic, wrote in the magazine *Mercure de France* in June, 1905], a scandal which should have awakened Berlioz in his tomb to the memories of his own personal experiences which he described in his memoirs with such a sharp and sarcastic pen.

How could this trio of asses manage to sneak, in their threefold and notorious impotence, into a position from which they have the power to rule and decide at the jealous whim of their debility and their own interest, assisted by old cadgers and neo-arrivists and by the unwitting complicity of the weak?

To be a moron is not prohibited by law since it is a congenital defect. But those who are afflicted by it usually are given treatment, and modern therapy has made considerable progress thanks to the *"trepan"* and to thyroid extract serum. They are usually left at liberty to dirty themselves, to play with ribbons, decorations, and other little playthings. If, however, they become mean, they are put under cold showers, but certainly never would anyone dream of putting them in charge of awarding prizes and distributing funds after having passed judgment on merits.

Envious, petty, or simple, their stupidity would become too easy a prey to shrewder acolytes.

In these times when the kings of oil and smoked pork, the rulers of Congo rubber, the princes of sports, the lords of the cafés, not to mention the knights of industry, are multiplying, in these times when a spontaneous mania for business is leading us gradually to the most idiotic barbarism, between the stupid and arrogant Croesuses and their exhausted slaves, an institution of this kind may yet turn out to be the best safeguard of a Nation's Art.

It remains yet to be seen, however, whether in this country at present and for all future times these benefits can be extorted by intrigues or awarded by imbeciles by refusing admission to the final competition to a musician who has reached the age limit but who could teach them all. The majority of the jury committed an act which resembles so closely a petty villainy that the only thing we can hope for is that it was committed without the necessary deliberation. Assuredly, the dilemma is an unpleasant one to their pride. Their repeated exploits are even more damaging to our national art, which is delivered into their hands without protection. For the sake of the future of our music, it is high time to sweep out this clique of . . . .

a string of strong words ended the article.

The "scandal" did not repair the irreparable, the decision taken by the jury was not revoked, but the outburst of the critics and public opinion did have an effect. The director of the conservatory, Théodore Dubois, as well as

M. Lenepveu, the leader of the opposition against Ravel, resigned and Gabriel Fauré was nominated as the head of the institution. Many reforms followed but none to affect Ravel.

Ravel had to accept the final blow as far as the Prix de Rome was concerned. But his friends rallied around him and at this trying moment in his life he was invited by the Edwards to join them on a yachting trip to Holland. True to his habit, Ravel was late for the departure and the yacht sailed while Ravel was in a haberdashery, choosing the new outfits which he deemed indispensable for such a trip.

Chapter Five

Ravel Changes His Style

FORTUNATELY, Ravel caught up with the yacht *Aimée* just as it was going to be taken through the lock at Soissons, some sixty-five miles northeast of Paris. He brought with him all his navigating paraphernalia, including a new yacht-man's cap with which he was particularly pleased. But this time he left behind, in Paris, the score of his latest work, the *Introduction et Allegro*, a septet, a sort of concerto for harp with pedals, accompanied by flute, clarinet, and a string quartet. It was commissioned by the Érard piano company, the principal manufacturers of the traditional harp. Érard was at that time competing with another piano company, Pleyel, who had introduced a new chromatic harp, perfected by Gustave Lyon (1903). This commission almost stood in the way of Ravel's accepting the invitation for the cruise. However, after eight days of desperate and intense work and three sleepless nights, he finished the composition for "better or worse," as he said, only to leave the manuscript on the counter in the haberdashery and to discover his loss weeks later.

"The joy of this journey! And this is only the first day! The nightmare of the last days is forgotten! . . ." Ravel wrote these few lines to Maurice Delage.

No wonder. For the first time Ravel tasted the life of a rich man. His host's manner of living would have matched that of any prince living on the European continent. Alfred Edwards, besides inheriting the wealth in money as well as costly jewelry which his father brought home after serving for years as a doctor to the sultan's harem in Constantinople, made his own fortune after founding *Le Matin*, a daily with the largest circulation in Europe, and investing in several successful enterprises. He owned a château at Corbeil, kept stables, and had the most beautiful carriages, cars, and horses for his personal use, but to please his new wife, formerly Misia Natanson, thirty years his junior, he had had built this yacht for her.

Misia wanted a "houseboat," as she explained to Edwards, and *Aimée*, "the beloved one," was just that. One hundred and five feet wide, so that it could get through the river locks, it had ample space accommodations: a large dining room, a sitting room, five cabins with two or three beds in each reserved for their guests and finally the most beautiful room, the Edwards' own bedroom, where Misia had her piano, which during the day was turned into another sitting room. Because of its perfect acoustics this little salon was a favorite of Caruso, the singer, an old friend of the Edwards'; he felt that the wood-paneled walls gave his voice the sonority of a violin.

The yacht was manned by five men and a captain, but the presence of a certain M. Apak was indispensable, for Edwards, being a rich man, never carried a penny in his pocket. M. Apak's sole function was that of a purser who paid all bills regardless of their size. Edwards treated his guests royally; everything they desired was served to them on board and whenever they put into port their excursions were assisted by M. Apak's magic wand.

Edwards had a passion for collections, all kind of collections; he bought jewelry, trinkets, souvenirs, statuettes . . . Misia's cupboards and shelves in their Paris apartment were filled to capacity with them, still he could not refrain from collecting more. Perhaps it was on this trip that Ravel was contaminated with this rich man's hobby, for he, too, later in his life could not resist the window display of a curiosity shop.

Three weeks later, when the yacht put into port of Amsterdam, Ravel wrote again to Delage. "We have been here for three days and I have not yet been in the museums. There are so many things to see! Yesterday, an excursion to Harlem. Some Franz Hals' which are a revelation. On the way, a magnificent spectacle: a lake bordered with windmills. In the fields, windmills as far as the horizon. Whichever way you look, you see nothing but revolving wings. You end by feeling that you yourself are an automaton in the midst of this mechanical landscape. With all this, I do not need to tell you that I am doing absolutely nothing. But

I am storing up, and I think a lot of things will come from this voyage."

In another letter, written on the same day to a friend in St. Jean-de-Luz, he described with even more enthusiasm the beautiful journey he was making, confessing that "the life of a grand seignior is not at all disagreeable": he had seen many picturesque and magnificent cities, the port of Anvers, an exposition at Liège, Dordrecht, Maestrield, etc. But although he spoke with great relish of the anticipated second part of the journey: sailing on the Rhine, recrossing Belgium, and the return home via Ostend, the open sea, and Trouville, in the same letter he remembered to repeat the account of his misfortune with the Prix de Rome. He was obviously pleased with Fauré's nomination to the director's post at the Conservatory, and spoke with proud satisfaction about "the noise" his own name was causing. "It's not all over yet," he wrote, "because they are preparing something very important for me as soon as I return. On the whole, it does me more good than harm: this scandal has given me more publicity than if I had been awarded the first prize. And besides it has given me the opportunity of making this splendid voyage, which I have been enjoying for almost a month already."

For a man who delighted in affected childish naïveté, for a man who could miss an important appointment because he could not decide which shoes, cravat, or shirt to wear, this is rather an astute appraisal of the situation. And as for the "something very important" that was in preparation for his return, there is no record left anywhere showing what that may have been. The plans must never have materialized, except, of course, for a hero's welcome upon his return to Paris, which he received among his friends, who stood by him like a bodyguard. Possibly, Ravel was aware that his friends were trying to find him a publisher and thus provide him with at least a part of that financial independence which he sought from the Prix de Rome. It came about in the most unexpected way.

In the previous year, 1904, Dmitri Calvocoressi had been asked by Pierre Aubry, the journalist, to suggest someone who could sing a few Greek folk songs at a lecture which Aubry was to give on short notice at the École Hautes Études Sociales. The lecture was to be propaganda in favor of the oppressed Greeks and Armenians in Turkey, and Aubry wished to use the songs as an illustration. For some reason Aubry did not like Bourgault-Ducoudray's well-known collection of Greek folk songs, and therefore it was decided that Calvocoressi would teach the singer, phonetically, a few songs from Hubert Pernot's "Popular Songs from the Isle of Chio," published in the *Rapport d'une mission scientifique en Turquie.*

Calvocoressi chose Louise Thomasset for the performer and called on Ravel to write the accompaniments, explaining the reason for haste. They chose four songs from the collection and added the fifth, *Quel Galant!,* from a group of songs published in Constantinople. Calvocoressi translated the lyrics for Ravel and, to his great surprise, Ravel was for once on time. Thirty-six hours later he was ready to coach the singer, with Calvocoressi correcting the pronunciation.

"I was amazed," Calvocoressi said, "at seeing what he,

who had never before turned his mind to harmonizing folk songs, had been able to achieve. Tunes and accompaniments simply seemed to have grown together."

Now, in 1905, when Ravel returned from his journey, Jacques Durand, the owner of the largest music-publishing company in France, offered to be his publisher, and as at that time Ravel had nothing ready for publication except these *Cinq Mélodies populaires grecques*, they became the cornerstone on which a lifelong association was established between the firm A. Durand et Fils and Maurice Ravel. At last Ravel could enjoy a certain amount of financial independence. For an option on all his forthcoming compositions Durand et Fils proposed to pay him twelve thousand francs a year as an advance on his royalties—the same amount paid to Debussy. But as Ravel explained, he preferred to take only six thousand francs, "so as not to risk feeling compelled to turn out a greater quantity of work."

According to Calvocoressi, there is no reason for the assumption that Ravel was particularly attracted by Greek subjects just because of this choice for his first experiment in harmonizing folk music and the fact that one of his most important works, *Daphnis et Chloë*, is based on a classic legend. Since neither subject was of Ravel's own choice, the whole matter is a pure coincidence.

Calvocoressi was instrumental in one more of Ravel's works—the *Sonatine*. In 1903 he was a contributor to the *Weekly Critical Review*—an Anglo-French magazine founded in Paris by Arthur Bles. The magazine was devoted to literature, fine arts, and music, and many prominent men, such as Arthur Symons, John Runciman, Remy de Gour-

Ravel at six

Joseph Ravel with his sons, Edouard and Maurice

Ravel (far left) and Ricardo Viñes (fourth from right) as students. At the piano (with beard). Charles de Bériot.

Ricardo Viñes   Ravel at thirty-three

Studio of Les Apaches, with Maurice Delage. Originally the studio was less
ornate.   (*Courtesy Maurice Delage*)

Contestants for the Prix de Rome, 1901. Ravel is at the far right.

A group of Ravel's contemporaries. Left to right, Ricardo Viñes, Mme Jane Mortier, Robert Mortier, L'Abbé Leonce Petit, Maurice Ravel.

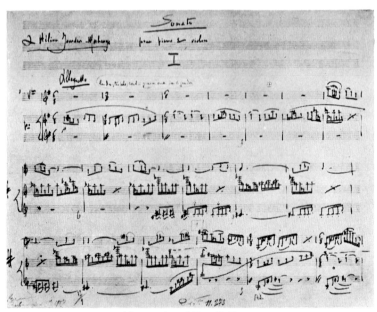

Manuscript of Ravel's *Sonate*

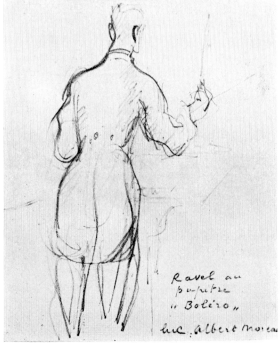

Ravel conducting *Boléro*

Ravel on the balcony of his house at Montfort-l'Amaury near Paris

(Courtesy Comte Joel de Croze)

Ravel at work

(Courtesy Comte Joel de Croze)

Ravel at the piano

(*Lipnitzki*)

One of the last photo-portraits of Maurice Ravel   (*Lipnitzki*)

mont, and Ernest Newman, wrote for it. Arthur Bles himself was a music lover and, to promote a larger circulation for his weekly, he announced an international competition for a best first movement of a piano sonatina. He stipulated that in length it should not exceed seventy-five bars and offered one hundred francs (twenty dollars) as first prize. Calvocoressi suggested that Ravel join the competition. Ravel did and even delivered his piece in time. But he did not receive the prize and this time it was not Ravel's fault.

Since no other composition arrived at Arthur Bles' desk, but instead a pile of notes threatening the magazine with bankruptcy (Bles was, according to Calvocoressi, over-generous with his contributors, while the magazine lacked sufficient public support), he called off the competition and sent back Ravel's manuscript, which, incidentally, was longer by two bars than the prescribed seventy-five measures.

Upon his return from the cruise Ravel first of all retrieved his composition for the harp from the haberdashery and completed the *Sonatine*. One should not be misled by the diminutive title: it is not one of the "little pieces for small hands." The exquisite miniature is one of Ravel's major works. When it was first performed by Gabriel Grovlez on March 31, 1906, at the National Society of Music, it had a mixed reception and some people in the audience booed. The general public was still somewhat hostile to each new composition by Ravel, but the *Sonatine* made rapid steps on the road to popularity and soon took its place next to the *Pavane* and *Jeux d'eau*, and with far more merit.

Almost at the same time, Ravel composed *Le Noël des*

jouets. He wrote his own text, precise and elegant, passing from irony to tenderness with a flexibility entirely his own.

Le Noël des jouets

Le troupeau verni des moutons
Roule en tumulte vers la crèche,
Les lapins tambours brefs et rêches
Couvrent leurs aigres mirlitons.

Vierge Marie en crinoline,
Ses yeux d'émail sans cesse ouverts,
En attendant Bonhomme hiver,
Veille Jésus qui se dodine,

Car près de là sous un sapin,
Furtif, enveloppé dans l'ombre
Du bois, Belzébuth, le chien sombre,
Guette l'Enfant de sucre peint.

Mais les beaux anges incassables
Suspendus par des fils d'archal
Du haut de l'arbuste hiémal
Assurent la paix des étables.

Et leur vol de clinquant vermeil
Qui cliquette en bruit symétrique
S'accorde au bétail mécanique
Dont la voix grêle bêle: "Noël, Noël!"

It is a matter of conjecture whether Ravel's compositions after his return from the cruise were a product of the impressions he had "stored up" or of the fact that the music "gushed out of him like water from an open tap." One thing is certain: the immediately following years were the most productive in his life.

Ravel was thirty years old, free from the Conservatory's shackles, free to compose as he pleased, and with a small annuity from his new publisher to give him at least some degree of independence. He was back among the Apaches on the Rue de Civry, when Ricardo Viñes came in obviously excited after a visit with Debussy. Debussy told him, Viñes explained, that he was possessed by an idea: to write music that would sound as if it were improvised. Instead of objecting, as every one expected, Ravel said that that was just the problem which he was trying to solve in his latest composition. (Another example of an idea occurring simultaneously to two men, without any grounds for suspicion of plagiarism by either of the two.)

Ravel said that this latest work, which, he expected, would baffle the musicians who were used to the way he had been composing in the past, was a product of his harmonic evolution.

And indeed, Ravel confused even the Apaches when he played his *Miroirs* to them, particularly with the second piece out of the group of five—*Les Oiseaux tristes*. Their confusion, for they could not grasp what Ravel was after, upset the composer himself and he played the piece to them over and over again. "This one," Ravel explained, "is the most characteristic of them all. In it I evoke birds lost in the torpor of a somber forest during the most torrid hours of summer." Some of the Apaches, including Roland-Manuel thought that Ravel preferred to "paint" rather than to "express emotion." But on the whole it was not clear to them. "Ravel was hawking about," Paul Sordes said, "holding on his extended finger two forlorn little birds with whom nobody would bother."

Ravel dedicated the *Miroirs* to the Apaches, inscribing each piece to a different member of the group: to Ricardo Viñes *Les Oiseaux tristes*, because, he said, "it was fun to dedicate to a pianist a piece that was not in the least pianistic"; to Fargue *Noctuelles*; to Delage *La Vallée des cloches*; to Calvocoressi *Alborada del Gracioso*; and to Sordes *Une Barque sur l'Océan*.

Ricardo Viñes played the work on January 6, 1906, at the National Society of Music to a bewildered audience. Out of these five descriptive pieces *L'Alborada del Gracioso* (Morningsong of the Jester) won favor with concert pianists because of its virtuosity. Its Spanish flavor, imitations of the guitar, and quotations of fragments of songs held, for a while, the attention of the audience which was bewildered by the impressionistic and slow-paced *Oiseaux tristes* and the architectonic complexity of *Une Barque sur l'Océan*.

Ravel had made several attempts at compositions for the stage, but each time he had, for one reason or another, he abandoned the project before halfway through with it. According to the Apaches, Ravel wanted to please his father, who was old and failing in health, with a theatrical production by his son. Gerhardt Hauptmann's *The Sunken Bell* was Ravel's choice.

The five-act play had had no success with the Parisian public when it was presented for the first time in the spring of 1897. It was considered to be too heavy and confusing.

But that spoke neither for nor against the play, as far as Ravel was concerned. He made his decision when, rummaging through the secondhand books on the quai along the Seine, he came across the French translation by A. Fernand Herold of *The Sunken Bell*. With a letter of introduction from his professor, André Gédalge, Ravel went to André-Fernand Herold for the permission to use the translation. Herold readily granted him his request, and although Ravel never mentioned it again when they met, Herold suspected that Ravel was working on this new project. And indeed he was.

Nine years later, in 1906, Ravel revisited Herold and told him that at last he knew how to make a musical drama out of *The Sunken Bell*. Herold became his collaborator: leaving intact the original Gerhardt Hauptmann text (that is, in the French translation) they made all the cuts necessary to make out of the original play a fairy tale, "pleasant, as well as cruel."

During the summer months, when the heat in the Levallois, where Ravel lived with his parents, becomes almost tropical, Ravel remained working at home without going out to see his friends or even answering the anxious letters and telegrams from the Apaches.

Finally, on June 12, 1906, Ravel wrote to Maurice Delage:

> . . . For the past two weeks I have not left the grind. Never have I worked with such frenzy. Oh, yes, at Compiègne but there it was less amusing. It is fascinating to do a dramatic piece. I would not say that it comes by itself, but

that is exactly where the beauty of it lies. By Jove, in a few days I will be sure of the whole thing!

Ravel was experiencing one of the rare moments of satisfaction and happiness in his work for, as he said:

> The apathy, the depression, the bitter reproaches to my parents that they did not see to it that I had a profession by which to feed myself—all this does not really matter. In this blackguard of a trade, there are some marvelous moments. . . .

Two months later, in August, while accompanying his father to Switzerland in the hope that the old familiar places of his father's childhood would revive his failing health, Ravel wrote to Delage from Hermance on Lake Geneva that he had already done a great deal of the second act and ended this message with a facetious quip: "Would you like an opera in five acts? You will have it within a week!" And that was the end of the project for a musical drama after Gerhardt Hauptmann's *The Sunken Bell!*

Despite his playing it often to the Apaches and their enthusiastic encouragement, despite Durand's signing for the publication of this work, and despite its announcement by the Théâtre des Champ Élysées, as late as 1914, on the list of forthcoming productions, Ravel never completed the score, although periodically he returned to work on it up to the outbreak of World War I, when he put it away and never touched it again. (Some of the material, however, he used later—twenty years later—in the second act of his *L'Enfant et les sortilèges:* "the tree" and "the frogs' chorus.")

It is a pity for, according to Herold, Ravel planned to develop his dramatic action not in a little blacksmith's shack in the midst of a German forest but in an immense modern factory with all its noises of hammers, saws, files, and sirens. Perhaps Ravel felt that the problem of preserving Grimm's fairy-tale atmosphere in an up-to-date factory was far more difficult to solve than he indicated in the initial outline of the piece, and therefore he turned again to the illustration of some poems with his music—a task for which he already had sufficient experience.

The language of Jules Renard, the poet, always held a particular fascination for Ravel. He felt that the text of his poems imposed a declamation directly related to the inflection of French speech. As was the case with Tristan Klingsor's *Shéhérazade*, Ravel again chose those of Jules Renard's poems which were the most difficult for musical adaptation. But apparently Ravel did not consult Renard, as the following entries in the poet's Journal show:

> November 19, 1906. . . . Thadée Natanson [Misia's first husband and Ravel's old friend] said to me: "A musician would like to put to music some of your poems from *Histoires naturelles*. It is a musician of the avant-garde in whom there is a great belief and for whom Debussy is already an old bore.[1] . . . What impression does this make on you?"
> —"None."
> —"But this must interest you?"
> —"Not in the least."
> —"What should I say to him?"
> —"Whatever you like; say thank you."

[1] Either Natanson's own opinion or Renard's misquotation, for obviously Ravel did not feel that way.

—"Wouldn't you like to hear his music?"

—"Oh no. No."

Jules Renard's disinterest in the project might have disconcerted any composer except Ravel. According to Tristan Klingsor—and he spoke from his own experience with the composer—Ravel did not need an author's collaboration: did not Ravel, after asking Klingsor to read to him his *Shéhérazade* over and over again, reverse the inflection of the voice once he put it down to his own music? Unlike some musicians who at first live the life of Siamese twins, with their collaborators, only to quarrel to the death after the first performance of the work, Ravel preferred to do his work by himself, undisturbed.

However, when Ravel completed his composition, he called on Renard. This interview also was recorded in Renard's Journal.

On January 12, 1907 . . . . Monsieur Ravel, the dark, rich, and delicate musician of the *Histoires naturelles* insists that I should come and hear his songs this evening. I told him of my ignorance in music and asked him what he had been able to add to the *Histoires naturelles*.

"My intention was not to add, but to interpret."

—"But in what way?"

"To say with music what you say with words when, for example, you stand in front of a tree. I think and feel in music, and I would like to think and feel the same things that you do."

And then Ravel, as if unconsciously, confessed the apprehension he had toward the National Society of Music, which under the influence of d'Indy had become reactionary.

There is music that is instinctive, sentimental—my own, and also music of the intellect: d'Indy [continues Jules Renard in his Journal, obviously misquoting Ravel, but still conveying the gist of what Ravel was saying.[2]] Tonight there will be nothing except d'Indy. *They* do not allow emotions which they do not want to explain. I do. But they find what I do interesting. And this is very important for me, this proof, I mean.

These were the first signs of the discord which eventually alienated Ravel from the old generation of musicians. The National Society of Music, where from the days of his youth he had received a remarkable hospitality, was now in Ravel's eyes a seat of César Franck's puritanism (d'Indy was a pupil of Franck and a Franckist). Ravel was always certain of being misunderstood by these *adeptes moroses*, as he called them, "of this neo-christianism." A stranger to their notion of a musical Trinity, Beethoven as God with Wagner and Franck at his sides, and even more of a stranger to their personal lyricism, too subjective for his taste, Ravel did not wish to appear as a disciple, however ingenious, still inferior to, say, Claude Debussy.

When on January 12, 1907, Jeanne Bathory performed the *Histoires naturelles* for the first time, the National Society of Music was shocked, and the furor of discussion unleashed such a polemic in the press that it was called the second *Affaire Ravel.*

[2] Jules Renard admitted that he was ignorant in music and therefore his records suffer from obvious misquotations when he speaks of Ravel's remarks about his own music.

Chapter Six

The Second "Affaire Ravel"

MAURICE RAVEL was, without doubt, *l'enfant terrible* of French music in the beginning of the twentieth century. Two years had hardly elapsed since Ravel had divided his countrymen into two warring camps because of the Prix de Rome. But now, in 1907, the controversy over his music (which had been brewing for some time) split the musicians into two hostile groups.

The scandal of the Prix de Rome and the performances of Ravel's latest works after his return from the cruise constantly kept his name before the public; Ravel was the most talked-about musician in France. Each performance of a new composition provoked heated discussions; with each performance he could count as many new admirers as enemies. And now the performance of the *Histoires naturelles* caused a new uproar; some shouted bravo, while others started a brawl—so incensed were they by performing a work on such a subject in a concert hall.

The first of the group of five songs, *Le Paon*, the peacock, portrays the disappointment of the proud bird who expects every day to get married, only to find that his fiancée "Leon" fails to come to the ceremony.

Le Grillon, the second in the group, is about a cricket who returns home after a stroll. He spends the rest of the day between tidying up his home and taking short naps after consulting his tiny watch. Then he locks the door of his home and listens. Outside all is quiet. He descends to the bottom of the earth.

The third song, *Le Cygne*, is the swan who floats on the water and watches the reflection of the clouds in the pond. He dives after them, trying to catch them with his beak. He would die of starvation if he did not catch a worm at each dive. He grows as fat as a goose.

Le Martin-pêcheur, the kingfisher, is a little poem about a fisherman who does not catch anything, because he does not want to disturb the bird who lands on his fishing rod. "They did not bite tonight, but I am carrying away a rare emotion."

La Pintade is a poem about a guinea hen who is mean; she imagines that everyone is laughing at her—at her size, at her bald head and her low tail. Her shrill cries stab the air like a barb.

Ravel succeeded in portraying these delicate little scenes realistically, giving the full weight of his interpretation to the vocal part rather than to the music which accompanied it. (Incidentally, those who knew Ravel personally could recognize Ravel's own way of speaking in the peculiarities of cadence of the phrases.)

Such were the subjects and the interpretation of Ravel's *Histoires naturelles*. But, on that first night of the performance, not many in the audience were calm enough to quote from *Le Martin-pêcheur:* "They did not bite tonight, but I am carrying away a rare emotion." The concert hall was a raging tempest. Screams of bravo and demands for the repetition of the songs accompanied a score of enthusiasts who in their demonstrative way invaded the stage to congratulate the performers, while frantic cries of "throw them out of the house" were heard above the general din in the hall.

"There has been no other such frenzied success in the annals of the old National Society of Music," Louis Laloy reported, but in the eyes of most of those in the audience and those who heard about it, it was a regular scandal, a *lèse-majesté* crime.

"How could this young musician," they cried, "who is not particularly popular anyway, but who is accepted as a serious man although not especially interesting, how could this man of good manners and presumably of good society," they demanded, "allow himself such an intolerable effrontery, which shows a complete lack of respect for music itself? How could he dare to use the art of Beethoven and Mozart for a display of such impishness?" The newspapers readily took up the discussion.

There is another *affaire Ravel* [Gaston Garraud announced on February 5, 1907, in *La Liberté*]. After having been generally acclaimed, now in the past two weeks his name has been unanimously dragged through the mud, because he presented a bit of tomfoolery out of the zoological garden at the National Society of Music. Let me say this, please: this is idiotic—French art is in no danger on account of it. The Érard Concert Hall is not a sacred temple. Oh, gentlemen, I beg you, let us not be like the geese who saved the Capitol! . . .

Nevertheless, in the immediately following lines of his article Gaston Garraud did not fail to express his views on Ravel's *Une Barque sur l'Océan* which had been given its first orchestral performance by Gabriel Pierné on February 3, 1907, at the Concert Colonne, two nights previous to the publication of this review.

I recognize that *Une Barque sur l 'Océan* is a rather disconcerting composition. . . . It seems that the idea is entirely concentrated in the sounds [Garraud said]. It is like a series of brush strokes of color applied over a design which has hardly been sketched. But these colors often have richness, vitality, and astonishing validity; these sonorities evoke, with force and remarkable precision, I would not say impressions, but visions. It is a pity that these visions change all the time; this is not a picture, but rather a bewildering kaleidoscope; one does not even know what sort of weather there is on this ocean—which lacks a bit of grandeur.

There was a real quarrel in the French musical family and the subject of the dispute ceased to be only *Histoires naturelles*, it encompassed all of Ravel's works as well as the general public's attitude toward new music. They reviewed and argued and reargued Ravel's whole musical career, as well as the general development of French music in the past thirty years. One could see them heatedly discussing *l'affaire*

Ravel all over Paris, from Montmartre to Montparnasse, and from Arcueil, the seat of Erik Satie, to Rue de Civry, the "home" of the Apaches, these groups of young men, musicians, painters, sculptors, and music lovers, gathered around tables in cafés sipping their *apéritifs* or cordials after dinner.

Those who professed to be Debussy's great admirers played on his sensitive and suspicious nature and succeeded in estranging him from many friends. To please him they were "against" other composers, with Ravel as the first in line—all of which only fostered prejudice against Debussy. It is reported that when an old friend said to him, "Listen, Claude, these Debussyites annoy me," Debussy replied, "Annoy you? They are killing me!"

(Perhaps I should say here that, never too close, the relationship between the two composers finally deteriorated when Debussy discovered that Ravel had joined Breval and Misia Edwards in providing financial assistance to Debussy's first wife. Misia Edwards no doubt carried the major part of the support, but Debussy never forgave any of them.)

The Ravelites jeered at their opponents:

Oh, the eternal wrath of the so-called Doctors of the Temple against the delightfully spontaneous spirit which, born in the minds of the cultured, safeguarded through the ages the existence of this one of the most endearing expressions of our nation! . . . Oh, musicologists, crouching behind dusty texts, who in each generation attempt in the name of indigestible rubbish to stifle the constant surging of life, oh, all these decrepit guardians of the great traditions and the great principles, who cover their faces in shame but whose hair is standing on end! . . .

In their rare more sober moments the Ravelites admitted that they displayed an exaggerated ardor in defending *Histoires naturelles*, but they felt that this should be excused because of their exasperation with those others who claimed a monopoly over everything "serious." Nonetheless, they argued, whether one did or did not like this kind of wit, there was in these compositions enough originality and skill to save them from ridicule and disparagement. And to those musicians who declared with contempt that Ravel's work should be considered as a mere inconsequential joke, they pointed out that this kind of joke was not the product of an ordinary intellect, that it demanded a sure and precise hand and that it should be rather admired than scoffed at.

After more than a quarter of a century an "unthinking" layman may still confuse Ravel's works with those of Debussy, but at the beginning of his career Ravel had to travel a steep and twisting road before the coexistence of the two original talents was formally recognized and accepted.

The controversy reached its climax when a month later, on March 19, Pierre Lalo took up the subject in his Sunday column in *Le Temps* and aired more than one thought, which he had had on his mind for some time.

> We have heard in the past season several new works by Maurice Ravel [Lalo wrote]. I have kept you informed about this young musician, one of the most representative of his generation, just as much on account of the strange mixture of his qualities and faults, as because of the unnecessary and dangerous noise made by his indiscreet friends; he would do better to have wise enemies.
>
> The pieces which he presented for the first time offer us

an occasion to consider the case of Ravel in particular, as well as another question of a general nature, which is not without interest for the present as well as the future of French music: I mean the question of "Debussysm."

At the National Society of Music, Ravel offered five songs on a text of Jules Renard's *Histoires naturelles: Le Paon, Le Grillon, Le Cygne, Le Martin-pêcheur,* and *La Pintade.* To set to music *Histoires naturelles* is an astonishing idea in itself. There are few subjects that are more foreign to music than these little pieces of precious and dry prose, these figures of animals which are laboriously constructed as if they were made of wood. But M. Ravel does not feel this way about it. He saw lyricism in Jules Renard's *La Pintade* and *Le Paon.* It seems to me that this subtle musician has never been more mistaken.

I admit, of course, that he succeeded in finding music which suits the text of his choice: music which is also as laborious and precious and dry, and also almost as lacking in real music—a collection of industrious rarities and a succession of reversed and complicated chords. This composition seems to have presented no end of difficulties: a sort of dance on a tightrope with a "sarcastic smile," to quote the author of *Histoires naturelles.* M. Ravel's compositions have the same little air of self-satisfaction as Jules Renard's prose. And when these two meet, when M. Ravel finds in the text a particularly significant point or word, the piano stops, the complicated harmonies keep quiet, the voice alone launches the idea. Then, the piano takes over again and a succession of chords twists around all over again. This makes one think of a music hall, a music hall with a ninth chord. I would be tempted to prefer the music hall as it is.

Benevolent judges, it is true, thought that one should not attach any importance to such little products and that one should not see anything except entertainment in them. It is difficult to argue with their opinion, first of all because of the indiscreet friends, of whom I spoke above, who desired to make an important event out of the appearance of *Paon*, *Grillon* and *Pintade*, and then, of course, because the character of these songs presumes that they should not be taken for anything but an unpretentious amusement.

However, they lack good-naturedness, abandon, and simplicity; they have an icy seriousness, a stiff pedantism which never loosens up. M. Ravel remains grave with the barnyard animals; he does not laugh, he is lecturing on *Paon*, on *Pintade*. One has to speak seriously about serious music.

M. Ravel also offered a piece called *Une Barque sur l'Océan*, originally written for piano and now orchestrated. But the orchestra does not add anything to this piece. The orchestra is a very capable one and is accustomed to instrumental effects and to piquant combinations in tone coloring. Ravel's composition, one would say, is a series of examples for a study in orchestration, examples of all kinds which show how to alter the original sound of an instrument. For in Ravel's music no instrument has its natural sound: he does not know any other trumpets than muted trumpets. And with all this he does not evoke anything, he does not create a sensation of nature. There is no barque, no ocean; there are only the notes, the instruments; there is not a moment of the sea. But at least this composition is a musical one and I can not say as much about *Histoires naturelles*.

Had Pierre Lalo contented himself with these criticisms at that time, which by then not only did not surprise anyone, but rather were expected from him, the Ravel matter would have rested right then and there, as had happened many times in the past. But this time Lalo went further, and, by bringing Debussy's name into the discussion, he started a fight to the finish, at least he must have thought so, on the whole question of Ravel and "Debussysm."

In each of these pieces one hears without end a special echo of Debussy's music. You know well, that Ravel is not the only one. It is an incontestable fact that a great majority of the young French composers write "Debussyst" music.

The theoreticians have been carefully considering this work and now they have come up with a thesis which was put forth this year for the first time and which was greeted with alacrity by all the composers whose music resembles that of M. Debussy and by that part of the public which thinks of itself as most refined [Pierre Lalo wrote in the same article]. It is, and I would like to warn you, the elegant opinion which should be held at the present time about "Debussysm." This opinion can be summarized as follows: "M. Debussy was the most eloquent speaker for a whole generation of musicians who, nourishing the same intentions as he, have been writing for a long time in silence and obscurity his most successful discoveries."

In other words, M. Debussy did not invent anything. Whatever he discovered, a crowd of others discovered at the same time as he did; he only was fortunate to be the first to publish the discoveries which belong to all. The young French musicians do not owe a thing to him. Between them and him there is no question of influence, or imitation, but that of coincidence and of a natural similarity. It is an error and pure injustice to maintain that they resemble M. Debussy; one could just as well say that Debussy resembles them. . . . .

It would be not entirely wasteful to pause and consider this new theory. No doubt, most musicians who belong to this group are at the beginning of their careers and their reputation does not transcend the narrow limits of their own little coterie. But they represent the future, and it is they who will make the music of tomorrow in France.

One must tell them at once: their theory does not seem to me to be anything but an impudent mockery; it cannot be

justified either by the dates of the works or by the character
of the compositions: neither by history nor by aesthetic
values.

Let us take history first. Debussy's first works are already
twenty years old. *La Damoiselle élue* and *The Spring* are of
1888, *Les Ariettes* of 1889, *Baudelaire's Five Poems* of 1890,
L'Après-midi d'un faune of 1892, *Les Proses lyriques* of
1893, and at this time *Pelléas et Mélisande* was already begun.
From that time on, that is, more than fifteen years ago,
Debussy's personality was completely formed. Where was
the generation of the young musicians then, who today pre-
tend that they owe nothing to him, and that they invented
at the same time as he did the art which is in error attributed
to him? In what languages, in which cradle did their inspiration then slumber? In what languages, in which cradle did
they themselves take their rest?

M. Ravel, the senior of all of them, has hardly reached
the age of thirty. In these fifteen years, what did he produce? What have his rivals and their successors produced
that could give them even a shadow of some kind of reason
to claim a part in the foundation of the art which they now
practise and to dispute the right of Debussy to his glory as
its creator?

On one detail, a small one, an utterly insignificant acces-
sory detail, a small doubt is permitted. It is not entirely impossible that certain of Maurice Ravel's compositions, published five or six years ago, offer the first example of a special
technique in the art of writing for the piano and of a new
virtuosity. But this business of virtuosity and the mechanism
of writing touches but indirectly the music; it has no more
interest than any organ point in a concerto; it is something
similar to the "rain of pearls" which enchanted our grand-
mothers, only a little more complicated; instead of falling
directly, the "rain of pearls" crisscrosses itself and falls in

all directions, but it never amounts to anything except a "rain of pearls."

For all that is essential in art M. Debussy created his own. The others came ten years after him and all they had to do was to make an effort to read his works; it is true they have killed them in their zeal. This is a bit of mockery at the world to wish to pass Debussysm as a collective phenomenon, where M. Debussy has no more place than anyone else: the dates are there.

As for the character of the music, the presumption of these young people is no better founded than when the question was put to the test of history. All that is precious and admirable in Debussy's art, all that makes his a profound originality—is a new sensitivity, a sensitivity marvelously intense and delicate, a sensitivity toward Nature, which lets him evoke the soul of things without any descriptive anxiety; in *L'Après-midi d'un faune* the ardent joy of the day, in *Nuages* the light silence of the night, the movement and the shadows of the clouds which pass over the moon; in *Pelléas et Mélisande*—be it the melancholy and the bliss scattered in the air of the setting sun and the beauty of the evening sparkling in the streams, or be it the hollow beating of the waves in the darkness, the quivering, the trembling of the wind and the water, the mystery of the night and the sea; the sensitivity to people's actions and emotions; remember that penetrating emotion, that profound humanity which forms the beauty of the final scene in *Pelléas*.

What is there in common between this art, which flowed from the very source of poetic sentiment, and the art of the diligent little composers who claim this art as their own? They do not feel nature in the least: in none of their works have they succeeded in evoking nature. They have no human feeling. They have never expressed an emotion or passion of a human soul. They do nothing but write notes, combinations of chords, and the tone coloring of different instruments; they have in common with Debussy only the technique of composing. And this technique they have borrowed directly from him.

It is possible that they might have been endowed with the same sensitivity as Debussy, and that in fact there was one way of feeling for a whole epoch; but it is impossible, it is absurd, to suppose that a whole generation of composers should have rediscovered in themselves, should have spontaneously re-created a technique invented exactly fifteen years ago by a musician they all know exceedingly well. One must remind them once again: the dates are there.

These young people, by the way, do more than just claim a part in M. Debussy's art. They have recently begun to push M. Debussy out of "Debussysm," they have begun to isolate him, even to discard him altogether, to point out to him that his part in it is finished, that he has, hereafter, nothing to do with this business, since he never did have much to do with it of any importance. "The house belongs to us and it is up to you to leave." They let him know that his own "Debussysm" is today a bit primitive, that he has been by-passed, that now everybody is "doing Debussy" better than Debussy himself.

This is terribly funny, one can not go much further in the grotesque than these youngsters do, these conceited, pompous simpletons, industrious copyists of the only exceptional, original and spontaneous musician among them, these composers of little songs and melodies, of little pieces for piano, of little pieces for orchestra, painfully, laboriously, and industriously harmonized or orchestrated, which they dare to put next to *Pelléas et Mélisande*, like placing next to a magnificent palace a dainty reproduction made of spun sugar.

The trouble is that by their debasement of M. Debussy's ways of composing they make them little by little tedious and hackneyed. His special style of composition is not the best part of Debussy's art. He has created it, it is the expression of his sensitivity and to be marveled at. But in itself it is extremely restrained and limited and it would not be hard to learn. Utilized unsparingly and without mercy by the composers for whom it is not a natural medium but a language which they have acquired, it soon becomes monotonous; one gets tired of it and this regrettable impression of boredom and monotony which is due to the imitations may prejudice one against the original.

It seems to me that only a few years ago, when speaking of the first works of the counterfeit "Debussyites," I pointed to the dangers for M. Debussy himself. The results already have proven that I was right. I hope that I will not be even more right in the future. I hope that the vulgarization and exploitation of "Debussysm" by clever and mediocre composers will not make too ephemeral the future of a delightful art and will not turn us away from loving the exquisite music of an exquisite musician as his work merits.

Pierre Lalo's article had the effect of a bomb shell. If for years his criticisms were read as a point of view or impressions of merely another music critic, even though of an authority with powerful influence, this latest exposé was a verdict which "the insulted and injured" could not accept without protest. But, while they were sharpening their wits for a counterblow, Ravel himself stepped into the fighting ring.

"We owe truth to the dead." So goes the French proverb. Yet the French proved to be rather poor creditors in Ravel's case. For some strange reason they have concealed more than one piece of information concerning his life and in the record of his reaction to the development of his career. The biographers and music critics, who have written more than half a dozen books and innumerable articles about him, have stuck to a rather sentimental but banal picture of an artist who never took any part in the controversies aroused by his works and who remained aloof in his working room creating the next masterpiece.

Nothing can be further from the truth. Ravel was very sensitive to both criticism and praise and, as to his behavior on his own behalf whenever the occasion permitted, the facts repudiate any arguments. During the Prix de Rome affair, at first with his comrade contestants he signed the protest against the jury's decision, which, it is true, he retrieved later on. At that time Ravel tried to see the Minister of Public Education to present his personal protest, only to be advised against it, but he did succeed in making a public statement through an interview in *Le Temps*, calling on public opinion to judge his case.

Ravel was also quick to react to reviews of his works, and showed his gratitude for favorable criticism in a letter to the critic—rather an unusual procedure. "It is not because of the eulogies (and yet, I must admit, partly on account of them), but above all because you have better (than others) understood my intentions," Ravel wrote on February 7, 1906, to Jean Marnold. "Oh my word—'delicate, refined, quintessential.' I did not think I could be so mistaken about myself. You have seen other things in my last compositions and it is for this that I am grateful to you."

Now Ravel lost no time (either on his own or ill advised —this is another question) to call Pierre Lalo to account.

Monsieur le Directeur [Ravel wrote to the editor of *Le Temps* on April 9, 1907], an article published in *Le Temps* of March 19 has been brought to my attention, an article which very much concerns me. M. Pierre Lalo, with the consummate competence for which he is known, takes pain, once again, to show that I completely lack personality of my own. But what is far more grave is that he attributes to "certain musicians" peculiar remarks about an artist of genius, Claude Debussy.

Following his custom, M. Lalo does not give the names of the "young musicians" whom he rather frivolously accuses. But since my name is mentioned rather often in the article, a regrettable misunderstanding might occur, and readers who are not forewarned could easily think that he meant me. A little more clarity is necessary. I would not like to accuse M. Lalo of prevarication without good grounds, or to challenge him to produce at least one witness who had heard me utter such absurdities.

I do not care if I am taken for an arrogant plagiarist by those who know my work only through the reviews. But it does not suit me to pass for an imbecile even with those people.

It is to your courtesy, Monsieur le Directeur, that I appeal in asking you to publish this letter in *Le Temps* in the same place and in the same way as M. Lalo's article.

Please receive . . .   Maurice Ravel.

Ravel must have forgotten that a year before, he had written to Calvocoressi asking his advice about the "two missives intended for Pierre Lalo" which he included: one just a postcard, the other a letter. "In the letter I appeal," Ravel explained to his friend, "not to a critic's judgment, as you can see, but as politely as possible to his good faith. Post the one, throw the other into the waste-paper basket. I leave it entirely to you."

In vain Calvocoressi, a journalist and a music critic

himself, argued against this move, pointing out that "as a rule, critics are adept in the art of twisting their contradictors' utterances and appearing always to be in the right." Ravel had made up his mind and the letter was sent.

Now, over twelve months after the receipt of the letter Lalo made use of it.

M. Maurice Ravel has no right whatsoever to have his letter published [Pierre Lalo wrote in *Le Temps* a week later, on April 16, 1907].

He declares it himself: I have nowhere attributed to him the opinions which today he disavows with such uproar. He maintains that a "regrettable confusion" could occur; this is a personal judgment and an arbitrary fear which does not authorize him to demand the publication of an answer. Thus, if I did reproduce his letter, it is because I like it so much.

M. Ravel defends himself without having been accused. He proclaims that he does not belong to the group of musicians whose "peculiar remarks" I have quoted. But these remarks are not remarks thrown into the air, the echoes of conversations or gossip, and M. Ravel is wrong to think that I was speaking frivolously.

I did not want to make a case out of this, although it would be natural, because of the authenticity of my quotations from articles published in the newspapers and musical magazines. M. Ravel must know them better than I, because in them he is referred to as a *"Maître"* and is given (in these articles) a glory radiating over future generations. But he is not the author of these articles. To my knowledge he has never written an article about music. Therefore it was not he of whom I wished to speak.

But M. Ravel wishes to be spoken about: I acquiesce.

I have reproached a group of young musicians whose music has a great resemblance to that of Debussy for maintaining that they do not owe anything to the author of *Pelléas et Mélisande*, and for insisting that between him and them there is no case of imitation, but only of coincidence, and for claiming from him their right of originality.

M. Ravel defends himself as never having said anything of the kind and challenges me to prove that he ever "uttered such absurdities." M. Ravel has not often written to me. But I quote a few lines from a letter which he addressed to me on February 5, 1906.

"I would like to call your impartial attention to the following point. You expatiate at some length upon a certain type of writing for the piano, whose invention you ascribe to Debussy. But the *Jeux d'eau* appeared at the beginning of 1902, at a time when there were only 'Three pieces for piano' composed by Debussy, for which, I do not need to tell you, I have a passionate admiration, but works which from a purely pianistic point of view did not bring anything new. I hope you will excuse this legitimate claim."

M. Ravel has not often spoken to me. But some time after he had sent this letter to me, I met him by chance and he himself explained how the relationship of his music and that of Debussy was not the result of an influence, but of an inborn similarity. It is M. Ravel who is a little too frivolous in his challenge.

M. Ravel expresses himself with a singular vehemence against the presumptuous Debussyites according to whom Debussy did not invent anything. The words "absurdities" and "imbecile" are his. These are severe qualifications. I did not use them in the article which aroused M. Ravel. But I do not contradict them in the least.

But Ravel was not going to let Lalo have the last word. Six years later, in February, 1913, in an article in *Cahiers d'aujourd'hui*, he denounced Lalo, saying that his sole aim was to oppose new tendencies in music, and accused him of "sowing seeds of dissension among young composers." And twenty years later, in an interview published in *Les Nouvelles Littéraires* in April, 1927, Ravel repeated once again that, "It is not the first time that M. Lalo assumes the posture of the saviour of music.[1] Let us hope that once again he will fail to save it. His methods are as stereotyped as his aesthetics. He tried to crush Debussy under Wagner, then me under Debussy, and now he is trying to crush that charming composer Marcel Delannoy under poor me."

One might be so "frivolous" as to presume that these two Frenchmen did not like each other. If these two principal characters in this musical play could indulge in such spirited argument in print, one can easily imagine the general temperature of the atmosphere in the *affaire Ravel*. Out of a medley of personal accusations, heavily argumentative technical reviews and articles filled with "oh's" and "ah's," one was asked to decide whether Ravel was a great musician or a little one, a successor to Debussy or one of his pale imitators. There were some who advised waiting for a final judgment, saying that Ravel had not written enough, while others declared that his was the art of tomorrow, that his work, like that of Schumann, was the beginning of a new music for the piano.

It was agreed that Debussy had a certain influence on Ravel: some saw it in his *Quartet*, others in his *Miroirs*. But examining his works up to this time, the *Pavane, Jeux d'eau, Quartet, Sonatine, Miroirs*, and *Histoires naturelles*, can

---

[1] Ravel was referring to Lalo's attacks against young composers, particularly Honegger, Milhaud, and Delannoy.

one not decide whether Ravel did or did not show personality of his own?

The amateurs, comparing Debussy and Ravel, spoke in vague terms, attributing to Ravel the "attempts" at presenting pictures rather than emotional states, "attempts" at caricatures and miniatures in his songs, rather than tending toward the erotic, as in the case of Debussy. And, while they described Debussy as a sensualist who expressed his own voluptuous nature in his music, and pointed to Ravel's cold intellectuality in interpreting only his "perception of things," the four most able music critics—Jean Aubry, Jean Marnold, Louis Laloy, and Dmitri Calvocoressi—wrote articles based on more solid theoretical grounds.

Dmitri Calvocoressi for one, "really took up the cudgels," as he said himself, writing for the *Grande Revue* an article entitled "Maurice Ravel et l'imitation Debussyite." He said that he deliberately had chosen this ambiguous title so as to lure his opponents into reading it in the hope of finding in it a confirmation of their assertions. "I did my best," Calvocoressi said, "by comparing idiosyncrasies of style, idiom, texture, and structure to show that the allegation was utterly unfounded."

But of far more importance and fraught with far more significance was Léon Vallas' (the author of the well-known biography of Debussy) invitation to Jean Marnold to express his views on the *affaire Ravel* to be published in the *Revue musicale de Lyon* of which Vallas was then the director. Jean Marnold at that time enjoyed the reputation of a specialist in the science of musical theories and was active both as music critic of the magazine *Mercure de*

France and as the founder and the editor of *Mercure musicale*. The invitation, coming at such crucial moment from a man like Vallas who was a stanch Debussyite, certainly was a challenge.

Under the title *L'Affaire Ravel. L'Opinion de Monsieur Jean Marnold* his response was published on May 1, 1907, in a form of a letter addressed to Léon Vallas.

Dear Monsieur Vallas—

Since you honor me by calling upon me in connection with what you refer to as the *affaire Ravel* and place me among his admirers, allow me to profit by this occasion by making a few observations.

With regard to the so-called *affaire,* I must confess that I do not understand much about it. Prompted by a composition which may be debated, the *affaire* has suddenly turned into a discussion of "Debussysm," which seems to be much confused if not utterly useless.

The question of "Debussysm" is a complex one and interesting to elucidate from the purely musical point of view, the only one appropriate to the subject, in my humble opinion.

Nothing could be more childish than the way it recently has been presented in many instances in the musical press. It is just as absurd to maintain that Debussy *invented* nothing, as to imagine that he *invented* all the harmonic material which he uses and in which lie the most important and most marvelous characteristics of his art.

Thus, for instance, innocent journalists recently have lamented the death of "M. Curie, the famous inventor of radium." One does not invent a chord any more than one does a color, shade, or tint, otherwise one would commit an impudence of the imagination, both arbitrary and sterile. Just as in the case of radium, all this pre-exists in nature and must be felt, contemplated, or discovered. The harmony emanates from the *sound*, an objective phenomenon, deciphered bit by bit, and dissected by our critical faculties into its original elements. And this natural harmony has regimented the whole evaluation of our music according to the physical laws of acoustics. It is this logical imperturbable evolution which is splendidly pursued in Claude Debussy's compositions and which gives beauty to his prolific work.

Actually, the so-called present "Debussysm" is only a phase of the eternal process between the consonance and dissonance. Therefore, one who would consider intervals of a fourth or sixth as consonant intervals, or who would introduce the interval of a third in a final chord, is already in his own way "doing Debussysm." Does this mean that one is imitating Debussy or is doing as he does? Can one be accused of having plagiarized his "technique"?

There is a similar naïveté in reproaching our young musicians in making use of "Debussyite" harmony. At all times artists have legitimately exploited the harmonic resources which they owed to a predecessor's genius, whether far or near. But, on the other hand, our musicians have the best reason to practice "Debussyite" harmony, that is, without simply copying it. They could not make use of any other kind and they should make use of this particular one.

Harmonic evolution, as a matter of fact, is strictly *determined* by the nature of the phenomenon of sound. From the time of the origin of our music this evolution has followed a progressive march from the most simple to the more and more complex, while the gradual familiarization of our senses with the correspondence of different intervals—at first known as dissonance, and later accepted as consonance— has rigorously followed the order of the series of the constitutive harmonies of the musical sound.

Then the hour of "Debussyite" harmony was struck. It would have been impossible to put this in practice some hundred years ago. Today Debussy's claim is inevitable. Certainly, the glory belongs to Debussy for having penetrated the surrounding vibrations of the sound. Without his genius we may have had to wait much longer for the liberating revelation. It could have come much more slowly and imperfectly, for Debussy's gesture is without comparison, without precedent, no matter how far back we go in the history of sound. But was the author of *Pelléas* not born at a time when we were somehow "doing Debussy" without knowing it?

And it has always been that way. Masterpieces are factors, unconscious as well as conscious, in the evolution of music. Exploring this evolution one will find that in each epoch the material of the art work is always different, but is determined by the harmonic development of the preceding one and is common to all contemporaries, and what is interesting to note, that the more one withdraws from the present, the more the originality of the creator pales. Have you observed how hard it is to discern distinctly the diverse personalities among the Gallo-Belgian contrapuntists or the masters of Palestrinian polyphony before they acquired the familiarization which eventually becomes their "culture"? Similarly, people who lack this musical culture do not know the least difference between the illustrious heroes of the classical period, for to their uninformed ears Haydn, Mozart, or Beethoven—"it is all the same thing."

It is very likely that the lack of familiarization of this kind may currently lead some to a confusion of Debussy and Ravel and none can boast of having escaped this initial impression. Thus it would be appropriate to be on one's guard against hasty and bold judgments.

One can not prevent the future generation from using its own language, different from that of yesterday, and from speaking spontaneously after having received the secret of a man, a man of genius, to tell the truth. After Hugo's "Alexandrine," to go back to Corneille or Racine would be an artificial fabrication. Our poets have followed their instinct and continued in the Hugo style, thus spontaneously achieving the evolution of our poetry.

It was in this sense that I wrote in July of 1904 in the *Mercure de France*. One need not fear to appear as an imitator of Debussy. Without copying him, one should follow him. Claude Debussy's art does not consist solely in his harmony; it also lies in his particular way of using it, which belongs only to him, it is made of something that only he could "create" and from which the radiant beauty disdains time and imitators.

Debussy's genius put a period in the middle of the evolution of music and turned a new page. There is already music "before Debussy" and music "after Debussy." The first is that of the past, based on more or less arbitrary theories; the second, on the other hand, is of the future, because it originates from unknown or ignored virtues, but essential nevertheless and inevitable as the laws of nature. Tomorrow's sensibility will not hear any other language spontaneously. One should follow Debussy. For those who succeed only in imitating him, the misfortune is not great; they would have imitated another, they would always have imitated someone or something.

I apologize for quoting myself, but I am doing this only for the record. I wrote this on the subject of one of Ravel's new works—his *Quartet* which, then unpublished, induced me to say; "One should remember the name of Maurice Ravel. He is one of the Masters of tomorrow." And, since there is an *affaire Ravel*, I would like today to add something else.

When I praised the *Quartet* and the *Miroirs* I had only heard the music. Since then these works have been published and I, like anyone else, have had the opportunity to study them more closely and my conscientious admiration has become even more sure. Yes, the composer of *Miroirs* is someone, and if his harmonies appear undeniably "Debussyite" by coincidence or by their origin—it could not be otherwise, because one does not choose one's own year of birth—his personality is nevertheless integral. He differs from Debussy as Mozart from Chevalier Gluck, Beethoven from Mozart, Wagner from Weber, or César Franck from Liszt. Thus, if the word "genius" has a meaning, surely Maurice Ravel is a musician of genius. I am grateful to you for giving me the opportunity to announce this as of this spring in 1907—just for the record. It is very pleasant, later on, to be able to prove with proper documentation that one was not an imbecile.

Please believe me, dear M. Vallas, your very cordially devoted Jean Marnold.

Chapter Seven

L'Heure espagnole.
Gaspard de la Nuit

THE CONCLUSION of Jean Marnold's article was rather sudden and surprising, although certainly to the point, and Léon Vallas did not fail to show his astonishment in the few paragraphs which he wrote in answer to Marnold's article. After paying tribute to Marnold as a music critic, Léon Vallas, despite his personal bewilderment by Marnold's unexpected resolution, nevertheless expressed his sincere hope that this prophecy (even if a bit exaggerated) coming from such an authority as Marnold, would draw attention to the wrong attitude toward Ravel and would induce others to share Marnold's opinion.

This concession on the part of Vallas was important, for it was the first sign of Ravel's winning to his side a critic from the arch-Debussyite camp. It added weight to Marnold's flat declaration of Ravel's genius. Thus, at last, at the age of thirty-two Ravel reached the goal of recognition. At last his name was spoken with the same respect in the salons which he visited as had previously been accorded the names of Debussy, Fauré, d'Indy, and other well-known and admired composers. And the frequent quotation of the closing sentence in Marnold's article, ". . . if the word 'genius' has a meaning, surely M. Ravel is a musician of genius. . . . It is very pleasant, later on, to be able to prove with proper documentation that one was not an imbecile," fell pleasantly on his ear.

Yet as far as Ravel was concerned, at this time such recognition was not quite sufficient because of the attitude of his father, who was old and ill and who belonged to that generation of Frenchmen which saw the proof of a musician's success only in a theatrical production.

Ravel worked for a time on Gerhardt Hauptmann's *The Sunken Bell,* and then toyed with the idea of adapting Maeterlinck's *Intérieur.* But in the month of May he suddenly began to work feverishly, as though racing against time, on Franc-Nohain's *L'Heure espagnole,* a one-act play which had had more than one hundred performances since the opening night on October 28, 1904, at the Odeon Théâtre.

Ravel obviously was attracted by the farcical plot of the play, laid in Boccaccio fashion in Señor Torquemada's clockmaker shop in eighteenth-century Toledo. The comedy, based on elementary psychology, held the public's interest entirely through the spirited sequence of situation and dialogue.

While Señor Torquemada is out examining the government clocks, his pretty wife Concepcion receives, in close succession, visits from her two lovers. Not knowing how best to conduct the traffic, she hides the men in the old-fashioned clocks and thus creates a sort of Charlie Chaplin situation with an innocent muleteer (who happens to come into the store to have his watch repaired) as her blind accomplice. He carries the clocks back and forth between her bedroom and the clockshop without realizing why his burden is so heavy. Finally Concepcion gives her preference to the muleteer because his calm, sure ways and his strong biceps attract her more than Gonzalve's poems and Inigo's "lack of romance and decision." She orders the muleteer to leave both clocks containing the lovers in the clockshop and go up to her bedroom.

When Señor Torquemada returns and finds his wife's two former lovers in the shop, he sells them the timepieces at an exorbitant price. The play ends with a chorus of all the characters singing together "Boccaccio's moral."

> Among lovers the one who is efficient succeeds.
> In the pursuit of love there arrives a moment
> When a muleteer has his turn!

Considering that this was Ravel's first dramatic work, and first score for a full-size orchestra as well, he completed the task in a rather short time. In September he called on Franc-Nohain and gave him as adequate a preview of it as he could. He sang all the parts in his own "composer's voice" and accompanied himself on the piano, hoping that Franc-Nohain would supply the rest from his musical imagination. Unfortunately the author lacked this capacity. After

Ravel played the last chord of his composition, the old play-wright looked at his watch and said, "Fifty-six minutes." This was his only comment.

Not in the least discouraged, Ravel offered his work to Albert Carré, the director of L'Opéra-Comique. But the performance was postponed for four years, from one season to the next, because Carré was afraid of the libretto. It seemed to him too risqué, too full of double meaning, at times bordering on the pornographic.

However, the fate of Ravel's *L'Heure espagnole* was decided by Mme Jean Cruppi who is reported to have been an excellent musician, a woman of influence to whom Ravel dedicated this work. When her husband became a minister in the French government she intervened personally with the directors of L'Opéra-Comique and at last The Spanish Hour struck on May 19, 1911.

The public again was divided in its opinion. The Ravel-ites, of course, applauded *L'Heure espagnole* as charming and witty and, while admitting that it did not mark a date in the history of French music, as was the case with De-bussy's *Pelléas*, nevertheless, they thought it an amusing work, conceived in a profoundly French spirit by a musician of extremely marked individuality, which therefore merited more attention than some heavy symphonies or some too-well-written quartets. But Pierre Lalo was still after Ravel.

He said that Ravel's humor was dry, *précieuse* and bit-ter, that his little superior air chased away all the gaiety and destroyed all the animation in the play, that his characters were like automatons, mechanical dolls who go through the gestures, speak or sing, come or go, but never leave an im-

pression of spontaneity or give an idea of being alive. Lalo
felt that while the orchestral part of the composition was
the best, charming, and full of subtle coloring, it reminded
him of that of Richard Strauss, only a Strauss who worked
in an infinitesimal medium. Lalo also said that some of it
somehow reminded him of Wagner: he even traced some
passages to those in The Ring but, and this apparently was
what he wanted to say above all, that Ravel owed his harmonic substance and technique to Debussy, except for the
soul of the music which, as he said, "was absolutely different: Debussy—all sensitiveness, Ravel—all insensitiveness."

Yet, in closing his review Lalo made one concession.
He said: "In *L'Heure espagnole* and in the pieces from
L'Histoires naturelles where all sentiment is absent, Ravel's
own, peculiar nature, subtle and ingenious, comes forth and
his insensitiveness gives him a personality. This personality
may please or not. But it is there."

This was not the kindest way Ravel's arch-opponent
could have put it, but probably it was the best Lalo could
do, considering that in the four years since *l'affaire Ravel*,
Ravel's stock of compositions had been enriched by such
works as *Ma Mère l'Oye, Rapsodie espagnole, Gaspard de
la Nuit,* and *Daphnis et Chloë.* Ravel in 1911 was not the
Ravel of 1907, but Pierre Lalo remained the same Pierre
Lalo.

L'Heure espagnole survived the criticisms, and although
it was not produced again in France until 1945, it made a
successful trip around the Western world: fifty cities including New York, Chicago, Brussels, London, Vienna,
Berlin, Prague, and Buenos Aires applauded this musical

comedy. But Ravel's father, to whom the success of his son was dedicated, did not live to hear it. Joseph Ravel, stricken with general paralysis, died in Levallois on October 13, 1908.

Ravel is quoted to have said that his *Histoires naturelles* prepared him for the writing of *L'Heure espagnole*. By the same token *L'Heure espagnole* prepared him for his *Rapsodie espagnole*, his first entirely orchestral composition. He either was working on it at the same time as on *L'Heure espagnole* or wrote it immediately afterward, for it was ready for performance at the beginning of the following year, 1908.

Since there are no reliable dates available for this composition, it is also possible that he worked on it in August, when, to escape the summer heat in Levallois, he installed himself on the Edwards' yacht, *Aimée*, which was moored at Valvins. There, presumably, undisturbed except by the sea adventures related by the old captain with whom he shared his lodgings, Ravel wrote the *Rapsodie espagnole* in thirty days.

Was the unusual speed with which Ravel completed this work influenced by the fact that Debussy was at that time in the midst of composing his *Ibéria*, which he started in 1906 but did not finish until 1908? As Ravel no doubt was aware that his new composition, an important one (his first orchestral score) would be compared to Debussy's work, did he want to beat him to the punch? Who knows if he did not choose to include his *Habanera*, although orchestrated, because it brought afresh the memory of the incident with the *Habanera* manuscript which occurred in 1895 and which caused accusations of plagiarism by Debussy.

Ravel said on more than one occasion that he thought that Spanish music was one third Italian and the rest Moorish. This might explain why, in addition to the *Prélude à la nuit*, *Habanera*, and *Feria* he introduced in the *Rapsodie espagnole* the *Malagueña*, a dance of Arab origin.

On March 28, 1908, at one of the Colonne Concerts at the Châtelet Théâtre, Ravel's first orchestral composition made its début under the direction of the aging Edouard Colonne. As usual, those in the boxes and the orchestra seats remained luke-warm, while the enthusiasts in the galleries, with their cries of *Bis!*, called for the repetition of the *Malagueña*. For a moment the growing murmur of protest in the orchestra seats held the fate of the piece in the balance, when suddenly Florent Schmitt's imperious voice from the gallery: "Play it once more for those below who have not understood!" decided the success of the performance. Except for this there was no demonstration, no catcalls, no fire-spitting, and name-calling by the neighbors in the audience. It could have been regarded as Ravel's triumph. The newspapers also showed kindness toward Ravel, although the criticisms of the new work were still colored by the general attitude toward the unresolved dispute over Debussysm.

Jean Marnold, accepted after his declaration of Ravel's genius as Ravel's foremost champion, said in his article (*Mercure de France*, April 16, 1908) that the *Rapsodie espagnole* was a fairyland of new sounds but, some critics, on the other hand, pointed to the lack of form in the composition and its "vague outlines," and Pierre Lalo, with the persistence of Cato the Elder, condemned the composition as an example of shallowness and narrowness of mind.

Nevertheless *Rapsodie espagnole* has withstood the severest test—time. The composition can not be discarded as a mere product of youth. On the contrary, like other Ravel works, it is stamped with his distinct personality. Ravel's orchestra can be recognized by its specific sound, its brittle *forte* and transparent *pianissimos,* its dry texture and up-surging spirit. All these qualities were present already in his first orchestral composition. Nor is the *Rapsodie espagnole* inferior in workmanship—nothing was left either to chance or to the influence of the performer. Everything was carefully calculated, and while with the works of other composers, including Debussy, performances in the hands of different interpreters might create different impressions, Ravel's composition needs only to be played as indicated by the composer.

As for the sources of influence which might be discovered in the score of *Rapsodie espagnole,* the French music critics have been so long embroiled in the constant accusation and defense of Ravel *versus* Debussy, that they seem to have forgotten that in his youth Ravel was as enthusiastic an admirer of Rimsky-Korsakov, Borodin, and Mussorgsky as he was of Debussy, and that Debussy himself was not entirely free from the influence of the Russians.

Plagiarism, and "influence" even more, are elastic terms which have been applied and still are frequently used, particularly in musical criticism, with complete disregard for common sense. When Ravel said that he wanted to find a way to set French speech, with all its peculiarities, to music, he was only repeating what Modest Mussorgsky said some forty-five years previously about his intentions with regard to the Russian language, and Mussorgsky in his turn was only echoing the words of Alexander Dargomijsky when the latter began his opera *The Stone Guest*, which incidentally is considered as the prototype of Debussy's *Pelléas et Mélisande*. It is quite possible that Debussy saw a production of Dargomijsky's *The Stone Guest* in Moscow, and was well acquainted with the score, but it is equally probable that Ravel never heard of it.

It was not so much the influence of one composer on another or of the music of one country on the music of the other as a general trend against the old Italian operas, against the arias with interminable high Cs, against German influence, the Romantics, Wagner, that should have been taken into account. The rebellion in both countries, Russia and France, followed the same paths, even if half a century apart. It is not surprising to find evidence of Russian influence in Ravel's work, for he and the Apaches were the musicians best acquainted with the works of their Eastern colleagues. Actually Ravel was most influenced by Rimsky-Korsakov, though he felt himself to be more of an adherent of Mussorgsky—and there was a definite resemblance in personal traits between Mussorgsky and Ravel.

When Mussorgsky died, Ravel was only six years old, and even at the age of thirty-two Ravel could not have known much about Mussorgsky as a man, because it was only then that Calvocoressi began collecting material for his future book on Mussorgsky, and there was little information available even in Russia. Thus without stressing the point, one might find it interesting that both men, in regard to their art, were driven, as if possessed, to everything new, to progress—to quote Mussorgsky, "On to new shores! Fearless through storm, shallow water and reefs—on to new shores!" Both men were freethinkers, negated dogma and tradition. To both, artistic integrity was as their own flesh. Their personal lives remained an enigma to the rest of the world. Both composers preferred the company of men. With women their relationships remained those of adoring sons and devoted but platonic friends. Although, unlike Ravel, Mussorgsky was never suspected of homosexuality, both men remained adolescent in their emotional relationships. Ravel always spoke of seeking solitude, yet he was as much afraid of being alone as Mussorgsky, who in the latter part of his life was terrified of spending a night by himself. Both men were the most sociable "animals," to quote Mussorgsky again, both loved homes, family, and children, yet neither ever married. For both the houses of their close friends were like their own homes. "I always return, like a cat," Mussorgsky said. At first Ravel's second home was with the Apaches on the Rue de Civry, then the homes of the Edwards and Cipa Godebskis in Paris, and the Gaudins in St. Jean-de-Luz, and later there were many others.

The Godebskis spent their summers at *La Grangette* (the Little Barn) at Valvins, a house they inherited from Père Godebski, who had bought it to be near Mallarmé. For years it was Misia and Thadée Natansons' summer home where Toulouse-Lautrec used to come regularly on Saturdays to stay until Tuesday and where in the autumn Mallarmé joined them every day for dinner and stayed till late hours while Misia played Beethoven and Schubert for him.

Then, when *La Grangette* became too small for the large number of their friends, Misia and Thadée moved to Villeneuve to a house, a former country inn, on the banks of the river Yonne and they let Cipa use the old Little Barn for his family and their friends.

At that time one had to take a train to Fontainebleau and from there, either by carriage or on foot, cross the forest which separated *La Grangette* from the Fontainebleau station. Most of the Godebskis' friends preferred to walk. The new arrivals were usually met by their hosts or the other guests somewhere in the forest halfway along the road which led to the villa. The Apaches' rally call— the theme out of Borodin's Second Symphony—served as the signal of their whereabouts in the forest. It was at *La Grangette*, while visiting the Godebskis, that Ravel composed his enchanting children's suite *Ma Mère l'Oye*, which later, in 1912, he orchestrated and made into a ballet.

Whenever Mussorgsky visited a house where there were children, his arrival was a signal for endless games, singing and dancing and general carousing, so that the parents in despair felt like fleeing their own home. Ravel had a similar relationship with children; one might think he too felt happier in their world—a world which combines the fantastic with reality. He was devoted to the Godebskis' little Jean and Mimie, with whom he spent hours, either playing games or telling stories, "Once upon a time . . ." Those who knew Ravel, while perplexed themselves, told me that Ravel's delight in playing with the children, crawling with them on the floor, romping from one room to the other and his amusement with the children's toys, were genuine. "In fact, although he always brought toys to the children as presents," Mlle Gaudin told me in St. Jean-de-Luz—Ravel loved to play with her niece Annette, as he did with the little Godebskis—"he really bought these toys to amuse himself."

Jacques Durand, the publisher, one day surprised Ravel by calling at *La Grangette* at a time when the composer was in the company of his little friends. On this occasion Ravel made the children play a duet for the unexpected guest, a piece which he had composed for them on the previous day. The performance must have intrigued the publisher, for he made Ravel promise to do something more with this idea. Ravel did. *Ma Mère l'Oye*, a suite of four pieces for four hands, was the result of the game into which Jacques Durand intruded.

Ravel dedicated the composition to the two Godebski children, but they were too young to appreciate the honor and instead saw in it only an obligation to practice the piano and to learn the pieces, for Ravel wished them to play the composition at the first public performance. This scheme particularly terrified the little girl Mimie and, despite Ravel's coaching, the plans for a public appearance of these two performers had to be abandoned. When it was heard for the first time on April 20, 1910, at the Salle Gaveau it was played by two little girls, Jeanne Leleu and Geneviève Durony (aged six and ten) from Mme Marguerite Long's[1] piano class.

But the summer of 1908 has far more significance in Ravel's story. At home in Levallois, after the visit with Godebskis, Ravel wrote one of the outstanding composi-

[1] The famous French pianist and professor at the Paris Conservatory.

tions in the modern piano literature. The French musicologists and critics like to refer to this period in the composer's activity as a sudden change from White Magic, meaning *Ma Mère l'Oye*, to Black Magic, meaning *Gaspard de la Nuit*. After writing short pieces for children of six or seven, Ravel turned to compositions of "transcendant virtuosity," as he told Maurice Delage, "to be more difficult than Balakirev's *Islamey*." He was inspired by a small volume of poems Ricardo Viñes had brought him.

In 1841 the manuscript of *Les Histoires vermoulues et poudreuses du Moyen Age* was found beside Aloysius Bertrand's[2] deathbed. When it was published in 1842 it was said that Victor Hugo read the small volume with as much interest as he read *Andrea Chenier*. It was republished in 1863 and then completely forgotten until 1895 when the *Mercure de France* brought out a third edition—the one which came into Ravel's hands.

Ondine

List, list! It is I, it is Ondine who touches with spray the resonant panes of your window, lit by the wan rays of the moon: and behold, in black robe, the mistress of the château, who contemplates on her balcony the beautiful starlit night and the beauteous sleeping lake.

Each wave is a water sprite swimming in the current, each current is a path that winds its way towards my palace, and my palace is built aqueously at the bottom of the lake, in a triangle of fire, of earth, and of air.

[2] Bertrand Louis, better known as Ludovic and Aloysius, French poet, born 1807 at Céva in Piemont (France), died in Paris in 1841. He spent his life "polishing" his short fantasies *à la manière de Callot et de Rembrandt*. After his death Saint-Beuve and David d'Angers, published the single manuscript of his poems and prose under the name of *Le Gaspard de la Nuit*.

List, list! My father strokes the croaking water with a branch of green alder tree, and my sisters caress with their arms of foam the fresh isles of grasses, of water lilies, and of irises, or mock at the frail and bearded willow fishing with a line.

Her song murmured, she begged me to place her ring upon my finger signifying my marriage with an Ondine, and to accompany her to her palace, there to reign as king of the lakes.

And when I replied that I loved a mortal, she, pouting, vexed, shed some tears, burst into laughter, and vanished in a sudden shower which trickled in white rivulets the length of my blue window panes.

The Gibbet

Ah! those sounds I hear, would it be the north wind that moans in the night, or the hanged man who breathes a sigh on the forked gibbet?

Would it be some cricket that sings, sconced in the moss and sterile ivy with which, through pity, the woods cover their feet?

Would it be some fly ahunting that sounds the horn for ears deaf to the fanfare of whoops and halloos?

Would it be some beetle that plucks in its wayward flight a bloody hair from his bald skull?

Or would it be some spider that embroiders a half-ell of muslin as a cravat for this strangled neck?

It is the clock that tolls from the walls of the city, beyond the horizon, and the corpse of a hanged man that is reddened by the setting sun.

Scarbo

Oh! How many a time have I seen and heard him, Scarbo, when at midnight the moon shines in the sky and like a silver shield on an azure banner sown with golden bees.

How many a time have I heard his laughter humming in

the shadow of my alcove, and his nail scratching the silk of my bedcurtains!

How many a time have I seen him descend from the ceiling, pirouette on one foot, and roll about the room like the spindle fallen from the distaff of a sorceress!

Did I think him vanished? The dwarf grew taller between the moon and me, like the tower of a gothic cathedral, a golden bell shaking on his pointed cap!

But soon his body became blue, diaphanous as the wax of a candle, his visage paled like the wax of a candle-end; and suddenly, he was extinguished.[3]

That Aloysius Bertrand was endowed with a rather weird sort of imagination can be seen from the notes which give his advice to the artist who might illustrate his little book.

"The general character of the design should be of the Middle Ages and fantastic." Here are the subjects as he describes them:

A fire which rocks a dead child to sleep.

A young man asleep whom Scarbo, the dwarf of the nightmare, adorns with the snake's skin.

The moon combing its hair, from which fall glittering poems.

A cat who pisses into a violin.

Gallows with the one hanged.

To this he adds a selection of locales for the dramatic action: dungeons, old castles, turrets, belfry, pointed arches, church candles, Gothic weathercocks, etc.

The haunting romantic content of Bertrand's poems is

[3] *Gaspard de la Nuit* translated from the French by Irene Miles Downes.

wonderfully portrayed in Ravel's short tone pictures. All of Ravel's genius for purely pianistic effects is displayed in a super-Lisztian manner—not like Liszt of *Liebestraum* but of *Mephisto Waltz, Feux Follets*, and the sonata *D'après une lecture de Dante.*

When Joseph Ravel died in October, 1908, Maurice Ravel felt this loss deeply. He was devoted to his parents and his sorrow was so great that some French musicians ascribe the sudden pause in his productivity to his emotional state following the death of his father. The family moved to new quarters at 4 Avenue Carnot near L'Étoile which was to be their last home. Only one composition dates from this period in Ravel's life. Ravel joined a group of French composers, Debussy, Dukas, R. Hahn, d'Indy, and Widor, in commemorating the centennial anniversary of Haydn's death, and wrote the little *Menuet* based on the name of the composer.

The interruption in Ravel's composing was not, however, entirely due to the family's mourning. The season of 1908-09 was one of the most exciting and stimulating in the recent musical history of France, and Ravel played no minor part in its preparation. It was the second season of the "Russian cultural invasion" under the leadership of Sergei Diaghilev, a season of Russian music culminating in a production of Mussorgsky's opera *Boris Godunov*, "the equal to which has never been seen since," according to the Apaches. Maurice Ravel's relationship with Diaghilev, his adjutants, and the Russian Ballet were an important chapter in his career, inspiring as well as disappointing both in his personal and artistic life.

To be associated with Diaghilev and the Russian Ballet was a distinction; to have one's work performed by this glamorous group of elite artists was a unique opportunity and an honor, and to be able to observe their work at close range, or still better, to be able to take a part in it was an unforgettable experience. For Diaghilev, from 1906 on, with his constant "new discoveries" and the almost legendary presentations of their work for more than twenty years wielded the most powerful influence on the trend of artistic activities in the Western world.

A unique figure in the history of the dance, Diaghilev was a complex personality. His irresistible charm and ability for organization won him countless admirers and devoted friends, while his autocratic manner, often bordering on foolhardiness, estranged just as many men of value. Endowed with many talents, but none developed to a professional degree, he might have remained a mere dilettante with excellent taste. But his tremendous energy and his genius for choosing the right men to help him changed him from a mere *bon vivant* to a patron of art *par excellence* and a super-Barnum rolled into one.

For once Ravel was not late for an appointment with his destiny.

Chapter Eight

The Russian Ballet. Daphnis et Chloë

RAVEL MET Diaghilev sometime during the winter season of 1906-07 through Calvocoressi, on whom Diaghilev called almost as soon as he made his plans for the "historical concerts of Russian music." Diaghilev had asked Calvocoressi to translate the works which were going to be performed and to prepare program notes for the forthcoming events together with Walter Nouvel, one of Diaghilev's assistants. Diaghilev also invited him to the rehearsals, and it was not long before he listened to Calvocoressi's advice on program-making to suit the Parisian taste.

Maurice Delage remembers well how the Apaches met Diaghilev for the first time in Calvocoressi's apartment. Diaghilev pulled a few Russian scores out of a large yellow

139

leather brief case hoping to stun the assembled French
musicians with their originality and novelty, only to be
completely taken aback when the Apaches offered to play
them to him from memory. But Diaghilev did have a surprise for the Apaches: he was well acquainted with most of
Ravel's music, having heard it at the Contemporary Music
Evenings Nouvel and Nourok had organized in St. Petersburg. A pleasant surprise, indeed, because not long before
this meeting took place, Balakirev, after many years of
correspondence with Ricardo Viñes and Calvocoressi, had
expressed an interest in seeing some works by contemporary
French musicians. Calvocoressi sent him what he thought
was most likely to be of interest to him. "Ravel's music,"
Balakirev declared, "showed genuine talent," but he found
"the harmonic cynicism of it unbearable." "I advise you in
all friendliness," Balakirev wrote in a note returning the
parcel, "to cease boosting this stuff."

On his arrival in Paris Diaghilev was not yet thinking
of using any but Russian music at his performances, and the
discussions were centered on the choice of a Russian opera
for Paris production. Ravel explained to Diaghilev that the
Parisian public was ripe for better operas than, for instance,
Tchaikovsky's *The Queen of Spades*, and the Apaches also
overruled Diaghilev's suggestion of another Tchaikovsky
opera, *Yevgeny Onyegin*.

"Ah, but you don't know how delightful a thing
Yevgeny Onyegin is with Sobinoff[1] in the title part,"
Diaghilev persisted. "A dream! Nobody could resist it!"

"Oh, yes, they could! . . ." the Apaches shook their

[1] Lyeonid V. Sobinoff (1872-1934), a famous Russian tenor.

heads. They told Diaghilev that the French did not care for Tchaikovsky any more than they did for Brahms and that was all there was to it. "Now, the works of The Mighty Five? Mussorgsky? That is another story," they explained. They were proud to remind Diaghilev that it was France and not Russia who first recognized the genius of his compatriot. And in discussing this matter with him, they discovered that by a curious coincidence the man who introduced Mussorgsky in France was also in a way responsible for Diaghilev's decision to present Russian Ballet to Western Europe.

In 1896 Pierre d'Alheim, in a small hall in Paris, gave a series of lectures devoted entirely to Mussorgsky and his works, in collaboration with his wife, the singer Marie Olenine d'Alheim. D'Alheim, a journalist, a writer, and a poet, "managed to speak of Mussorgsky," according to the Apaches, "and to describe his works relevantly and convincingly, speaking with childlike simplicity and faith" while Marie Olenine, who made Mussorgsky's songs known throughout Europe, "evinced from the first the keen musical intelligence, the perfect sense of style and proportion, the straightforwardness and pregnancy in interpretation that have won her a place entirely her own among singers." The Apaches had never missed a performance and became closely associated with the couple. It was Pierre d'Alheim's book on the Russian Ballet, *Sur les pointes*, that first gave Diaghilev the idea of launching the Russian Ballet in the rest of Europe.

And now in 1907, at the beginning of his ambitious enterprise, Diaghilev found himself in Calvocoressi's apartment, facing the friends of the d'Alheims, the Apaches who told him—a Russian—that he did not seem to realize that Mussorgsky's *Boris Godunov* was not just another Russian opera, but a masterpiece which stands apart from anything he ever heard. The Apaches were amazed that not only Diaghilev, but also his two Russian advisers Nouvel and Nourok preferred Mussorgsky's *Khovanshchina* to *Boris,* and that if they considered the production of *Boris* at all, it was on account of the success Chaliapin had scored in the title role in Russia in 1904. To the utter surprise of the Frenchmen, the Russians were regarding the opera in the same terms of title roles, star singers, ballet, and chorus as they would apply to other more conventional operas and seemed completely to miss the true significance of Mussorgsky's *Boris.*

But Diaghilev was not easily persuaded. He liked arguing; it was his way of getting acquainted with the Apaches and their views. He spoke of Rimsky-Korsakov's *Sadko,* which he wanted to produce, and it took all the eloquence and arguments Ravel and Calvocoressi could muster to finally convince him to agree to their choice: Mussorgsky's *Boris.*

The Apaches soon realized that this Russian, despite his genuine interest in new ideas, had to be approached at the right time and by the right people. Fortunately the Apaches, and particularly Maurice Ravel, had an invaluable assistant in Misia Edwards, of whom, twenty years later, shortly before his death, Diaghilev was to say that she was his greatest friend, and that if he ever could have loved a woman, she would have been his choice. Thus Ravel's relationship with Diaghilev began with an unselfish collaboration for the sake of Russian art, a relationship which provided him no end of personal enjoyment and excitement as well as inspiration for the creation of a masterpiece—the best among his works—*Daphnis et Chloë*.

Diaghilev emerged on his world career as an impresario in 1906, when he organized an exhibit of Russian art in Paris at the Salon d'Automne. In twelve rooms, and a garden reserved for sculpture, seven hundred and fifty items were shown, including a collection of ikons occupying a separate room. Many pieces for this exhibition were lent to Diaghilev from the Imperial palaces, museums, and private collections in Russia. A great showman, Diaghilev was a past master at presenting his wares in the best possible light. He organized a patron's committee composed of artists, writers, and, of course, men of wealth and influence as well as the leading members of Paris society and the Russian nobility. Through his friendship with Grand Duke Vladimir, Diaghilev enjoyed unlimited financial support, and his enterprise benefited also from the political situation of the time: France and Russia were moving closer toward the Entente Cordialle and every manifestation of Russian success in France was both encouraged and welcomed by the French government. The exhibition was a great success and it was only natural that Diaghilev should exploit the ground he had so carefully cultivated. He immediately started plans for the next season: to follow it up with a presentation of another branch of Russian art—music.

The Russian Season of 1907 or "Russian Music Through the Ages" as it was called, was offered to the Parisians in a series of five concerts at the Opéra. The elite among the Russian musicians took part in this National Festival of Music. Feodor Chaliapin was to make his debut in the Western world. Two choruses were imported from Russia to support him in his singing of fragments from the operas. Diaghilev preferred to have the composers conduct or play their own works; he engaged Rimsky-Korsakov to do his symphonic suite from *Tsar Saltan* and the submarine-kingdom scene from *Sadko*, while Rachmaninoff was to play his *Second Piano Concerto* and to conduct his cantata, *The Spring*, and Glazunov, Felix Blumenfeld (of the Imperial Opera of St. Petersburg), and Arthur Nikisch (the great exponent of Tchaikovsky's music) were to share the conductor's desk in the programs which included Glinka's overture and the first act from *Russlan and Ludmilla* and his *Kamarinskaya*; Tchaikovsky's Second and Fourth Symphonies, excerpts from Borodin's *Prince Igor*, Mussorgsky's "Song of the Flea," and the second act from *Boris*, Balakirev's *Thamar*, Glazunov's Second Symphony, and César Cui's "Romantic Piece" from his opera *William Ratcliff*.

Hundreds of eminent musicians and artists from all over Europe came to the French capital. Never before was there such a conglomeration of stars of the musical world than at that time in Paris. At last the curtain at the Opéra rose for the first night of Diaghilev's season. "If the theater were to burn down tonight, the best artistic brains and the most elegant women in Europe would perish," Diaghilev is reported to have said. It has never been ascertained after which première he made this remark, but it was virtually true of all the first nights of his presentations from 1907 to 1929.

The concerts at the Opéra surpassed every expectation. The Russians were dined, wined, and feted by their West-European fellow artists. But while the French composers showed their admiration far beyond the usual call of hospitality, the Russians remained indifferent to their hosts. There was less intercourse between the Russian and French artists than one might have expected. The little free time the Russians had, they spent among themselves, sitting in the Café de la Paix and listening to arguments which might have been settled just as well at home in Russia between Rimsky-Korsakov and Scriabin about the relationship of sound and color (the latter explaining his *Prometheus* for which he planned a color keyboard), but seem never to have shown any curiosity about the idea of the relation of sound to perfume with which the French composers were preoccupied.

Felix Blumenfeld and Rimsky were the only exception, but not a sufficient one to excuse the Russians. Blumenfeld called on Calvocoressi in order to see for himself "this French stuff Calvocoressi praises so highly." There he surprised his host with his prodigious sight-reading of Debussy's *Reflets dans l'eau* and Ravel's *Alborada*, to mention just two of the compositions Calvocoressi showed him. "After each piece—and often while playing—he gave vent to sundry grunts and other expressions of disapproval," related Calvocoressi. Finally, after he played through a whole pile of music by Ravel, d'Indy, Debussy, Fauré, Schmitt, and others, Blumenfeld departed, saying that he did not think much of Calvocoressi's taste in French music. (A year later when he returned to Paris Blumenfeld asked whether he could take another look at "all the nasty stuff" Calvocoressi had shown him the year before.)

Rimsky with his family enjoyed their stay in Paris, but he did find time to see *Pelléas et Mélisande*. He did not like it. He thought it was an example of "unintelligible developments" and added with a wry smile, "I will have nothing further to do with such music, lest by misfortune I should develop a liking for it."

When the Apaches cornered him about his rather free editing of Mussorgsky's works, Rimsky merely shook his head, "You young people in France go picking out just the specks of dirt in Mussorgsky's music and then you put them all on an altar and worship them." This time he was replying not only to their remarks concerning his own rewriting of Mussorgsky's *Boris*, but referring to "certain particularities of idiom and methods in the music of Debussy and Ravel." But what amused the Apaches most was Rimsky's attitude toward his own *Sadko*, which was not given at the Paris Opéra because of its length.

"Yes, it is long, I know," Rimsky said, "but why not give it in two halves, the first one evening, and the second the next?"—this remark coming from a man who had disfigured Mussorgsky's masterpiece by the most appalling cuts and changes, but who could not admit that a single bar of his own music should be cut.

Yet none of these Russian personal peculiarities cooled the ardor with which the Apaches and particularly Maurice Ravel and Calvocoressi urged Diaghilev to produce Mussorgsky's *Boris*. They were disappointed when Diaghilev explained the virtual impossibility of giving *Boris* in Mussorgsky's original version. First of all he doubted that he could find the original score, and then even if he did obtain it, he was sure that the singers of the main roles as well as the chorus would refuse to relearn their parts. Considering that Rimsky tampered with keys and time signatures as well as harmonies and even, though less often, with melodies, it was hard to argue this point with Diaghilev. The Apaches were even more disappointed when they discovered later on that Diaghilev had asked Rimsky-Korsakov to expand the coronation scene in *Boris* for the Paris production in order to have more opportunity for pure pageantry, thus completely destroying the very essence of Mussorgsky's idea, "the atmosphere of strain, depression, and gloom which spreads over the whole ceremony, because of the officially enforced rejoicing."

But the Apaches felt that even a mutilated *Boris* would be better than none—"half a loaf is better than no bread," they said. They hoped that the success of *Boris*, even in Rimsky's version, would lead the way to a production of the original. They were fanatically devoted to Mussorgsky's cause and could never have suspected that the success of *Boris* would pave the way to a turn in Diaghilev's plans which was to benefit French artists, and Ravel one of the first.

At that time, as I have said, although Diaghilev himself was far more interested in the music written outside of Russia than the others of his group, he never thought of using the contemporary French music. Only after the success of *Boris* in 1908 and his decision to bring the Russian Ballet to Paris did his mind open to the possibilities of including the French composers in his undertaking, which by then had ceased to be purely a Russian national propaganda forum. For in 1908 Diaghilev's fortunes had changed considerably.

His patron, the Grand Duke Vladimir, died in 1908, and with his death and the triumph of the intrigues against Diaghilev at the Russian court, the subsidies on which Diaghilev's enterprise flourished came to an end. Fortunately Diaghilev's personality and success as an organizer commanded such respect that a number of influential and wealthy people were willing to back his projects. Thus, when in the following year (1909) he presented his Ballet Season, although the programs were still one hundred per cent Russian, his organization was already sponsored by non-Russian capital and Diaghilev was his own master. It was then that he turned to the West-European composers for collaboration, with Ravel's name heading the list of his choice.

Years later Ravel, in an autobiographical sketch, gave 1907 as the date when he was commissioned by Diaghilev to do *Daphnis et Chloë*, but he was mistaken by two years. It was in 1909, at Diaghilev's apartment in the Hôtel Hollande in Paris, that the decision was made. After various librettos were offered to Ravel, in conference with Diaghilev, Fokine, Bakst, Benoit, and Calvocoressi, it was finally agreed that Fokine would write one to Ravel's satisfaction. This meeting must have taken place sometime during the summer or early fall of 1909. At any rate it must have been after Ravel saw the Russian Ballet and Nijinsky, for it is evident from Ravel's score of the ballet that Nijinsky had inspired many passages in *Daphnis et Chloë*.

The Russian Ballet arrived in Paris in 1909 at the end of April and set feverishly to work, for they had only three weeks before the scheduled opening night. It may be that the Ballet had more glamour than a group of opera singers or composers, but in any case the enthusiasm for the forthcoming productions engulfed the whole Parisian artistic world—"The very air was intoxicating," as Diaghilev put it, and everyone was ready to help them as best as he could. As best as he could, for the Russians, the "barbarians" as the French affectionately referred to them, were all *un peu maboule*—a little mad.

This time the performances were to take place not at the Opéra but at the old Châtelet Théâtre. Diaghilev did not like the large orchestra pit; he cut it in half and had a row of boxes instead. The stage was inadequate for the Ballet because the floor was uneven, the trap door always jammed, and the whole interior of the theater had to be improved and renovated to suit Diaghilev's group. They could not present masterpieces of art in a barn or stable. Diaghilev spent money as if it were water. He ordered the entire theater recarpeted and a whole army of carpenters (some of them imported from Russia) were sawing and hammering away in every part of the hall, while the members of the Ballet rehearsed with their directors and choreographers, who shouted themselves hoarse in order to be heard above the general din. Then to the exasperation of the Russians—every minute was dear to them—the French workmen would stop for two hours—the sacred lunch hour. The Russians never stopped working. Diaghilev would order food brought in from the restaurants—roasts, fish, fowl, salads, and desserts were placed on packing cases and devoured by the young dancers between *entrechats* and *pirouettes*. "What do you expect? They are savages!" the French smiled and shrugged their shoulders. It was new, gay, and exciting, even to the Apaches, who made their first acquaintance with the Ballet there at these first rehearsals at the Châtelet Théâtre.

Diaghilev firmly believed in advance publicity to stimulate public interest in the forthcoming performances, and he invited writers, critics, artists, musicians, and journalists to come and watch the work in progress, so that stories of the Russian artists' endurance and their devotion to art for art's sake were told in the papers long before the opening night. The unmistakable signs of success were in the air, although no one except a Russian could fathom how any production could come out of the three weeks' hysterical, convulsive cataclysm of squabbles called "rehearsals."

But not even the best well-wishers, the closest friends of the Ballet, could have predicted what was going to happen on that first night, May 19, 1909. "Something akin to a miracle," Tamara Karsavina, the famous prima ballerina, said later, "the stage and audience trembled in an unison of emotion." Countless reports with the most flattering accounts of the Ballet have been published speaking of the feats performed by each member of the group and of the coordination of the whole. But none could ever describe the effect which was produced by Nijinsky's famous leap into the air.

The *Pavillon d'Armide* was the first ballet on the program that night. The audience was quietly watching the *pas de trois* performed by Tamara Karsavina, Nijinsky, and his sister Bronislava Nijinska. Then, when Nijinsky was supposed to leave the trio in order to return on stage for his solo, the audience witnessed an unrehearsed and unheard-of feat of virtuosity. A few yards from the wings, Nijinsky leaped, describing a parabola, floated through the air, and vanished from sight. No one in the audience saw him land. The public gasped and broke into such a storm of applause that the orchestra had to stop. Ravel and the Apaches were in the audience, but not merely as spectators. They had been so closely associated with the Diaghilev group right from the start that they shared their triumph; and, as for Nijinsky's virtuosity, this leap which Ravel witnessed that night inspired many passages in his *Daphnis et Chloë* score—patterns characterized by a run and a long pause (page 26 and after in the piano score) in a dance of Daphnis providing opportunities for similar leaps.

Although Ravel began working on *Daphnis et Chloë* almost immediately after it was commissioned, and was so engrossed in his work that he paid no attention to a flood threatening the little house near Fontainebleau where he was working at the time, the performance of the ballet, originally scheduled for the following year, had to be postponed from one season to the next. Difficulties arose right from the start. Fokine, the choreographer, and Leon Bakst, the stage designer, had a conception of Greece different from that of Ravel.

The libretto was based on an ancient myth, translated into French by Jacques Amyot (1559). Bakst visualized the ballet developed against the background of archaic Greece, while Ravel pictured "a vast musical fresco, concerning itself less with archaic fidelity, than with fidelity to the Greece of my dreams, which in many ways resembled that imagined and depicted by the French artists of the end of the eighteenth century." Fokine's choreography did not suit Ravel. He demanded constant changes, and Fokine and Bakst in their turn asked him to compromise—leading to a not too harmonious result. Finally in 1912 Ravel delivered his score to Diaghilev who, although impressed by its musical merit, hesitated to produce the ballet. Diaghilev went so far as to express his misgivings about Ravel's score to Jacques Durand, Ravel's publisher. Then suddenly, during their conference, either out of whim or prompted by a mischievous idea in the back of his mind, he declared as if persuaded by Durand's arguments that he would put on *Daphnis et Chloë.*

Lengthy conferences and rehearsals followed in Durand's presence, but he was unable to assist in Ravel's behalf because the vehement arguments among Fokine, Nijinsky, and Diaghilev were carried on in Russian. What actually was said has never been recorded, but from the violence with which they expressed themselves it has been presumed that the discord was serious enough to be considered as the starting point of Fokine's break with the Russian Ballet. Whether this means that Ravel's way prevailed has never been ascertained.

There were also purely technical difficulties in the score retarding the progress of rehearsals until Ravel himself helped to solve them. Even such an experienced dancer as

Tamara Karsavina needed coaching in one of her dances, with the rhythm: 1, 2, 3—1, 2, 3, 4, 5—1, 2. On the morning of the performance Ravel worked backstage with Karsavina until she finally could "dismiss mathematics and follow the pattern of the music." When the *corps de ballet* ran into the predicament of 5/4 time in the finale, Ravel came to their rescue by suggesting that they omit the customary counting of 1, 2, 3, 4, 5—1, 2, 3, 4, 5 and substitute the syllables of Diaghilev's full name: Ser-gei Dia-ghi-lev. Since Ravel dedicated the ballet to Diaghilev this seems especially appropriate.

Finally the ballet, badly prepared, was given on June 8, 1912, at the end of the season. It had only two performances. On the following morning (June 9) Robert Brussel wrote in *Le Figaro:*

> A most accomplished and poetic work we owe to the artistic enterprise of Sergei Diaghilev . . . . usually we are dazzled by Maurice Ravel: but this time we are stirred; stirred not because his manner is aggressive or haughty, but because it is infinitely gentle, fresh, and tender as befits such a subject.
>
> Ravel's art is astonishingly consolidated in this systematically plastic score [wrote Émile Vuillermoz a week later in the *Revue S.I.M.*]. The composer has allowed the shape of his design to emerge in clear-cut lines . . . . everything points to a balanced and consumate art. The last part of the work reveals a happy carelessness, a kind of nonchalant mastery, sufficient to enrapture musicians who with consternation have seen a certain harshness and affectation become normal to the ironic Muse of *L'Heure espagnole*.

And Jean Cocteau, the French poet and dramatist, as

if to summarize the general impression, remarked that "*Daphnis et Chloë* is one of the creations which fell into our hearts like a comet coming from a planet, the laws of which will remain to us forever mysterious and forbidden."

Fokine's choreography of *Daphnis et Chloë* was considered one of the best things he ever did and yet. . . . Ravel's *Daphnis et Chloë* was not a success. To the general public, unaware of backstage intrigues, it seemed that Ravel's ballet did not live up to the unique opportunities offered by the Russian Ballet. It did not, as they said in Paris, mark an event in the annals of French art. It was eclipsed by the success of another ballet given on May 29, only a week before the première of *Daphnis*, a ballet which had the true, the traditional, Parisian "success—scandal" with the audience brawling, the newspaper headlines screaming across the front pages and men and women insulting each other whenever the subject was mentioned. Intellectual Paris was divided into two camps. Editorials attacking or defending the production carried on the fight which involved the most eminent figures in the French artistic, literary, and political world, including the Russian Embassy, until it was talked about everywhere—as far as Berlin, Constantinople, St. Petersburg, London, and New York.

It was as if Ravel was doomed to this fate: *L'Après-midi d'un faune* was the name of the ballet. Claude Debussy was the composer.

The scandal was caused not by the fact that *Eclogue*, Mallarmé's poem, was used for a ballet set to music by Debussy, but by what Gaston Calmette, the editor of *Le Figaro*, described in his editorial as "a faun, incontinent, with vile movements of erotic bestiality and gestures of heavy shamelessness . . . of the too-expressive pantomime of the body of an ill-made beast. . . ."

In 1895 when *L'Après-midi d'un faune* was first performed, Edouard Colonne, the conductor, did not dare quote Debussy's own description of what his music sought to evoke. "Too many girls attend my concerts," said Colonne.

Debussy's description was "The successive scenes in which longings and the desires of the faun pass in the heat of the afternoon."

At Diaghilev's performance Nijinsky went a bit too far in his zeal for absolute accuracy to conform with the composer's interpretation. Calmette, in his article, referred to Nijinsky's final scene in which the dancer substituted for a parting kiss what appeared to be an act of onanism. Nijinsky "espoused the veil" which he took from the nymph, as Misia Edwards discreetly put it.

The tragic coincidence of the performances of the two ballets was not maliciously prearranged, as it might seem if one followed Ravel's career. It just happened that way. Ravel was slow in the preparation of his score. Constant alterations as the result of conferences with Fokine, Bakst, Nijinsky, and Diaghilev delayed the final version, while many changes took place in Diaghilev's entourage as well as in his plans.

Nijinsky in the interim had become Diaghilev's favorite. Diaghilev firmly believed that Nijinsky's genius should not express itself only in dancing, but that given an opportunity it would also manifest itself in Nijinsky—the choreographer. That Nijinsky lacked every endowment necessary for a choreographer—education, culture, taste, but above all,

vision and the ability to communicate his ideas to others—
was obvious to every one except Diaghilev, who was sure
of his own Svengalian power.

In 1911 (while Ravel was still working on the score of
Daphnis et Chloë) Diaghilev took Nijinsky to Venice for
the summer vacation. One day as they sat in a café on the
Piazza San Marco, Diaghilev suddenly was struck by an
idea. Nijinsky was to create a ballet to Debussy's *L'Après-
midi d'un faune!* Diaghilev then outlined to his friend the
whole synopsis of the production. Thereafter the two men
spent days in museums studying the plastic forms of the
past, and immediately upon their return to France the production of the ballet was put into work.

But because of Nijinsky's lack of experience in choreog-
raphy, to put it mildly, he had to be constantly assisted by
Bakst, who was in charge of the stage designs, and of course
Diaghilev himself—the two men who were actually the
authors of the ballet. It was up to Bakst to introduce to
Nijinsky the forms and images of ancient dancing depicted
on Attic vases, bas-reliefs, and sculpture, the same Bakst
who was working with Fokine on Ravel's *Daphnis et Chloë*.
It was not surprising that the two ballets laid in ancient
Greece showed a similarity particularly noticeable in the
frequency of movement in profile. And whereas *L'Après-
midi d'un faune* emerged as the hit of the season and a new
word in choreography, Ravel's *Daphnis et Chloë* remained
in its shadow.

Fokine blamed Nijinsky for the insufficient time left for
the preparation of *Daphnis et Chloë*, because Nijinsky
needed one hundred and twenty rehearsals for *L'Après-*

midi d'un faune. When the season closed Fokine resigned.

Thus Ravel's work was an innocent victim in the feud between Fokine and Diaghilev. Public attention which should have been focused on *Daphnis et Chloë* was obstructed by the controversy over *L'Après-midi d'un faune,* still raging in Paris during the performances of Ravel's ballet —a scandal in which Diaghilev reveled.

Was Diaghilev a fool or an ignorant ass to have two ballets by the two most competitive, most eminent French composers presented in the space of such a short time and in the face of their similarity? Or was Diaghilev neither, but an autocrat who trampled everything and everybody in his way while backing his favorite against Fokine, a man for whom he no longer had any use?

Where was Ravel? Where were the Apaches? Was there not a single man among them to stop Diaghilev's foul play? Not a murmur has been recorded, nothing is remembered except that on that first night Maurice Ravel was late for the rise of the curtain and that immaculately dressed he carried a present for Misia Edwards into her box—a gorgeously dressed Chinese doll.

There was no break in Ravel's relationship with Diaghilev. However, there was a definite cooling of Diaghilev's enthusiasm for further collaboration. Diaghilev was disappointed to find that Ravel's music did not correspond either with his own ideas or with those of the choreographers in his company. Ravel was not commissioned to do another ballet, but other non-Russian composers were, including Claude Debussy.

Chapter Nine

Stravinsky and Ravel

NOT EVERYTHING in Ravel's association with the Russians was entirely disappointing. During the year of 1910, at the "Home of the Song" on 22 Smolensky Boulevard in Moscow, the Apaches' old friend Marie Olenine d'Alheim organized a competition for the harmonization of European folk songs: French, Spanish, Italian, Scottish, Yiddish, Flemish, and Russian. Ravel joined the competition and for the first time in his life he won a first prize (five hundred rubles—at that time worth one thousand three hundred and twenty-five francs or two hundred and fifty dollars) in a country miles away from his native land, where his name was virtually unknown. He was awarded the prize for four songs: French, Spanish, Italian, and Yiddish. (The last of these Durand later brought out with two Hebrew songs which Ravel harmonized in 1914.) The four songs were published by Peter Jurgenson in Russia and Marie Olenine gave their first performance on December 19, 1910, in Paris at the Salle des Agriculteurs.

Of these four songs, there is no doubt that it was the Yiddish which aroused the most admiration. The harmonization of the song seemed so perfect that it was taken for granted by the Russian critics that only a Jew could have accomplished so authentic a work. This incidentally was the first time that the question of Ravel's Jewish origin came up, although this was to happen time and again during his life. Ravel paid no attention and only gave an answer much later in his life.

Less lucrative but far more important was another episode in Ravel's relationship with the Russians. Ravel met Igor Stravinsky. He heard about Stravinsky for the first time when the Apaches met Diaghilev and his collaborators in 1907. Discussing contemporary composers, the Apaches were curious to know who the young Russian composers unknown in France were that "really mattered," as Ravel put it. "One or two," the Russians replied, "especially one. We are keeping him back for the present for fear that some one might spoil him for us."

Two years later the Apaches heard from Robert Brussel that during his visit in Russia Diaghilev invited him to hear a new and unperformed ballet, composed by a young man— Diaghilev's latest discovery. *Firebird* was the ballet and Igor Stravinsky was the young composer. Diaghilev entrusted the unknown young man with writing the music after he lost patience with the well-known composer Anatol Liadov —the laziest man in the history of music—whom Diaghilev had originally asked to set the old Russian fairytale to music.

In 1912 Stravinsky came to Paris for the first performance there of the *Firebird*, and Ravel went to the rehearsals.

"Old man, you must take leave of your galoshes," Ravel wrote to Maurice Delage, who happened to be at his country place at the time. "This goes further than Rimsky. Come quickly. I am waiting for you to return to the *Firebird*. And what an orchestra! . . ."

Firebird had an immediate success with the Parisian public and the Apaches welcomed the thirty-two-year-old composer into their midst as one of their own. As a matter of fact he became the last member—the last Apache—to join their *cammerata* on the Rue de Civry. There were several reasons why Igor Stravinsky fitted into their group so perfectly. To the Apaches he represented first of all a symbol of the new and the original; he epitomized the contemporary trend in Russian music. His art was the continuation of that of The Mighty Five and particularly of Mussorgsky. Mussorgsky had taken Wagner's place in the eyes of the French and Stravinsky's attitude toward Wagner was in perfect harmony with that of the Apaches. Stravinsky also visited Bayreuth, heard the much talked about performance of *Parsifal*, and frankly expressed his feeling toward the whole Wagnerian cult.

"What I find revolting in the whole affair is the underlying conception which dictated it—the principle of putting a work of art on the same level as the sacred and symbolic ritual which constitutes a religious service," Stravinsky said. "And indeed, is not all this comedy of Bayreuth with its ridiculous formalities simply an unconscious aping of a religious rite?"

Stravinsky was more depressed than impressed by the

much advertised "atmosphere" of the Bayreuth performances—the signal for devoting oneself to contemplation given by a blast of trumpets, an "intermission" rewarded by two sausages and a glass of beer, another blast of trumpets for another period of contemplation, and another "intermission" with more sausages and beer, and still another blast of trumpets. Stravinsky felt that it was high time to put an end to this sacrilegious conception of art as religion and the theater as a temple. He offered the following argument to show, as he said, "the absurdity of such pitiful aesthetics."

One can not imagine a believer adopting a critical attitude toward a religious service [Stravinsky said]. That would be a contradiction in terms; the believer would cease to be a believer. The attitude of an audience is exactly the opposite. It is not dependent upon faith nor on blind submission. As a performance one admires or rejects, one accepts only after having passed judgment, however little one may be aware of it. The critical faculty plays an essential part. To confound these two distinct lines of thought is to give proof of a complete lack of discernment, and certainly of bad taste.

When Stravinsky first arrived in Paris there was much talk about Richard Strauss, highly praised by Romain Rolland, but neither the Apaches nor Stravinsky were particularly attracted by his music. They did not think he had anything new to say. The Apaches were rather amused when Stravinsky told them of the remark Richard Strauss made after hearing *The Firebird:* "You can not start it with *pianissimo,* you must start with a loud crash, so that the audience will sit up and take notice."

Stravinsky on the other hand shared with the Apaches

their curiosity in the manifestation of a new force coming into the musical world—Arnold Schönberg. Their interest was kept alive by the newspaper reports of the first performance of Schönberg's symphonic poem, *Pelleas und Melisande,* and later of the concert in Vienna given by the famous Rosé Quartet, when the members of the audience came to blows after hearing the first performance of Schönberg's *String Quartet*—so strongly were they divided in their enthusiasm and utter disgust. When in 1911 the Apaches received Schönberg's piano pieces (Opus 11) Stravinsky, Ravel, and Calvocoressi were fascinated by the "music which avoided tonality with as much fidelity as the traditional school maintained it," and two years later, when the performance of Schönberg's Chamber Symphony ended in a riot in the concert hall, the Apaches were in an uproar, just as if the piece had been composed by one of themselves.

Stravinsky visited Schönberg in Berlin and although Ravel did not do much traveling himself, he was kept well informed. For among the Apaches what was known to one of them was immediately communicated to all, and Calvocoressi's role was that of a roving reporter. Just at that time (1912) Calvocoressi set out on a trip to Russia and he too visited Schönberg in Berlin on his way to St. Petersburg.

This short visit, only a few days, with the composer was far more fruitful than his month-long sojourn in the Russian capital, which the Apaches expected to be of paramount value. The main object of Calvocoressi's journey to Russia was to collect material for his book on Russian music and to study the original score of *Boris*—so dear to the hearts of the Apaches. He had been planning to go to St.

Petersburg since 1906 when he was in correspondence with Balakirev. But by the time he finally made his trip, Balakirev had been dead for two years. Calvocoressi returned from Russia with the most pleasant memories of a whirlwind of social activities with musicians, mostly in the gastronomic field. He happened to be in Russia during Lent, when the traditional hospitality and gourmandism reach their zenith in a string of everlasting festivities, mountains of pancakes with caviar, and vodka. He saw Glazunov again, and the Rimsky-Korsakov family, and he met César Cui, the only one of The Mighty Five still alive. He visited with Liapunoff, Balakirev's disciple, Gretchaninoff, Siloti, and Prokofiev, then only a twenty-one-year-old beginner, but he did not get the much-coveted information about the Russian musicians and particularly about Mussorgsky. The Russians, with the exception of Nikolai F. Findeisen, a music critic and editor of *The Russian Musical Gazette*, who gave him a pile of copies of his magazine, were too busy playing host or trying to convert Calvocoressi to liking Tchaikovsky's music to find time to help him locate the material and information he needed—the sole purpose of his long journey.

Calvocoressi never did get to see the manuscript of Mussorgsky's *Boris* either because the Imperial Theatre, where the archives were kept, was temporarily closed for repairs or the custodian happened to be on vacation, or because many unpublished parts were torn out of the manuscript and were on the shelves in the libraries and no one seemed to know how to find them. Calvocoressi's trip would have been a complete failure had not Ravel found in

Findeisen's material a lot of information about the original scores of *Khovanshchina* and *Pictures at an Exhibition*, invaluable to the work he did later on.

On the other hand, Calvocoressi's report of his visit with Schönberg was far more concrete. It testified once again that there was a musician who should be reckoned with. Besides a most instructive and enjoyable talk he had with the composer, he attended a rehearsal of Schönberg's works where "Schönberg was surrounded by a number of young composers who clustered around him, not only because they found him a peerless teacher, but because his work was the very embodiment of something for which they had been longing and more or less consciously groping." At a concert in a small hall Calvocoressi heard Schönberg's piano Opus 19, his song set, *Das Buch der hängenden Gärten*, and the arrangement for double piano duet of three of the orchestral pieces. In the audience he met Feruccio Busoni and discussed Schönberg's experiments with him. Finally Calvocoressi brought back a copy of Schönberg's *Handbook of Harmony*, which was then just published and which fascinated the Apaches not so much by its technicalities as by its philosophy.

However, Calvocoressi's journey, and the information he brought back with him, was far more important and timely than it first appeared, for meanwhile Diaghilev had decided to follow up the success of his production of Mussorgsky's *Boris* in 1908 with another Mussorgsky opera —*Khovanshchina*. But as he was not satisfied with Rimsky-Korsakov's version (Mussorgsky himself never finished the opera) Diaghilev asked Stravinsky "to restore certain parts of the original score altered by Rimsky, to orchestrate the parts which were not orchestrated by Mussorgsky, and to compose a chorus for the finale, for which Mussorgsky had indicated only the theme—an authentic Russian song." When Stravinsky, busy on his own compositions, realized how much there was to be done he asked Diaghilev to divide the work on *Khovanshchina* between himself and Ravel.

Early in the spring of 1913 Ravel joined Stravinsky at Clarence in Switzerland. The two composers decided that Stravinsky would orchestrate two parts of the opera and write the final chorus, while Ravel would undertake to do the rest. Actually Maurice Ravel orchestrated the "Reading of the Ukases," "The Hymn to Prince Ivan Khovansky," the duet between Emma and young Khovansky in the first act, Marfa's song, and Kooz'ka's song with chorus.

When Diaghilev's announcement of the Stravinsky-Ravel project reached Russia, Rimsky-Korsakov's son Andrei justly pointed out that, "however much a fresh edition of *Khovanshchina* might be desirable, this should be carried out straight from Mussorgsky's manuscripts and not—as Stravinsky and Ravel were doing—partly on the basis of the Rimsky-Korsakov version." But according to Diaghilev's plan the Stravinsky-Ravel work was to be amalgamated with the rest of the score and as Stravinsky himself said, "Unfortunately, it made the mixture even more incongruously heterogeneous than Rimsky-Korsakov's version, which had been retained in all essentials, the only difference being a few cuts, a change in the order of certain scenes, and the substitution of my chorus for his."

Apart from this work, Stravinsky denied any responsibility for Diaghilev's version which, when compared with Mussorgsky's original, showed even greater liberties than Rimsky-Korsakov had ever dreamed of taking.

> I have always been sincerely opposed to the arrangement by anyone other than author himself of work already created and my opposition is only strengthened when the original author is an artist as conscious and certain of what he was doing as Mussorgsky. To my mind that principle is as badly violated in the Diaghilev compilation as it was in Rimsky-Korsakov's Meyerbeerization of *Boris Godunov* [Stravinsky said].

There is no doubt that this declaration could have been made jointly with Ravel, for was not Ravel the one of the Apaches who only a few years before was the leader in the campaign for producing the original *Boris*—not Rimsky-Korsakov's version—and for the same reason? Why then had Ravel anything to do with the work on *Khovanshchina?* This remains a mystery, unless again, as in the case of *Boris,* Ravel believed that it was worth a compromise to pave the way for further propaganda for Mussorgsky's music. Years later in 1922 he paid another homage to Mussorgsky when he orchestrated his *Pictures at an Exhibition.*

Ravel obviously enjoyed his stay in Clarence and working with Stravinsky, who also showed him a short song cycle for voice and a small ensemble of flutes, clarinets, strings, piano, and xylophone, *Trois poésies de la lyrique japonaise.* It was Stravinsky's latest composition and although it bears no resemblance to the morbid expressionism of Schönberg's *Pierrot lunaire,* it has been said that it was influenced by this Schönberg piece which Stravinsky heard on his visit to Berlin. Ravel was so fascinated by the use of certain instrumental devices and passages where the tonality can not be definitely defined that he also in his turn composed *Trois Poèmes de Stéphane Mallarmé*. The first of the songs, *Soupir*, written for voice, a string quartet, piano, two flutes, and two clarinets, he finished in Clarence; while the second, *Placet futile*, he completed a month later in Paris; and the third, *Surgi de la croupe et du bond*, in St. Jean-de-Luz in August of the same year. Once again, as in the case of *Miroirs*, Ravel surprised those who thought they knew his style of composition.

"I wanted to transcribe Mallarmé's poetry into music," Ravel said, "especially that preciosity so full of meaning and so characteristic of him."

Delicacy, refinement, and a wealth of new and attractive material in these compositions make up for the deliberate, remorseless limitation of emotional expression so characteristic of Ravel's writing, which is simple, hard, and original. Less popular than his *Daphnis et Chloë*, these three poems are considered by the experts as a pinnacle in Ravel's art.

But what must have caused a real surprise was the appearance in print during the same year of another *Three Poems of Mallarmé* out of which two, *Soupir* and *Placet futile* were the same poems which Ravel chose for his experiment. The composer of this other work was Claude Debussy. There is no record left to prove whether this was intentional or coincidental, but after fifteen years of rivalry, did it have to happen? On close examination of the two scores, once again the profound difference in the invention, style, and temperament of the two artists is evident. It is quite clear not only that Debussy influenced Ravel, but that both Frenchmen had an influence on Stravinsky, who in his turn influenced them, and yet the differences of their art are indisputable.

While in Clarence, Ravel had another exciting experience—Stravinsky showed him the manuscript of *Le Sacre du Printemps*, almost ready for Paris production. Ravel's enthusiasm is obvious in the letter he wrote on March 3 to Lucien Garban, one of his friends in Paris. "One must hear Stravinsky's *Sacre du Printemps*. I think it will be as important an event as the première of *Pelléas*."

Ravel was not mistaken in his prediction. The Apaches turned out in full force for the première of *Sacre du Printemps* under Pierre Monteux's direction on May 29, 1913 (Diaghilev was superstitious and chose the same date as that of the première of *L'Après-midi d'un faune*), for, as Delage explained to me, if the Apaches had any *raison d'être* at all it was to further the success of such compositions as *Pelléas et Mélisande*, Mussorgsky's *Boris*, and *Sacre du Printemps*. The famous brawl at the Champs Élysées Théâtre—the most fashionable theater in France—surpassed anything that had so far been witnessed at a theatrical performance in Paris, including the premières of *Pelléas et Mélisande* and *L'Après-midi d'un faune*. The smart audience behaved like hoodlums, booing and cheering. The violence with which the opposing groups attacked each other with their fists, canes, and umbrellas turned the occasion into a riot. There was such a bedlam of noise that one could not hear the orchestra, which continued to play. In the midst of catcalls and applause, men and women jumped to their feet and yelled their instructions as to how to perform the work. Some were so excited that they drummed the rhythm of the music on the heads or shoulders of their neighbors, who were too numb from the tense excitement to notice it. People whistled, yelled, and insulted one another; one beautifully dressed woman in an orchestra box got up and slapped a young man hissing in the next box, while another prominent society lady spat in the face of one of the ballet enthusiasts, and an old princess left her box crying, "I am sixty years old, but this is the first time any one has dared to make a fool of me."

The Apaches were right in the thick of the battle, while Diaghilev ordered the lights turned on in the hall, and then off again. Florent Schmitt's roaring voice was heard above the deafening noise, calling the ladies in the boxes "whores from the fourteenth *arrondissement*" (a fashionable district in Paris), and Ravel was treated to a "dirty Jew" by one of these ladies, because he implored her to keep quiet.

Ravel's own *Daphnis et Chloë* was "revived" and presented again during that season, but it did not fare any better than it had a year before. This time it was outshone by Stravinsky's *Sacre du Printemps*. Although it was taken off the repertory of the Russian Ballet, Ravel later carved two suites out of his score, and in this form *Daphnis et Chloë* has become known around the world.

Ravel bore no grudge against anyone and remained a faithful friend to Stravinsky. When three days after the scandal of *Sacre du Printemps* Stravinsky fell seriously ill with typhoid fever and his life was in danger, the Apaches never left their comrade. Ravel wept by his bedside.

Eventually it was Stravinsky and not Ravel who became Diaghilev's ballet star. Altogether, over a period of twenty years, Diaghilev presented eight ballets to music by Stravinsky, in addition to two operas, an oratorio, and a symphonic tableau.

The Ravel-Stravinsky friendship lasted until the middle twenties when they ceased to see each other, although, presumably, their mutual esteem was in no way destroyed. Ravel never said a word, even to his closest friends, about his break with Stravinsky, and Stravinsky never went to see the Apaches again.

Today Igor Stravinsky says he did not know Maurice Ravel very well.

Chapter Ten

St. Jean-de-Luz

DURING these years of Ravel's most prodigious productivity not all his work was connected with his new friends—the Russians.

As early as 1907 there was a schism among the members of the National Society of Music. The discord had been brewing for some time in the previous years. The old organization had become so reactionary that a mere incident caused the final alienation of a whole group of musicians, among whom were Aubert, Caplet, Dukas, Schmitt, and Ravel.

The organization provoked their wrath by refusing to perform *Conté par la Mer*, a work by Maurice Delage. Already then, with Gabriel Fauré on their side, these musicians were scheming to establish their own society which would adhere strictly to the principles on which the old

National Society of Music had been founded but unfortunately had failed to honor.

In 1910 the new organization came into being under the name of *La Société Musicale Indépendante*, the S.M.I. (or, as some called it, *La Société de Musique Invertébrée*), with Maurice Ravel as one of its founders. The Society was inaugurated at the Salle Gaveau with a concert on April 20, 1910. The program included Fauré's *Chanson d'Ève*, Caplet's *Septette*, Dukas' *La Pastorale pour orgue*, and the first public performance of Ravel's *Ma Mère l'Oye*.

At this concert, either to emphasize the principles of the new organization and its complete impartiality in the choice of compositions and performers, or possibly because of Ravel's personal desire to put an end to the years-long dispute, Ravel himself played Debussy's *D'un Cahier d'esquisses* with its *Soirée dans Grenade* which, with Ravel's own *Habanera* was the subject of the dispute in 1903.

Throughout his career as a composer, Ravel was always ready to help others get their works performed, rather an unusual trait among composers. He used his influence in propagandizing Mussorgsky's works and now he took the first opportunity to pay homage to Satie, to whom, as he said, he owed a great deal for the inspiration of his own early works. Ravel gave a successful concert entirely devoted to the works of Satie. He played Satie's second *Sarabande*, the third of the *Gymnopédies*, a Prélude from *Les Fils des Étoiles*, and, with Ricardo Viñes, *Morceaux en forme de poire*. But not all the concerts of the newly organized society turned out satisfactorily for Ravel.

During the same year of 1911 the committee of the

S.M.I. announced a concert with a rather unusual procedure
—a sort of quiz program: the audience was to guess the
names of composers from hearing their pieces played.
Except for the members of the committee and the composers who were present in the concert hall, only the performers were let in on the secret. The committee felt there
was too much prejudiced criticism, particularly on the part
of snobs, who posed as the arbiters of French art and music,
and many well-known contemporary French composers
were willing to participate in this rather dangerous game.

Among several compositions played on that night one
was accompanied by particularly loud hoots and catcalls.
Ravel was sitting in a box surrounded by a group of society
dilettantes who ordinarily would have swooned over the
first few chords of a composition which carried Ravel's
name. It must have been disconcerting to Ravel to hear the
loudest sneering and expressions of ridicule come from these
young people. Obviously by their behavior they were
courting Ravel's good graces, only this time they did not
realize that they were jeering at Ravel's latest composition,
Les Valses nobles et sentimentales. The general public reaction was almost as disappointing. Some listeners attributed
the composition to Zoltán Kodály, the young Hungarian
composer, or Erik Satie, while others missed it by an even
larger margin, ascribing its paternity to Mozart, Chopin,
Gounod, Mendelssohn, or Wagner.

It is interesting to note a certain parallel in Ravel's account of the reception of his composition to Mussorgsky's
of the want of success of the first performance of his opera
Boris Godunov. "The opera had a stupefying success—a

complete triumph for the author," wrote Mussorgsky in his autobiographical sketch, which was as short as that of Ravel and written for an almost identical purpose. Less flamboyant, Ravel said *Les Valses nobles et sentimentales* were recognized as his "by a minute majority." Actually, according to the French critics' records, only three per cent of the audience guessed the name of the composer correctly.

"The title *Les Valses nobles et sentimentales*," Ravel said, "sufficiently indicates that I was intent on writing a set of Schubertian waltzes. The virtuosity which formed the chief part of *Gaspard de la Nuit* has been replaced by obviously greater clarity, which strengthens the harmony and sharpens the contrasts. . . ." Ravel also said that his pieces had no motive beyond the "delicious and ageless pleasure of a useless occupation."

However, the critics who found the waltzes charming or annoying, banal or distinguished, intoxicating or somniferous, were unanimously in favor of the composition when later, orchestrated by the author, it came back for a return engagement—this time in a form of a ballet.

It was given at the Châtelet Théâtre, the same theater where the Russian Ballet had made its début; but not by Diaghilev's troupe. The work was presented by a French ballet, organized by Jacques Rouché, then the director of National Academy of Music.

This group of French dancers began its career on January 28, 1912, at a small theater on the Boulevard des Batignoles—Théâtre des Arts—with a performance of Musset's *Fantasio*, Couperin's *Les Dominos ou les Folies Françaises* and Ravel's *Ma Mère l'Oye*, which he orchestrated and provided with a libretto for the occasion.

Dresa's (André Saglio) exquisite décor and costumes and Jane Hugard's choreography left an unforgettable impression of this version of *The Sleeping Beauty*. Delighted by the spectacle, Nijinsky said to Ravel, "It's like dancing at a family party," and Natalie Troukhanova, the prima ballerina, immediately suggested dancing to the *Valses nobles et sentimentales*.

Three months later at the Châtelet Théâtre, Troukhanova with L'Orchestre Lamoureux gave four performances (April 22-23-25-27, 1912) of *Adélaïde ou le langage des fleurs*—the rechristened *Valses nobles et sentimentales*. At last "the symphony and the dance have formed a love union in France," the French critics announced. Four French composers, d'Indy, Dukas, Schmitt, and Ravel, represented by their work the strength, nobility, grace, and audacity of their nation. As if to follow Diaghilev's precept, each composer was asked to conduct his own work. For the first time since the performance of his *Shéhérazade* in 1899, Ravel conducted his own composition. To his friends who were a bit apprehensive about his ability he said, "It is not difficult. It is always in three time . . . but when I get to that point there, I just go around and around."

The ballet portrays an amorous intrigue among the beautiful courtesan Adélaïde, her aspiring lover Loredane, a young poet, and an old duke who offers her wealth. Love, devotion, deceit, disappointment, hope, and despair are communicated between them by the flowers they present to each other. In the course of the ballet, the poet's passionate love conquers Adélaïde's fickle heart, as the curtain falls on the last chords of the seventh waltz, the last in the group of the *Valses nobles et sentimentales*.

The four performances of the ballet at the Châtelet failed to conquer the Parisian public. During World War I, on April 7, 1916, it was revived at the Opéra and again did not kindle public enthusiasm. Ravel was, of course, disappointed, but by the time it was decided not to give any further performances of the ballet, he was far away from Paris and was having other troubles with another Adélaïde . . . an Adélaïde of a different metal.

In summarizing Ravel's life and his work before World War I one must remember that just as Ravel's work was not all connected with one organization or another, so not all of his compositions were written in Paris, where his home was, or were the product of the inspiration and influences of the capital.

After the Ravel family moved to Paris in 1875, whenever they had an opportunity to get away from the city they went to St. Jean-de-Luz for their summer vacation. A few still remember seeing Mme Ravel on the streets of St. Jean with her two little boys in their large straw hats with bright ribbons, such as are worn nowadays by Venetian gondoliers rather than Basque fishermen. Around six or seven o'clock in the evening it was fun to go to the pier of the small harbor of St. Jean-de-Luz, to walk among the peanut, balloon, or ice-cream vendors to the accompaniment of the distant sound of the merry-go-round in the nearby square, to watch the fishermen return in their bright blue vessels, to see the large tuna still covered with blood thrown on the scales, and to hear the old timers discuss the catch. Later, when the boys grew up, they were remembered racing with their friends through the countryside on bicycles, picnicking in the hills back of Ciboure, or, from the top of the old tower of the Abbey of Bordagain, watching the sunset over the vast panorama of the slopes of the Pyrénées, St. Jean-de-Luz' harbor, and the faint outline of the Spanish coast.

During the last years of Ravel's father's life the family remained in Paris, but from 1910 on, whenever Maurice Ravel's work permitted, he would take his mother for a vacation to St. Jean-de-Luz. A devoted son, he made a great fuss over Mme Ravel, bought her a new dress after the first performance of each new work, helped her select her wardrobe, and loved to give her advice while she dressed for a party. Ravel's love for his mother was equaled only by Mme Ravel's love for her son. She was probably the only person never to lose patience with him, and was always ready for his call. "I am waiting for Maurice," she said, whenever Ravel was not at home.

Ravel always complained that it was difficult for him to work in Paris because of the social life there. In St. Jean-de-Luz he was sure to be able to work undisturbed. During the summer months of 1911 he virtually rewrote the finale to *Daphnis et Chloë* after he had first abandoned the idea of having a chorus join the orchestra—an idea inspired by Borodin's *Prince Igor*. At the same time he was also pre-occupied with Mussorgsky's opera, *The Marriage*, left by the author in the form of a vocal score. Rimsky-Korsakov intended to orchestrate it, but his death prevented him from writing more than one page. Unfortunately Bessel and Co., the Russian publishers of the original score, were not generous enough to encourage Ravel in his plans. In St. Jean-de-Luz, during the summer of 1913, Ravel wrote the third and last of his Mallarmé poems, but while his desk was covered with unfinished scores and sketches and plans for future work, it was in St. Jean-de-Luz that he relaxed.

Ravel was not a sportsman. He neither played *pelota* nor had he ever been seen in a bull ring. But as a spectator he enjoyed the elegance of the former and the pageantry of the latter and always joined the enthusiasts of these shows. Nor would he miss watching the merrymaking of the natives—the picturesque but always dignified Basque dances and their choral singing. In his yellow-and-black-striped bathrobe and a red Basque beret he was a familiar figure on the streets and beach of St. Jean. Besides swimming and diving (he excelled in the first rather than the second form of the sport) he loved to organize all sorts of excursions into the surrounding country by car, on bicycles, or on foot. Ravel could outwalk anyone. These trips familiarized him with the Basque country, on the French as well as the Spanish side, and were the source of inspiration for a composition he had been talking about for some time.

After visiting the Basque villages in Navarra and Arragon, after traveling to Pamplona and Estella by the mountain roads of Lescar and returning home via Ronceveau, St. Jean-Pied-de-Port, and Mauleon, Ravel brought with him a detailed plan for a composition for piano and orchestra: Basque in its character and with a Basque title—"Zaspiak-Bat," that is, Seven—One, the motto of the Basque nationalists, which refers to the unity of the seven provinces: Biscay, Guipuzcoa, Alava, Navarra on the Spanish side and Labort, Bas Navarre, and Soule on the French side.

Gustave Samazeuilh, a music critic and an old friend of Ravel, who went along with him on these trips, told me that he had seen parts of the score, already well advanced, but that at that time Ravel was still hoping to find a satisfactory middle part—a link between the first movement, inspired by a spring morning in Ciboure, and the last—a festival at Mauleon.

It has often been said that when Ravel wrote Hebraic melodies he was more Jewish than a Jew and when he wrote an Arab tune he was more Arab than an Arab—it would have been interesting to see the result of his work on a Basque piece, since he so strongly felt he was Basque himself. But the piece was destined never to be finished. The declaration of World War I caught Ravel in the midst of his work on at least two musical scores and several sketches for different projects, among which "Zaspiak-Bat" was the first casualty.

Chapter Eleven

World War I

IN 1914 RAVEL was of "territorial age," meaning, in the language of the French army, that because he was underweight and undersize he was good enough only to do some auxiliary service, such as working in various depots or doing guard work on railroad stations well behind the front lines. He volunteered and was rejected. Both the military authorities and his friends advised him that he would do his country a better service by remaining a composer. But this was no consolation to him; he felt differently about it.

Besides, the behavior of the Germans prevented Ravel from following this advice. "Must I before acting, wait, until a couple of *uhlans* arrive in the as yet non-existent garden of my dream-villa at St. Jean-de-Luz?" he wrote to Roland-Manuel. He was referring to Alberic Magnard, a composer ten years Ravel's senior, who was living a quiet idealistic life seeking neither publishers nor performers for the work he was doing, when in September, 1914, he found two German *uhlans* in the garden of his villa at Baron (Oise). He shot at the invaders and was shot in return, his house being burnt to the ground with all his manuscripts.

Ravel was no longer Basque. He could not remain neutral like his friend Ricardo Viñes, a Spaniard. Maurice Ravel was first of all a Frenchman and a patriot. He was determined to join the fighting forces—no matter what.

But instead of returning to Paris at the end of the summer vacation, as he usually did, he stayed in St. Jean-de-Luz to finish the work on the Trio begun during that summer. By September 26 the Trio was ready.

"I have accomplished in five weeks as much as would ordinarily have taken five months," Ravel remarked, and he was eager to complete all his other unfinished scores before trying to enlist again. However, he could not continue the work on "Zaspiak-Bat," because he had left most of the sketches for it in Paris. Nor did he now feel particularly inspired by Hauptmann's *The Sunken Bell*, to which he had returned sporadically in the past few years. The play was of German origin, and now that fact decided its fate. Instead, he turned again to Maeterlinck's *L'Intérieur*. "It would be a touching gesture toward France's ally," Ravel said, but most of the sketches for this composition were also in Paris and thus he decided to work simultaneously on two series of pieces for piano. One of them was to be a French Suite—but without *Marseillaise*, he warned. It was going to have a forlane and a gigue, but no tango. As for the second suite, it was to be a *Romantic Night*, "full of spleen, with a hunt in hell, an accursed nun, etc. . . ." He worked for a while on the former of the two suites, the one which, after the war, became *Le Tombeau de Couperin,* but the second suite never materialized, for Ravel could not keep his mind on his work. He felt that he should be doing something useful. If he could not be in the army, the least he could do, he thought, was to offer his services at the hospitals.

"It is amazing," Ravel remarked, "the number, if not the variety of needs forty fellows could have during one night."

But taking care of the wounded was not really what he wanted. Deep in his heart he refused to accept the army's rejection as a final "No"—he was sure that in Paris he would be able, through his friends, to pull all the necessary strings to reverse the authorities' decision. Early in November he went back to Paris. Upon his return home the feeling of "being left behind" weighed even heavier on his mind. His brother Edouard had gone to the front. Most of his friends were called into the army or volunteered. Every day brought news of another Apache being sent to the front. Roland-Manuel, Florent Schmitt, Delage, and Klingsor were in the army, Calvocoressi was in England where he joined the British Army Intelligence, Diaghilev's group was dispersed all over Europe. Nijinsky was caught in Hungary. Stravinsky was in Switzerland. Alfred Edwards, lost to his friends for some time because of his love affair with a certain Mlle Lanthelme, a young actress of doubtful reputation who broke up his marriage with Misia and eventually wrecked his life in dissipation, died just before the outbreak of the war. Misia was doing war work. She received an authorization from General Gallieni to form a convoy of ambulances to serve at the front. With her third husband José Sert, the Spanish painter, she organized a team of volunteers including Jean Cocteau, François de Gris, Gautier-Vignal, and Mme Rumilly, the only professional registered nurse among them.

The war was less than three months old when Ravel received his first blow from gruesome reality. The two Gaudin brothers from St. Jean-de-Luz were killed. Jeanne and Marie Gaudin, the sisters of the boys, were probably the closest friends Ravel had in St. Jean-de-Luz. They practically grew up together. Ravel seldom allowed himself to express in words so deep an emotion as in this letter to Marie Gaudin:

> My poor Marie—
> What a shock. . . . When I came home last night Maman, in despair, told me . . . You can imagine the night we have passed . . . We embrace you even more affectionately than ever and silently. . . . Oh, Lord, what can we say? That they have gone in a glory . . . this is true about them, but for you, for your poor parents, what a revolting horror. Maman is crushed. She does not cease repeating, "poor children! poor Annette! poor Monsieur Gaudin!"

This was war. It scarred Maurice Ravel in the most vulnerable spot of his whole being. He had a horror of death. He adored his mother. He loved family and children, the growing up "young beings." "How lovely it is to be alive," he had often said.

And yet nothing would stop Ravel from trying to get into the army. He was examined three times and three times he was rejected. Then, since he was so light in weight, he naïvely decided he could become an aviator. He spent the next year and a half following up every bit of advice, every opportunity that his friends could provide with the military authorities. Finally in the first days of 1916 he was accepted as a truck driver in an auxiliary branch of the military service at 156 Rue de Vaugirard in Paris.

My dear Marie [Ravel wrote to Mlle Gaudin on January 19, 1916]. Alas! My silence has an excuse. But it is not because of the all-absorbing service, but rather because of inaction. From time to time I do some uninteresting errands with my truck. But most of the time I remain whole days in the garage doing nothing. It is the depression that takes every desire for action away from me, even the will to take a pen into my hand. Last week I was supposed to have been sent to the front, but at the last moment I was told to remain where I am. I have received no answer for my last application for aviation. It seems we are 13,000 aspiring aviators, each one using more influence than the next. I am convinced that many a man who was accepted tried as much to stay at home as I did to do something in the army. Patience is the only thing left to me. And besides, it would hardly be more dangerous in an airplane than in my charming American truck, in which the other day I just failed to lose my skin.

Edouard, who has returned to us intact after more than a year of constant danger, and who suffered incredible exhaustion through all this time, now begins to pay for it. For the past fifteen days he has had neuralgic pains and angina and now it looks like an inflammation of the lungs. . . . We hear that fortunately your little Annie is unbearable. In your misfortune what happiness you must find in this little being who forces you all to live. . . .

P.S. As for any wishes . . . one could have only one, isn't that so?

But with the most passionate faith.

Maurice Ravel wished for peace and yet he could hardly wait to be sent to the front. Another two months that seemed to him like years passed in the dull life in the garage in Paris. He was getting used to the comic figure he cut in the long army overcoat which made him look even smaller than he already was and to his comrades' jibes who compared him to a bat as he drove his large army truck, looking like a ghost in the blacked-out streets of Paris, clutching the steering wheel, only his shiny eyes visible.

Then men were needed for work in connection with the heavy artillery. "Was it because of his size and weight," his comrades asked, "that Ravel was chosen for this project and sent to Verdun, where the worst battle of the war raged?" His spirit rose once again. He was full of braggadocio. In his letters to his friends (Ravel hated writing letters and never in his life wrote as many as during the time he was in the army) he said that although so far his activities brought no glory—he smashed his first truck and had an accident with his second—"it" (the glory) "was coming." He was burning with the desire to "really" use his helmet, not just sport it as though he were going to parade on the Champs Élysées, to use the gas mask which he carried in his pocket, to look the war square in the face.

At last Ravel had his wish. He saw "the magnificent fireworks . . . but black." And then a little later he heard back of his truck a whistling noise and an explosion. At first he thought a tire had blown out. "And to say that I will end up by being scared. . . . For the moment, I assure you, it amuses me very much. I am in the period of curiosity," Ravel explained.

Ravel was curious, for he was still only a spectator. He was still attached to an ambulance-dispatching service and he was rather happy there. Everybody knew him and besides, his outfit was stationed in a beautiful park of an old château. In the hall of the mansion Ravel discovered an excellent grand piano and on Sunday afternoons he played Chopin. It was there, he said, that he realized that Chopin was one of his favorite composers. Whether he knew it at the time or not he was still treated as Maurice Ravel, France's most eminent musician, and only the different sonorities "coming from afar which lulled him to sleep at night," reminded him of the danger that was ahead of him.

The pleasant country life in the park came to an end when Ravel was suddenly transferred to a company assigned to bring the broken remains of the so-called "75," the heaviest cannon in the French army, back from the front.

> It was then [Ravel said] that the true war began for me. . . . And what a duty! We had to go by the most incredible roads littered with stones and broken pieces of armor, passing over the shell holes in the midst of constant enemy bombs exploding on the right and left, in front and in back. During five days and as many nights, I drove without any lights. Whenever we had to stop to ask for directions we hurried for cover. And when the men who were with me would leave me alone, for there were places where the truck just could not get through . . . the waiting, all alone in the midst of these pleasant things! . . . It was good to have a cigarette, leaning against the slope . . . while waiting for my comrades to return. . . . Nothing serious happened to me. I escaped the shrapnel. . . . Except one morning, near a small abandoned railway station, an Austrian shell . . . *sciicion . . . pan!* sent the dirt and fairly disagreeable smell

straight into my face. . . . I have managed to resist fatigue but my poor truck, my Adélaïde, did not do as well. After almost failing me on the road in "the dangerous zone" right in the face of the *Boches'* batteries, she indolently let go one of her wheels. Fortunately it happened in the middle of a beautiful forest in front of the kitchen in the encampment of a truck company. And now while waiting for five days to be pulled out of here, I lead the life of my ancestors, performing my ablutions in a brook nearby, begging my food . . . and sleeping inside my truck rolled into animals' skins. During the first three days this rest in the forest was bearable; the weather was splendid. But two nights ago it began to rain and I could hardly sleep; it was so cold.

Ravel found the uncertainty of when he was going to be "pulled out" and the perspective of a dreary life in the barracks during the repairs on his truck even more cruel, "a boring life so far away from the adventurous existence at the front with its terrifying charm, but so luring to one who has tasted it."

Another five days passed, and then another week, and another and another and no one came for Ravel and his truck. He was getting used to the life of a man in a forest, for as he said:

I have plenty of wine, pernod, and snails. But this amusement which seemed to me at first very delicate, begins to lose its freshness. . . . I can still see myself smoking a cigarette in another forest, less quiet than this one, while a procession of four litter-bearers passed by carrying the dead bodies of Moroccan soldiers, one of whom was without his head. It seems to me as though years have gone by since I saw this. What I feel right now is not so much horror or fear, but on the contrary only the wish that my truck will soon be repaired. . . . And yet I am peace-loving; I have never been brave. But there it is: I am curious for an adventure. It has such a fascination that it becomes a necessity. What will I do, what will many others do, after the war?

Ravel received an answer to his questions much sooner than he expected. He was rudely interrupted in his reveries and reminded once again that he was a musician and of his duties to French art by a letter from Paris which reached him while he was waiting for the spare parts for his Adélaïde.

On March 10, 1916, that is, about the time when Ravel departed for the front, the National League for the Defense of French Music was organized in Paris with headquarters at 16, Rue d'Assas and included among its members Camille Saint-Saëns, Théodore Dubois, Gustave Charpentier, Vincent d'Indy, Xavier Lerous, Paul Meunier, and others. Two months later Ravel received the League's Charter comprising nine articles which stipulated the League's aim, the predominance of French music in France and its propaganda abroad, and the conditions for membership, from which every one of German or Austrian origin was excluded (unless naturalized longer than five years), and the following proclamation:[1]

> In all spheres of activities the constant goal of the triumph of our fatherland imposes on us the duty of collective action and of unity.
> Musical art, whose function is economic as well as social, should not remain a stranger to the use of the following measures of active solidarity.

[1] Ravel underlined the points which disturbed him.

The National League was born of this necessity of action. It is concerned with all the means of chasing, and later ferreting out the enemy, to prevent the return of his disastrous infiltrations in the future.

Since there can be no question of the repudiation by us and the coming generations, of the "classics," which constitute the immortal monuments of humanity, it is imperative to condemn modern Germany—the Pan-Germanists—to silence.

Our aim, therefore, is to unite and to create a front for our future by abandoning the small quarrels of diverse coteries.

First, after forbidding public performances for a long time of the works of our Austro-German contemporaries, which are not in the public domain, their interpreters, *kappelmeisters,* and virtuosos, their Viennese operettas, the cinematographical films with which they flood us, their phonographic records which are a camouflage, let us make their real intentions clear, demask the pseudonyms of their song writers, who even now succeed in fooling our censors, and watch that the enemy "shall not pass."

Then, after safeguarding the development of our music, let us watch out for the interests of our compatriots; safeguard our national inheritance, without discrimination of style or school, work with all the means available for the predominance of our art in France by publications and public performances, and create a basis for an exchange with our allies of the products of our art.

Our means of action, depending on the circumstances, will be: coalitions, controls, propaganda, interventions with the public authorities, reforms in our schools, struggle against the trusts which are suspected of being or are subversive and against all those who suggest a permanent desire of the enemy to obstruct our revenge.

Let us adhere to the League, and support it in large numbers, and with the will to make this [organization] a patriotic and an artistic creation which will <u>give one the right to count among those who wish to remember.</u> The large professional associations have assured the League of their powerful cooperation. The League calls for the cooperation of all musicians and friends of music, who within the limits of their capacity, inspired by the sublime effort of our brothers at the front, are interested in the destiny of our art and wish to act as Frenchmen.

FRENCH MUSIC FOR THE FRENCH.

Honorary presidents: MM Camille Saint-Saëns, Théodore Dubois, Gustave Charpentier, Vincent d'Indy, Xavier Lerous, Charles Lecocq, Paul Meunier, Lucien Millevoye.

The document was signed by at least one hundred musicians and directors of music schools and opera companies from all over France.

This was not the first outburst of patriotism by French artists. At the beginning of the war there were protests against performing Wagner's operas. Jean Marnold, fifty-six and too old for the army, remained in Paris and was one of the first to protest against this campaign, while Ravel was the first to congratulate him for his article, "The Case of Wagner" (*Mercure de France*, May, 1915). A year later, in January, 1916, Marnold, answering another campaign, this time to deny an artist who was not drafted the right to pursue his work during the hostilities, reminded his compatriots that "it was during the Peloponnesian war that Sophocles produced a trilogy sometimes accompanied by a satirical drama, every two years until his death. . . ."

Although Ravel could hardly have been accused of any particular friendliness toward German art since the declaration of the war—did he not abandon for good his adaptation of *The Sunken Bell*—still he could not remain indifferent to the sweeping measures proposed by the League.

Gentlemen [Ravel wrote on June 7, 1916, to the Committee of the National League for the Defense of French Music]. An enforced rest permits me to answer the declaration of your charter which reached me after a long delay. I beg you to excuse me for not writing sooner: diverse transfers and my service adventures have not left me much leisure up till now.

Please forgive me also if I can not adhere to your charter. After reading it carefully, I feel that it is prohibitive as far as I am concerned.

I fully approve of the "necessity of action" from which the National League was born. This necessity of action has been so strong in me that it made me leave civilian life, although nothing obliged me to do so.

But I can not follow you, when you declare that "the function of musical art is economic and social." I have never considered music nor the other arts in this light. I willingly abandon to you these "cinematographic films," these "phonographic records," and these "song writers." All these have only a distant relation to the art of music. I will even abandon these "Viennese operettas," although they are far more musical and are of more careful structure than our own similar products. This, however, also belongs to the domain of "economics."

But I do not believe that for the "safeguard of our national artistic inheritance" one has "to forbid the public performances in France of the works of our German and Austrian contemporaries, which are not in the public domain."

If "there can be no question of the repudiation by us and the coming generation of the 'classics' which constitute the immortal monuments of humanity," there must be even less question of "forbidding for a long time" interesting works, which might later on, in their turn, constitute "the monuments," but from which meanwhile we could gain useful information.

It would even be dangerous for French composers to ignore systematically the productions of their foreign fellow artists and thus to create a sort of national coterie; our musical art, so rich at the present time, will soon degenerate if it shuts itself within such bigoted formulas.

It matters little to me that M. Schönberg, for instance, is of Austrian nationality. He is nonetheless a musician of high merit and his interesting experiments have had a happy influence on some composers among our allies, as well as on our own. Furthermore, I am delighted that MM Bartók, Kodály, and their disciples are Hungarians and manifest this in their works with so much zest. In Germany, except for Richard Strauss, we do not see any but second-rate composers, for whom it would be easy to find equivalents without crossing the border. But it is possible that soon even there a crop of young artists will emerge who would be interesting to know. On the other hand I do not think it is necessary to "make predominant in France and to propagandize abroad" all French music regardless of its merit.

You can see, gentlemen, that on many points my opinion is fairly different from yours, so I can not have the honor of appearing among you.

Nevertheless, I hope to continue to act as a Frenchman and to "count among those who wish to remember."

Ravel sent a copy of this letter to Marnold.

I must tell you why I entrust you with this copy [Ravel wrote to his friend]. I am a fellow full of precautions. Later on a friend, even with good intentions, might quote small parts of a sentence, just so, just to be smart, and if I were no longer there to explain or answer, one can never tell where it may lead. . . .

Although obviously perturbed by his fellow artists' behavior, in the same letter to Marnold, Ravel confessed:

I suffer from another thing. In the past few days I have suddenly discovered that I can no longer live without music. This might be because I do not hear any. For almost two years I thought I had forgotten it and now it comes back as a sharp pain. Yesterday I received a letter from Delage, who offers to arrange a transfer for me to a service near his. He says that his duties leave him time for his own work and that *he has a piano*. Definitely, I am more musician than warrior. . . . I think I will accept it. . . . But what about this life at the front?!

Ravel's letter to the League must have enraged the Committee, for the president of the League did not take long to answer Ravel and say, "I was delighted to learn to what degree you appreciate the 'high merit' of the musician Schönberg, the 'zest' of MM Bartók, Kodály, and their disciples. The National League will be here at the opportune moment to advise the public of your admiration in the case of the eventual sacrifice, most unfortunate, of your own music."

"Imagine after this," Ravel wrote Marnold, quoting the president's threat, " 'the interventions with the public authorities' by such influential and well-known personalities as MM Saint-Saëns, d'Indy, Charpentier, Paul Meunier, etc. . . ."

Marnold was collecting material about the League for an

article he was planning to publish, and offered to include Ravel's letter.

My letter? . . . I hesitate . . . but I think you are right [Ravel replied on June 24, 1916]. Naturally these gentlemen would never publish it; it is even probable that it will never be read before the assembly, as you say. One would know only those who adhere to the League and ignore the names and the reasons of those who object and protest. After all, it's true, I am just as qualified as anybody else to speak in the name of French music. Although I have not been in the trenches I have done as much for the defence as those who stayed on the Rue d'Assas. The danger was not the same, that's all.

But let's not forget that I am a soldier and have no right to publish anything, particularly if it might cause a polemic. But this is serious. When we come back we might be obliged to curl up before an accomplished fact. Well! Publish my letter but without the signature—some insinuations will make clear to your readers what it is all about. The effect will be the same.

It is regrettable that these gentlemen will be able to make their propaganda at their ease: your *Mercure* reaches only the elite, while they easily will have for themselves the readers of the daily papers. . . . It will be a bit tough after having battled down the military principles of modern Germany to have to admire or be repulsed by orders at home.

What trenches we will have to clean up when we return! As for me I have decided to arrive on a horse—or twelve horses in the midst of the assembly on the Rue d'Assas.

But for one reason or other Marnold never wrote the article, and Ravel sat in his forest through the months of May, June, and most of July waiting for his Adélaïde.

Still hoping to get into aviation, Ravel passed another

physical examination. This was his first visit with the doctors since he had come to the front. Their verdict alarmed
him. Comparing himself to Adélaïde, Ravel observed: "It
is not only the carburetor that is affected. The motor itself
is hobbling about on three legs. Including the gear shift,
everything leaves much to be desired. . . . But let's hope
that the steering wheel will not likewise go wrong now."

There was not a chance of his getting into aviation.
Nothing came of Delage's offer. Ravel was lonely and depressed. He was worried about his mother and he hoped
she would never know about his health.

"I really suffer from one thing only, and that is not to
be able to kiss my poor mother . . . ," Ravel wrote in July,
1916. "Yes . . . and yet there is another thing: music. I can
think of nothing else. I am sure that I would have been in
the midst of a period of full production. . . ."

Ravel was indeed full of musical projects of all sorts:
symphonies, chamber music, ballets and he saw only two
solutions to his dilemma: the end of the war or his return to
the front. But there stood his Adélaïde rotting away while
waiting for the spare parts and he himself "fermenting," as
he put it, in his latest assignment "to stand guard over gas
and oil." The futility of his life drove him to despair. "I will
never be a character in the genre of Napoleon," he concluded.

The new address should not mislead you, my dear friend
[Ravel wrote Marnold]. I have not budged. The regiments
move, while I remain where I am. It will soon be two months
and a half since I arrived here hoping to leave at the end
of the week. The spare parts for my truck arrived at last

the day before yesterday . . . but now it seems that my radiator is ugly and they have decided to order a new one. It will be some time before . . . and I don't give a God damn. . . . They can ambush me, or send me to the front, or keep me here! . . . and I don't give a God damn. . . . This stupid, useless life has brought me to the point where nothing interests me . . . except, perhaps, music and the furlough which does not come. . . .

Finally, at the end of August, when Ravel had lost all hope of ever seeing a new radiator for Adélaïde, when from pure boredom and lack of action he developed insomnia, lost appetite, and had become completely *abrutis* as he put it, he received his furlough.

Ravel had a brief visit with his mother. He found her much better than he had expected. He thought that even the short time he spent with her had a rejuvenating effect on her, although he felt that she was aware of the dangerous service he was in. When he returned to his post he learned that he had been transferred to another station, but three weeks passed before his orders came through.

By way of St. Digier, Vittel, and Nancy, Ravel arrived in a miserable state at his destination near Châlons-sur-Marne. He had been suffering from dysentery for the past two weeks, of which the last two days had been spent in traveling—adding most singular charm to the journey. Ravel was annoyed at being put to bed upon his arrival, for his situation in the new service promised to be more attractive than the last, judging by the ovation with which he was greeted—they had been expecting him for more than a month. He was allowed to eat with the officers and later he was taken around and introduced to all the notables in the place. But after a few days he felt so ill that he had to be taken to a hospital.

One more complication crowned Ravel's troubles at the most inopportune moment. He had to have a hemorrhoidal operation and the ordeal terrified him, particularly since his comrades promised him "inconceivable, quasi-Chinese tortures," as he said. Ten days after the operation, while still in bed, his spirits rose high enough to report in his letters to friends that the operation had been successful, that he was sure now that he was of a Spartan type since he found the whole procedure *très supportable*, that chloroform gave him neither headaches nor colic nor nausea, and that on the contrary, as soon as he woke up he had to have a cigarette, because he was dying of hunger. Facetiously he advised his friends, who did not know the exact nature of his illness, not to fear "divination" as a sequel to his operation "because it was not on the same side." His one worry was to keep his mother from knowing anything about it. "She does not even know I am in the hospital," he said and he wanted to make sure no one would blurt it out.

Ravel spent many weeks in the hospital and finally in the last days of the year was discharged and sent to Paris to convalesce. He arrived home just in time to spend her last few days with his mother. She died on January 5, 1917, at the age of seventy-six.

The loss of his mother was the most terrible blow Maurice Ravel suffered in his life, for there was no one whom he loved as much. Nothing his friends could do would console him. He was as if in a dumb stupor. A few days later on January 11, Diaghilev, who had just returned from Italy, paid him a visit and proposed that he write the music for a new ballet. Ravel sat and listened. His thoughts were far away. But on the following day he wrote:

My dear Diaghilev—

In accordance with our conversation yesterday I accept your proposition to compose a ballet on the subject you showed me; the author Cangiullo, the Italian poet. This work, as far as the piano score is concerned, should be finished by the end of the year [1917] and the orchestration by April 1, 1918. The exclusive rights for the presentation of this work in all countries belong to you for five years after the first performance. I am to receive for this work 10,000 francs [$2,000] the first half payable upon the delivery of the piano score and the rest upon the delivery of the orchestral score. For the orchestral parts you can make an arrangement with my publisher M. Jacques Durand. You can have the rights of performance at concerts, but only after the ballet has been given in the town where the concert is to take place.

Devotedly yours,
Maurice Ravel

Was this contract the blow that finally destroyed Ravel's fascination with the war, the front-line life, the morbid adventure? For it seems that from now on Ravel's one desire, if and whenever he had one, was to return to civilian life. But it was almost as hard for him to get out of the army as it had been to get in. The hospital of the Grand Pallais recommended his discharge, but the higher authorities thought he could still do some work in auxiliary service. On February 7, Ravel returned to his company in Châlons-sur-Marne.

"Today, I wanted to write to my friends," Ravel wrote a few days later. "I have come across one of her [his mother's] letters; I have no courage to do anything, nor to see anyone. . . . Upstairs some one is practicing Carpentier's[2] method; the bells are ringing, I do not know what. It is all so lugubrious. . . ."

Ravel led a miserable existence in Châlons. He was weary of the army life, of men, good comrades, friendly and gay, but strangers to him, particularly in his present state of mind. He vegetated from day to day, from month to month.

An immense weariness that has come over me [Ravel wrote to a friend], stops me from writing. Yesterday I became forty-two years old. It seems to me as though I am seventy. Only a year ago—think of it!—I was leaving for the front. I was preoccupied with curiosity, a desire for an adventure. I did not know. . . . I did not want to know . . . the pain I was causing my poor mother. . . . Do you remember how we were almost happy then—when we read Edouard's letter to her. She kept smiling, but I saw her lips tremble a little. From that moment on, she was *touchée*. . . . And what joy—the quiet day—when Edouard returned! And she was to bear the anxiety of seeing me depart in my turn . . . and I went just the same. . . . This did not serve any great purpose, and I have killed her. . . .

Ravel's new status in the auxiliary service gave him the right to return into the interior zone more often and he was going to profit by his next furlough which was coming up on February 20, to take the necessary steps in Paris for his release and to take another physical examination.

[2] The boxer Carpentier, light-weight champion of the world.

I have a good chance to be discharged [Ravel said referring to the spots in his lungs which were discovered at his last physical examination]. If I am released, I must go to Italy to work on a composition which was commissioned for the Russian Season in Argentina, not later than June, where I am to go to conduct my works. . . . But I am indifferent to all this. I believe I will never do another thing. I feel that I am finished. Physically I do not feel so badly, although I am in bed at this moment. But it is nothing serious: my feet were frostbitten, and I am getting treatments. But it's the morale. . . . The only thing which keeps me sane is my poor Edouard's affection. How are you all? You exist, isn't that so? As I do. One does not really know why.

Ravel spent another six weeks in Châlons before he was transferred to Paris. There he was assigned to various depots until finally on June 17, 1917, he was "temporarily" discharged from the army.

Chapter Twelve

The Third "Affaire Ravel"

MAURICE RAVEL paid a high price for his "curiosity," his noble patriotic gesture, and the French victory in World War I. He returned from his military service in wretched condition. Ravel, who had never been ill before in his life, developed a heart condition, his nerves were shattered, he suffered from insomnia and general depression, and the doctors were not sure that he did not have tuberculosis. He needed a complete rest and care and he needed work to keep him from brooding and to get him well. It was a problem. At first he went to Lyons-la-Forêt in Normandy. There, after almost three years he hoped to pick up composing again where he had left off in St. Jean-de-Luz in 1914.

Ravel's first choice was to complete the already-started score of *Le Tombeau de Couperin*—a homage addressed not so much to the memory of Couperin, the composer, as to the French music of the eighteenth century. Ravel worked slowly, with difficulty, but by November he was ready to deliver the manuscript to his publisher. The separate pieces in the suite were all dedicated to friends who had been killed in the war, the *Rigaudon*, the fourth in the suite, to the memory of Pierre and Pascal Gaudin, whose death at the beginning of the war caused him his first war pain. On April 11, 1919, Marguerite Long played the work for the first time at one of the *Société Musicale Indépendante* concerts at the Salle Gaveau, but the piece disappointed even the most ardent Ravelites.

After the *Valses nobles et sentimentales* and the *Gaspard de la Nuit, Le Tombeau de Couperin* was certainly a step backward in his harmonic evolution. The composition would never have attained its position among Ravel's works had it not been for the new form in which it was presented two years later. At the suggestion of D. E. Inghelbrecht, the conductor, Rolf de Maré, the head of the Swedish Ballet, decided to use the music for a ballet and Ravel orchestrated it. In this new attire *Le Tombeau de Couperin* has been making world tours in concert halls ever since Rhené Baton conducted it for the first time at the Concert Pasdeloup on February 28, 1920. On November 8, 1920, the Swedish Ballet gave the first performance of the ballet with Inghelbrecht conducting. Three pieces out of the suite—*Forlane, Menuet,* and *Rigaudon*—were danced against the charming décor of a *fête galante* and were such a success that during the following years the Swedish Ballet gave one hundred and sixty-seven performances. In 1923 Ravel himself conducted the one hundredth performance of the ballet at the Champs Élysées Theatre.

But there was at least one man who did not think that *Le Tombeau de Couperin* was worth the paper it was written on. This time Pierre Lalo out-Pierre-Laloed himself with a caustic remark in closing his review on November 16, 1920. "Couperin's Tomb by M. Ravel, that's nice. But how much nicer Ravel's Tomb by Couperin would be!"

To return to the fall of 1917, after Ravel finished the original piano score of *Le Tombeau de Couperin* he felt so weary, so depressed, his health was so run down that for the following year and a half he did not do much except orchestrate works already composed. In one of his melancholy moments Ravel said to Claude Delvincourt (present director of the Paris Conservatory):

> I have failed in my life. . . . I am not one of the great composers. All the great [composers] have produced enormously. There is everything in their work: the best and the worst, but there is always quantity. But I have written relatively very little . . . and at that, I did it with a great deal of difficulty. I did my work slowly, drop by drop. I have torn all of it out of me by pieces . . . and now I can not do any more and it does not give me any pleasure.

He stayed for a while with his brother Edouard in Saint-Cloud, but his health was not improving and finally it was decided that he should go for at least three months to the mountains.

Ravel enjoyed the beautiful country, the radiant sun, fresh air, the tranquility in Mégève, Haute-Savoie. He was told to exercise and he was already planning to learn to ski. But he did not sleep well. His doctor at first blamed it on the high altitude—thirty-five hundred feet above the sea level—and then suddenly forbade him all exercise and ordered a complete rest. Ravel suffered from the cold, he was bored, the piano in the little pension where he stayed was out of tune, and he could not use it. He had moments of terrible depression and others when he just "did not give a damn." But not for an instant would he think of returning home before he felt better. He would do anything to get well.

"I will climb still higher if need be. Why didn't they want me as an aviator?" he said, pointing at the surrounding mountain peaks.

Ravel knew he had "spots in his lungs," but thought his condition was not too serious and was glad that at last he knew the reason for the apathy he had felt ever since he came to Châlons-sur-Marne.

After six weeks in Mégève, Ravel gained one pound and only, as he said himself, because for more than ten days he "never moved, drank milk between meals, and with the help of Valeronal went to sleep right after lunch, the way the fat gentlemen do." But his pulse and his temperature jumped in an "insane fashion." He still suffered from insomnia, yet he did not think he felt any worse on account of it. He thought it was all a matter of habit. He woke up thirsty, his tongue coated with white. . . .

Unnecessarily his doctor quite often reminded him that he had never promised to cure him.

In April, 1918, Ravel returned to Paris, bringing with him the orchestration of the two Hebraic songs: *Kaddisch* and *L'Énigme éternelle*—the only work he accomplished while at Mégève. Again Ravel met some of his friends who had come back from the war. Now they somehow saw

things in a different light. There were no more sessions on
the Rue de Civry, no more meetings with the Apaches.
Whenever they heard the theme out of Borodin's Second
Symphony it gave them only a nostalgic pain, it was no
longer their rally call. Not that they quarreled with each
other—they had just drifted apart. Maurice Delage, who
owned the chalet at 3, Rue de Civry, told me that their
weekly meeting ceased partly because most of the Apaches
by then were married, and the cardinal rule—to keep
women out of the place as much as possible—broke down
their formal association. Yet the main reason lay deeper than
the "likes and dislikes" of their wives. They themselves
were no longer the same men; what Léon-Paul Fargue had
said in the past, that "they all agreed in their opinions, for
you can not discuss a subject except with those who agree
with you, and then you actually dispute only the details"
was no longer true.

Debussy was dead. With a group of other composers
Ravel was going to compose a piece in his memory—the
old dispute between the Debussyites and Ravelites belonged
to a remote past. Now, in 1919 Ravel was criticized by
another group of musicians, led by Ravel's old friend Erik
Satie. When Ravel had returned from the army, he had
already heard of the caustic remarks hurled at his music:
"a worn-out art, old and sterile" and of the new "*politique*"
his old friend Satie was stirring up.

"Let us wish for them," Ravel said, "that the '*politique*'
will not stay in the way of the work of these truly 'new
youth.' As for myself, my incurable pride won't let me be
afraid of anything and I bear no grudge. . . . Only so far

I have not understood a thing. . . ." The "new youth," as Satie nicknamed them, were to become known a few years later as The Six, a group of young composers of whom Ravel was to hear more.

Meanwhile, probably urged by Ravel's old friend Misia Sert, Diaghilev asked him to write another ballet. This time Ravel sat down to a subject of his own choice, one he had nursed in his heart ever since 1906, when he first mentioned it in a letter to Marnold.

> It is not subtle—what I am undertaking at the moment [Ravel wrote then]. It is a Grande Valse (*sic*) a sort of *hommage* to the memory of the Great Strauss, not Richard, the other—Johann. You know my intense sympathy for this admirable rhythm and that I hold *la joie de vivre* as expressed by the dance in far higher esteem than as by the Franckist puritanism. I am so little a Catholic.

The sketches for *Wien* (Vienna), as Ravel called the composition, had remained on the shelf during all these years. To be alone and undisturbed, Ravel accepted an invitation from his old friend Herold with whom at one time he collaborated on his adaptation of Hauptmann's *The Sunken Bell*. Herold took him to his family's old house in La Praz in Ardèche Vallée and after arranging everything for Ravel's comfort left him there alone. Ravel remained in La Praz for six months. Once again he became completely absorbed by his work and lived in a fever of creative excitement.

It was at this time, when depressed and ill from the war, trying to find his way back to his pleasure in living, living with the images of his own imagination, dancing in the large ballrooms of the Austrian Imperial Palace in the year 1855, that Ravel was suddenly interrupted by a long-distance call from Paris congratulating him on being awarded the *Légion d'Honneur*—the highest tribute to merit paid by the state in France. Maurice Ravel declined the honor. Although many Frenchmen including André Gide, Monet, Vuillard, Bonnard, Pierre Curie, Mme Marcelle Tinayre, Valloton, and Roussel have refused the decoration, Ravel's attitude created a regular scandal, another, the third *affaire Ravel*.

On April 8, 1920, *Le Temps* published the following:

> On January 15, Maurice Ravel, the composer, had been promoted to the grade of the knight of the *Légion d'Honneur* on the recommendation of M. Léon Berard, the Minister of Public Education and Fine Arts. Not without astonishment have we recently learned through the *Journal Officiel* that the decree of promotion for Maurice Ravel has been canceled in the following terms:
>
> The President of the Republic of France on the report of the Minister of Public Education and Fine Arts.
>
> Regarding the decree of January 15, 1920, concerning promotions and nominations in the *Légion d'Honneur*.
>
> Let it be decreed:
>
> Article I. The decree of January 15, 1920, mentioned above is canceled as concerns M. Ravel (Joseph-Maurice), composer of music.
>
> Article II. The Minister of Public Education and Fine Arts and the Grand Chancellor of the *Légion d'Honneur* are instructed to execute the present decree.
>
> Paris, April 2, 1920.   P. Deshane.

The newspaper carried all the information about this delicate situation that could be obtained from the Ministry of Public Education and the Chancellery of the *Légion d'Honneur*. At the former it was explained that Léon Berard had made his recommendation without Ravel's consent; that Ravel, as soon as he heard about it, had sent him a telegram thanking him for his attention but declining the honor for personal reasons; that a mutual friend had tried, unsuccessfully, to persuade Ravel to change his decision and that therefore there was nothing left to do but to revoke the nomination. It was further stated, according to a spokesman at the Chancellery of the *Légion d'Honneur* that since Ravel was only nominated but not yet decorated—he had failed to fill out the necessary official papers—the decree was automatically canceled. However, the whole *affaire* brought up a question which had not been foreseen by the French law because of its improbability: could one refuse to be decorated?

On April 10, 1920, the newspaper *Excelsior* published an answer to this question, asserting that there was no law which could force an individual to accept the red ribbon. But probably to admonish Ravel for his unusual behavior, it reminded its readers that an army officer or a government employee might be punished for breach of discipline.

Three days later *Le Matin* disclosed the following statement by Edouard Ravel, the composer's brother:

"My brother has refused the red ribbon out of principle, as he would refuse all other distinctions of honor. He has always declined offers of this kind whenever they have been made to him, saying that he would never wear a decoration, because he does not need it."

Only the last five words in this statement may be considered as corresponding to the truth—Ravel certainly did not need it. For this was the first time that the state had offered him an award, and later in his life Ravel himself proved the fallacy of his brother's assumption. On March 5, 1926, after the brilliant success of his opera *L'Enfant et les sortilèges*, Maurice Ravel was awarded the Knight's Cross of the Order of King Leopold of Belgium. Ravel was present at the performance and contrary to his usual behavior in France, came out on the stage of the Théâtre Royal de la Monnaie in Brussels and was enthusiastically applauded. Five years later, in 1931, Ravel traveled all the way to England to receive the *Doctor Honoris Causa* at Oxford University.

Would it not have been more natural to presume that Ravel remembered well how shabbily the state had treated him at the time of his competition for the Prix de Rome, when he did need help, remembered well the *nota bene* in Romain Rolland's article written at that time: "Isn't there any way for the state at least to prove its interest in Ravel?" Years later Ravel himself admitted that he declined the *Légion d'Honneur* out of pride. Evidently the state's action came a bit too late.

"I have lost a whole day away from my orchestra," was all that Ravel said about the whole business, referring to the congratulating telegrams and telephone calls and the general excitement which interrupted his work on *Wien*.

This composition, rechristened *La Valse*, eventually became one of Ravel's most popular works. However, when Diaghilev received the manuscript he refused to produce it as a ballet. Diaghilev did not see any possibility in the score for a choreographic development of Ravel's own vision of the ballet. "Drifting clouds give glimpses, through rifts, of couples waltzing. The clouds gradually scatter, and an immense hall can be seen, filled with a whirling crowd. The scene gradually becomes illuminated. The light of chandeliers bursts forth. An Imperial Court about 1855. . . ." These directions appeared to Diaghilev prohibitive for purely financial reasons. Ravel took this refusal as a mortal offense.

When, five years later, in 1925, Ravel went to Monte Carlo for the first performance of his *L'Enfant et les sortilèges* and the two men met, Diaghilev, greeting him, offered his hand. Ravel ignored the gesture. Diaghilev felt insulted and challenged him to a duel. Apparently, friends intervened and the matter was dropped. Fortunately they never met again.

Chapter Thirteen

The Six

RAVEL'S FRACAS with Diaghilev was caused not so much by personal animosity as by Ravel's indignation at the lack of respect for him as a composer, from which he had suffered on several occasions since the end of the war. There is an old theory that wars are followed by violence in postwar civilian life, because men whose aim was to kill still want to destroy after all the killing is done. The former concept of right and wrong and respect for established reputations and authorities has been thrown into a melting pot on the battle-field, and both those who were actually engaged in the struggle and those who remained at home hoped for a "new life." Like so many others at the front who had time to think, compare, and decide about "things at home," did not Ravel warn of the "cleaning to be done" when he came home? Did he not declare in a rather cocky way that he would arrive on "a horse, or preferably twelve horses" in the midst of the assembly of "the National League for the Defense of French Music in France"?

But Ravel came home a sick man, far more seriously ill than he ever realized. The National League was forgotten. When the Apaches returned, their close association had lost its verve, their meetings lost the old meaning and purpose. *C'est la guerre*, men said during the war when they lacked essentials in food and clothing. *C'est la guerre!*, they said afterward, blaming the war for the "new human behavior," "new vogue in dress and taste," and the "new trend in the arts."

During the first two years of the conflict the arts remained stagnant, as if struck by a thunderbolt. But by February of 1916 signs of a new life in the arts became apparent. From a café in Zurich the Rumanian poet, Tristan Tzara, launched the Dadaist movement—a new aesthetic cult advocating "an utter nihilism in the domain of the intellect and the arts," and in Italy Jean Cocteau, in collaboration with Pablo Picasso, was working on *Parade*, a ballet for which Satie wrote the music. A year later on March 18, 1917, the Parisian public was stirred up by Diaghilev's production of this ballet, given at a brilliant gala performance for a war charity at the Châtelet Théâtre. The press was hostile toward the new work and accused Cocteau, Picasso, and Satie of being *Boches*. It created a minor scandal, minor because Paris was living through its most tragic days of the war and the general public's interest in art was only secondary. But the musicians, the literati, and the artists were divided into camps, as always happens in Paris.

Stravinsky is quoted to have said that *Parade* marks a date in the history of French art, as *Carmen* did, and Cocteau announced that the Impressionists did not like it because for once they were served music without "the sauce." But when Ravel saw one of the rehearsals he said that he failed to understand it.

However, a new group of musicians rallied around Satie. They saw in his *Parade* an expression of the "new spirit" and Satie in turn, pleased with his role of mentor, called them *Nouveaux Jeunes*, the new youth. Thus, as soon as the roar of the German cannon was silenced, this small group of French musicians made their official entrance on the artistic field under the patronage of Cocteau and to the accompaniment of bugles, brass drums, triangles, toy trumpets, whistles, clapboards, cymbals, and the scraping of sandpaper. They became prominent almost overnight, not so much because of their works of art but because of the "new ideas" to which they pledged their allegiance. "We have had enough of clouds and mists," they declared, enough of waves in the aquarium, enough "of all these ondines and perfumes of the night. What we need now is the music of the soil, the music of our daily life."

In France, as I have said before, each artistic coterie had to have a sort of label. And it would certainly have been too unwieldy to refer to the four, then-unknown musicians Arthur Honegger, George Auric, Louis Durey, and Germaine Tailleferre, who were a year later joined by Francis Poulenc and Darius Milhaud, by reciting all their names. Yet they had to be differentiated from the Impressionists, from Ravelites and Debussyites. They were not Dadaists nor cubists nor surrealists. They could have been called Satie-istes, but Satie would have objected strongly. Instead they were given a name which by its connotation set them on a pedestal much higher than they deserved. The music critic, Henri Collet, after meeting them at Milhaud's, wrote an article in *Comoedia*[1] and spoke of them as a "Group of Six," similar to the Russian "Group of Five." The Group of Six, or The Six became their official title.

And as if to accentuate the resemblance between the French Six and the Russian Five, Jean Cocteau took upon himself the role enjoyed by Vladimir Stassov in St. Petersburg, that of the intellectual leader of the group. The members of Diaghilev's company had called Cocteau *l'enfant terrible* because of his overvivacious behavior during the rehearsals when the ballet first came to Paris in 1908. Now in 1919 his little booklet *Cock and Harlequin* became the bible for his friends to think and to live by. This compendium of platitudes, delivered in typical Cocteau brassy style occasionally interspersed with original twists of old axioms, actually served as the source for The Six's *raison d'être* and quotations to *épater les bourgeois:* "Enough of hammocks, garlands, and gondolas, I want some one to build me music I can live in, like a house. . . . MUSICAL BREAD is what we WANT. MUSIC ON WHICH ONE WALKS. THE CAFÉ-CONCERT IS OFTEN PURE; THE THEATRE IS ALWAYS CORRUPT."

"Debussy is dead! Long live The Six!" proclaimed their ardent followers, cheering them long before their diverse personalities were clearly defined.

[1] "Les Cinq Russes, les six Français et Erik Satie," *Comoedia* (January 16 and 23, 1920).

"Out of six there are only five," Erik Satie later re-marked. For Louis Durey, the eldest in the group (born in 1888), was too Ravelite, "too respectable," to remain with them long.

"Out of five there are only three," Satie continued. Honegger, the most serious and hard-working among them, and Tailleferre—the Muse of Montparnasse—soon went their own ways: the former to become France's most emi-nent composer, and the latter almost the least.

"Out of three there is only one," Erik Satie concluded. Poulenc for a long time remained a composer of charming little salon pieces, while Milhaud, the most prolific of them, like Honegger developed a personality of his own. Thus, George Auric, the youngest among them (1899), was left as the only true spokesman for the so-called Six.

"I do not like catastrophes, tragedies, and ruins," Auric declared, "and I do not care to walk around the Acropolis. These famous landscapes are just as stupid as the souls of my famous neighbors—Dada, the Ninth Symphony, De-bussy. The lessons of humility depress me and I am bored by the *Sacre du Printemps*. I would prefer a shot of strychnine."

At the beginning of their careers The Six, like naughty children, wrote facile pieces in which raw colors, sarcasm, and impudence predominated whatever they wished to say. They quoted and burlesqued the old masters, the classics, as well as Wagner, Mahler, Strauss, and thumbed their noses at whomever pleased their fancy. In their composi-tions, like Auric's *Fox-trot—Adieu New York, Paris-Sport*, and *Le Quatorze Juillet*; Milhaud's *Soirées de Petrograd*, and *Les Mariées de la Tour Eiffel*, on which all six collaborated, one hears banal military marches, vulgar street songs, jazz and dance tunes of Negro and South American bands, and sounds of broken-down pianolas, reminding one of merry-go-rounds, country fairs, and movies. One hears tunes of all ages and all kinds, from pastoral eighteenth-century airs to the braying brass of jazz bands and imitations of exhaust pipes. Although sharp and jerky, full of violence and cruel mockery, nevertheless this music had a primitive charm, ill-mannered wit, and eccentricity which could not fail to attract attention, if not always to please. The brevity of these works was their cardinal virtue. Short pieces for ensembles as small as six, eight, or ten men, they were written in such popular style that they could be performed as well at the railroad station, circus, or country fair as in a concert hall.

The Six declared that Ravel's music was "arty," "excessively refined," and on the whole "outworn." For once Ravel kept aloof from their criticism, although he did not keep his ears closed to this new aesthetic cult. He disagreed with the very premises of their theory that the future of French music lay in drawing inspiration and material from folklore and street songs. He believed that French music had always been more subject to literary influence, and that Gounod, Chabrier, and Liszt were the sources from which the main stream of French music was derived. Speaking of Debussy's role in the development of French music, he refused to classify him as an Impressionist, for impressionism, Ravel said, was a term borrowed from a sister art, which had very little application to music, and he believed that Debussy achieved through intellectual perception what

Chopin had done from inspiration or intuition. Ravel admitted that he followed Debussy in the ideal of economy of material, but that he could not go along with him in his respect for forms and that in his own view of melody—that is, the melodic line as distinct from the *thème développé*—he considered himself as a Mozartian.

Ravel was convinced that while social evolution was moving toward internationalism, music was becoming more and more national. He thought that foreign influence, coming even from such a force as Schönberg, hardly touched the development of French music, which is essentially Latin in nature, and that the musical apathy into which the French musicians had fallen during the war had at last reached its end.

"At that time," Ravel concluded, "I was near despair. Now that we have likes and dislikes, we are alive again. At last, we will start again to battle."

Ravel's entrance into the fighting ring was not that of a contestant but of a champion who came to claim his title after a short period of retirement. To prove to the "new youth" that he was still the youngest among them he set himself a difficult musical problem. He worked at it diligently, but it was not to be solved until he had coped with another pressing problem, that of establishing a home of his own.

After the death of his mother Ravel never returned to their apartment at 4, Avenue Carnot; his friends persuaded him to stay away from the place where every object brought painful memories of his loss. For almost four years Ravel did not have a home of his own. When he was in Paris he stayed with Mme Dreyfus (Roland-Manuel's mother) or with his brother Edouard. The rest of the time he visited friends in the country.

". . . I am not particularly predisposed to solitude—a bit deadly, it's true, but it does not bother me," Ravel made this contradictory statement in his letter from La Praz to Mlle Marnold, the critic's daughter, on March 25, 1920. "Still I wish you would inquire about a little hut for me, but it must be at least thirty kilometers away from Paris."

Ravel wanted his future home to be in Ile-de-France, which stretches its fields and forests for thirty miles north of Paris. For years the gentle landscapes along the Seine and the Oise have been admired by poets, painters, and musicians who sought seclusion for their work, but who still wished to remain in the vicinity of Paris. Gounod lived at Saint-Cloud, Debussy at Saint-Germain, Zola at Médan, Flaubert at Mantes-la-Jolie, Corot at the lake of Ville-d'Avray, and Renoir, Millet, Cézanne, Sisley, and Claude Monet—all had their homes in this part of France. Montfort-l'Amaury where Ravel finally found a house is one of those little towns that still does not have a railroad station and has less than two thousand inhabitants. It is beyond Versailles on the road to Brittany, about twenty-five miles out of Paris.

After looking over several properties in the vicinity of the Rambouillet Forest, Ravel decided on a house which suited him as if it had been built according to his own plans. Who but Ravel would choose a house with one story in front and three at the back? A small ornate turret sits with an air of importance on the roof of this gingerbread toy house catching the visitor's attention as he climbs up the hill at the curve of the road to Houdan. *Le Belvédère*, Ravel named his house, perhaps because of this turret or perhaps because the little rooms are so unlike the halls of the Viennese Royal Palace.

It was his first home of his own, and the business of remodeling and furnishing it to his taste made Ravel extremely happy. In Montfort l'Amaury—with its medieval name, with its old Saint-Pierre church and its chapel Notre-Dame-du-Chêne, with the old dungeons of Guillaume de Hainaut (996) and a tower of Anne of Brittany (1498)—Ravel did not want a modern house, except of course for the kitchen and bathroom. For his interior decorating he chose his favorite period—the first half of the eighteenth century.

But by the time Ravel was halfway through he had a strange, fine, sometimes odd or even ridiculous collection of pieces of furniture, trinkets, and knickknacks: crystal candlesticks of Gothic-Restoration style, all sorts of colored boxes, glassware, seashells, a miniature white and orange chest-of-drawers with small glass candlesticks, a naval scene with painted waves under a globe, an inkstand in the form of cathedral and writing pens made of duck's feathers, a small Basque door knocker used as a paperweight, and a mechanical toy nightingale, whom Ravel called Zizi, in a gilded cage: the bird would sing and flutter its wings to the great amusement of its master. All these *bibelots* were arranged with care, just as the curtains, rugs, and the small bookshelves were well planned and carefully chosen. The bathroom, with its checkered black-and-white bath mats and towels with large initials showed that the owner of the

house spent an unusually long time on grooming himself.
A row of bottles containing various hair tonics and lotions
for shaving were displayed on the shelves and a most elab-
orate manicure set was laid out like surgical instruments on
a little table that stood by itself.

For a musician's house there was a surprising lack of
evidence of his work except, of course, for the grand piano,
but even this was covered with so many things that it could
have belonged to any drawing room. It was one of Ravel's
peculiarities never to leave any traces of his hard work—
books, music paper, or scores. Ravel's little house reminded
one of his friends of a ship divided into small cabins, another
thought it was done in such bad taste that it looked like
chamber of horrors, and still another compared it to the
house of a provincial old maid. Personally I do not think it
was as bad as all that, particularly if compared to the two
rooms in Victor Bonnet's[2] house in Paris, which several
years later were reserved for him whenever he cared to stay
there. These rooms, in contrast to Ravel's country place,
were "modern." One was a small crowded bedroom with
a single bed, *bar Americaine*, two high barstools cushioned
in bright red leather, and a cupboard containing various
collections of tiny knickknacks. The other was a work-
room, still smaller than the bedroom, with a wooden desk
facing a window, and two ugly aluminum chairs. Since the
only window in the room looked out on a rather prosaic
view of the chimneys and roofs of the industrial neighborhood of Levallois, an ingenious contraption of small round

[2] A former business associate of Joseph Ravel and a close friend of the
family.

metal disks covered the shutters so that the view was trans-
formed into a nightmarish picture of "things to come," as
suggested by the German moving picture, *Metropolis*, then
much in vogue.

Now, these rooms certainly would leave one with an
impression that whoever lived and worked in such surroundings was a weird fellow. But *Le Belvédère* did not
make such an unwholesome impression. The house at Montfort-l'Amaury was set in a small garden which Ravel trans-
formed into a Japanese garden and for which he was
constantly buying rare plants. He was going to prove, as in
his own musical compositions, that he could have everything landscaped on a small scale.

By the middle of May, 1921, Ravel had made such
progress in arranging his home that he wrote to his friends:
"The installation advances! In a few months I will be able
to have my piano." He was full of enthusiasm, full of the
joy of life, which he vainly had tried to recapture when he
first returned from the front, and yet three months later the
old depression seemed to gnaw at him once again.

". . . After all it matters little where I get bored: at St.
Jean-de-Luz, or at Montfort or anywhere else . . . I continue to work here, but this does not prevent my boredom.
Now that all the arrangements for my house are almost
completed, I would like to go somewhere else and start all
over again. I am a character in the genre of the romantics,
eh?"

Despite his protestations Ravel simply could not bear
the solitude. The novelty of arranging his house soon wore
off, and he still went back and forth to Paris or visited

friends who lived in the neighborhood, because he felt lonely at Montfort-l'Amaury.

Upon his return home Ravel would find his *Belvédère* "even more lugubrious" than when he left and he became even more depressed when he discovered the humidity of the country, the smell of the sewage pipes, and the howling of the wind. "My room, my winter room," he cried, "is icy cold. Whether I keep the windows open or closed, the cold keeps me awake, and yet it is mild outdoors." Mme Révelot, his faithful *bonne*, was to take care of him and *Le Belvédère* for almost fifteen years; and a small but "cumbersome" family of Siamese cats shared his new home. At first it was the kitten Jazz, whose place was taken later on by Mouni and Minon and their cousins, all playing "jungle," hiding in his rolls of music paper, arching their backs as though expecting a calamity to strike, and then suddenly walking calmly up to their master to lick the end of his nose as if the imminent danger had never occurred to them. Ravel loved cats, loved to watch their play, "to listen to them chatter in their foreign language, and to see these Indo-chinese," as he said, "in terror, when the North Wind trumpeted like an elephant at the door of my room."

At one point Ravel was ready to give up *Le Belvédère* and leave, but gradually he got used to it, although when-ever he could find a pretext for going to Paris he went there. "Ravel says that he lives in the Paris suburbs, yet it is easier to find him almost anywhere except at home," his friends used to say. But then again there were periods, sometimes lasting through many weeks, when he would "lock himself up," would not even answer the telephone, and would spend all his time at work. The *Duo*, a sonata for violin and cello, intended to prove to The Six that he was far from the *vieux jeux* they thought him to be, was completed during one of these spells. Ravel admitted that no other composition caused him so much difficulty. It took him a year and a half. "This devil of a *Duo* is giving me agony," he wrote on September 22, 1921, to Roland-Manuel, but a week later he said that he began to see a little light in the *Duo*. On February 3, 1922, he triumphantly announced that it was finished, and then he noticed that "the scherzo was much too highly developed, much too long and ugly, and so I started it all over again, using fresh material . . ."

Finally the *Duo* was ready for its first performance at one of the *Société Musicale Indépendante* concerts. It is a piece in the tradition of the eighteenth century when the combinations of violin with viola de gamba and with cello were popular. Ravel may have been inspired by Kodály's duet for the same combination of instruments. Although it was published only in 1922, it had already been composed in 1914 and Ravel no doubt knew about it, since he was always interested in Kodály's music. "The reduction to essentials," Ravel said about the *Duo*, "is carried to extremes. The fascination of harmony is disregarded." Was Ravel saying in his own words what Jean Cocteau called "without sauce"? No one had ever written a duo resembling this sonata in four parts: its texture harder than that of Schönberg's music and more devoid of embellishments, more "naked" than that of Satie. Some musicians felt that Ravel had risked his reputation in accepting the challenge of the new ideas; others, mostly his close friends, did not show much enthusiasm for the piece and regretted that he paid any attention at all to The Six.

On April 6, 1922, at the old Salle Pleyel, Ravel's friends, Hélène Jourdan-Morhange, the violinist, and Maurice Marechal, the cellist, played the *Duo* for the first time in public. But it had no success. There was a feeling in the audience that it was the fault of the performers—some one even quoted Ravel as saying that his work was "massacred," that more false notes had been played than were indicated in the music.

Ravel himself, on the contrary, seemed to have been perfectly satisfied with the performance, denied any quotations attributed to him, and insisted that the composition marked a turning point in his style, "in my evolution," as he put it.

Speaking of his work, Ravel often had said that as soon as a composition was achieved he lost his interest in it and turned toward new ideas. Whether this was always true or not it was the case with the *Duo*, for Ravel never had mentioned it again and returned to a composition which took him longer to finish than any he had ever written.

During the war Jacques Rouché had asked Colette to write a script for an opera. When the time came to choose a composer, Rouché suggested Ravel. Colette had vague recollections of meeting him at the beginning of the century at the home of Mme Saint-Marceaux, and remembered his pleated shirts, his double-breasted waistcoats, and gay neckties better than any conversation she had had with him. Afterward Colette had lost sight of him and only occasionally heard his music. A little apprehensively, since their styles were diametrically opposed, she agreed to have the manuscript sent to Ravel's army address. But it never reached him. When Ravel was demobilized, Rouché approached him again with Colette's *Le Ballet pour ma fille.* "But I don't have a daughter," Ravel said as he took the manuscript.

Five years went by before Ravel even spoke about it to Colette—his librettist. When he finally did come to consult her, all he wanted to know was whether she would mind if he changed the sound "mouao" to "mouain" in the duet of two cats.

Ravel believed that opera in the old style was dead and that the opera's future lay in the direction indicated by Rimsky-Korsakov's *Coq d'Or.* He believed that if he were to write an opera it should be a sort of lyrical fantasia which would be a mixture of every style from the purest lyricism to music hall. Colette's story suited Ravel's taste perfectly. It is about a boy who has a bad day: he does not feel like studying, is nasty to his mother, and goes berserk torturing his pets, destroying furniture, and ripping curtains to pieces. He even starts a fire, but eventually falls asleep. In his dream he sees a princess, his first love, but she turns away from him, and then all the objects which he destroyed and the animals he tortured come to life and turn against him. In the general scramble he is hurt, but despite his pain he takes care of a wounded squirrel. This wins the animals' sympathy. They want to help him, but do not know how. When the boy calls weakly *"maman,"* although the animals do not know the meaning of the word they call in chorus *"maman"* and the boy's mother comes to forgive him.

It is unfair to tell in so few words this touching fairy tale, one that might have deeper meaning, portraying the brutality of the human race as compared to the goodness of the animal world, a tale of a helpless human being whose first and the last words are "*maman.*" This was Ravel's world, the world of a child, of make-believe and dreams. For the adult world in which the dramatic element is based on love and death unfortunately was denied to Maurice Ravel. Human passions leading to bliss or despair and destruction were foreign vistas to him. His sophistication, his gentleness, his superior intelligence and sense of proportion —these were the qualities which made this "childish piece" a masterpiece.

Ravel worked slowly on *L'Enfant et les sortilèges*—the title under which the piece later became known—and with many interruptions; and if it were not for Raoul Gunsberg, the director of the Monte Carlo opera, who persuaded Ravel to sign a contract for a production in 1925, he would have lingered much longer. He was depressed, suffered from insomnia, and was in no mood to compose. He would "much rather orchestrate something," he said. Serge Koussevitzky's commission for an orchestration of Mussorgsky's *Pictures at an Exhibition* came at just the right moment. Ravel accepted it with joy.

Once again the collection of N. Findeisen's articles that Calvocoressi brought back from his trip to Russia provided Ravel with useful information about the changes from the original in Rimsky-Korsakov's published edition of Mussorgsky's *Pictures at an Exhibition*. Ravel wanted to work from the original version, but since this was impossible to obtain, Calvocoressi, who lived in London and whom Ravel had not seen since the outbreak of the war, sent him the first edition of this work.

During the summer of 1922 while visiting Roland-Manuel at Lyons-la-Forêt, Ravel completed this score—a masterpiece in craftsmanship. Then, with the sketches for *L'Enfant et les sortilèges* lying in the drawer of his work table, he took some time out to compose a piece for violin and piano—a *Berceuse* on the name of Fauré, in honor of his old teacher.

While he worked on the *Duo*, Ravel had often consulted Hélène Jourdan-Morhange on the instrumental possibilities of the violin and now as if looking for another excuse not to work on *L'Enfant et les sortilèges* he sent her a telegram: "Come quickly and bring the Paganini Etudes with you." This was the starting point for *Tzigane*, a super virtuoso Hungarian rhapsody which he wrote for Jelly d'Arányi, the Hungarian violinist.

L'Enfant et les sortilèges remained in the drawer of his desk. There were still other reasons for Ravel's slow progress on the score. Since the end of the war his popularity abroad had grown and he was invited to conduct in Amsterdam, Venice, Vienna, and London. Ravel loved to conduct, and although he never improved he was very pleased when he could report that according to the London newspapers he was "at least a good, if not a great conductor."

When Ravel returned from his travels, his life was even more social than before the war. Now that he had his own home he entertained his friends. Sundays were reserved for sumptuous lunches with Ravel playing barman. Cocktails were a new vogue in Paris and Ravel would emerge from the cellar of the house to surprise his guests with his latest concoctions, each christened with a fancy name—*Phi Phi, Valencia,*[3] etc. After lunch the guests had to see his garden (this was obligatory) to admire the new plants and the flowers, to walk by "a little foot-path" to "a little water fountain" in "a little pond."

Ravel took great joy in showing off every detail of his house. The element of surprise was as important to him in this ceremony as it was in his music. "It's an imitation," he would chuckle when he saw his friends admiring what they thought to be rare prints on the walls of his sitting room, and he was delighted whenever the illusionary effect fooled the visitor. Serious topics and serious discussions of musical problems were kept out of the conversation. Yes, he was working on an opera, but that was all Ravel would say.

After Sunday lunch he would take his friends on a long walk in the Rambouillet Forest where Ravel knew every road and every path, where he talked about the trees and the birds whose songs he could imitate to perfection. In the evening they returned to a little bistro in the square at Montfort-l'Amaury.

During the weekdays Ravel always found an excuse to go to Paris. He stopped at a little hotel on the Rue d'Athènes near the Godebskis. His favored night clubs in Paris were the *Boeuf sur le Toit* on the Rue Boissy d'Anglas and the *Grand Écart* in Montmartre. *Boeuf sur le Toit* was opened in 1919 and the snobs flocked there to see Cocteau. In a

---

[3] *Phi Phi* (short for Phidias), operetta by Henri Christine, first presented in Paris, 1918.

Valencia, a popular song by Padilla, made famous by Mistinguette at the Moulin Rouge in the early twenties.

small room crowded to the last inch of space the elite of the Parisian artistic world and the curious bourgeois gathered there to gossip, to see and to be seen to the accompaniment of Wiener and Douset, the pianists who introduced the latest jazz hits from America.

"What I like about jazz is that it cries of pain and you just don't give a damn about it," Eric Satie said, and the smart set and The Six quoted him with joy. At first they said that they hated jazz, then they laughed at it, and finally they ended by imitating it. The American postwar influence in music as well as in drinks and dress reached them through the *Boeuf sur le Toit*, which might just as well have been called *Tout Vas* (Anything Goes), like the famous Parisian gambling house, for, spiritually speaking, any stake no matter how high or low was accepted there, whether in the field of morals or aesthetics. It was hard to tell the male and female *Boeuf sur le Toit* habitués apart, so mannish were the suits of the women and so baggy the trousers of the men. The night club had a shallow atmosphere, where egotism reigned supreme, and it is puzzling how Ravel, who did not drink much, could have spent night after night there for years. With the last customers to leave *Boeuf sur le Toit* Ravel and his party would move to Montmartre where other friends were sure to join him after the theater or concert, and eventually all of them would wind up the evening at the central market place, Les Halles, for a bowl of onion soup.

Ravel dreaded the nights. He would do anything to escape insomnia. He would make the rounds of the night clubs and then walk his friends home before he walked home himself, no matter what the distance was. All his life he went to bed late and got up around noon, but after he returned from the war his insomnia kept him awake sometimes for days, so that he had to "take Veronal and sleep it out, sometimes for twenty-four hours, in order not to crack up," as he said.

With *L'Enfant et les sortilèges* still locked away in his desk Ravel again started on another work: a sonata for violin and piano for Hélène Jourdan-Morhange. "It won't be very difficult," he promised her, "and it won't sprain your wrist."

It was during this summer of 1923 that he signed the contract with Raoul Gunsberg for *L'Enfant et les sortilèges,* the score to be delivered not later than the end of the following year. In the spring of 1924, when he suddenly discovered that he had not progressed very far with the sonata and that the time for *L'Enfant et les sortilèges* was running short, he shut himself up again in his *Belvédère:* "I am going out just enough to prevent me from cracking up. If *L'Enfant et les sortilèges* doesn't get finished it won't be my fault."

"There is a bit of everything in it," Ravel said later, referring to the score. "There is a little of Massenet, of Puccini, of American music, and of Monteverdi." He was anticipating severe criticism for this mixture of styles, but he was sure that his collaborator Colette would not be perturbed by it, and as for himself he said that he did not give a God damn.

Long before the scheduled opening night, March 21, 1925, Ravel was on hand in Monte Carlo. He was very pleased to find a "really extraordinary conductor" in Victor de Sabata and an orchestra which he thought was "superior." Ravel was flattered by the genuine enthusiasm for his work, from Gunsberg, the director, down to the last usher in the hall, including members of the orchestra, the chorus, and the soloists—a good omen in his opinion.

The Monte Carlo performance was a success, but when a year later on February 1, *L'Enfant et les sortilèges* was presented at the Opéra-Comique in Paris it barely missed becoming a minor "scandal." At the end of the first act some in the audience began to giggle, and others voiced furious protest against the all too realistic duet of two cats. The stodgy "subscribers' audience" of the Opéra-Comique was just as hostile to what they considered music-hall effects in the concert hall as they had been to the "immorality" of *L'Heure espagnole,* given in the same theater some twelve years before.

However, this time the press, with only a few exceptions, was on Ravel's side and the future of *L'Enfant et les sortilèges* was in no way jeopardized by a lack of welcome at its birth. Ravel's *Lyric Fantasia* survived fifteen performances during the following two seasons at the Opéra-Comique, and was applauded in London, New York, Brussels, Prague, and Leipzig.

But Ravel had hoped to see it produced on the stage of the Opéra in Paris. In 1930 he wrote Jacques Rouché, who had originally commissioned the work: "I am taking back my child from the Opéra-Comique to give it to you." Rouché often promised to produce it and indeed did, on May 17, 1939. But once again it came too late. Maurice Ravel had been dead for a year and a half.

Chapter Fourteen

American Concert Tour.
Boléro

MAURICE RAVEL's contact with the United States, where today his works are played more often than anywhere else in the world including France, began with a cable he received during the summer of 1925 from Hans Kindler, commissioning a piece of chamber music for voice, piano, cello, and flute for the Coolidge Foundation. Ravel had heard of Mrs. Elizabeth Sprague Coolidge's musical foundation, which each year sponsored free concerts in public libraries, universities, and colleges throughout the United States, but he was particularly delighted by what he thought was "the exotic combination of instruments" in the prescribed quartet. He had just finished a voice and piano version of the first of the *Chansons madécasses*, inspired by the

French translation by Evariste Parny, and decided to offer this one song to the Coolidge Foundation. Within a month he was ready for Mrs. Coolidge's gala performance at the Hôtel Majestic in Paris in October of 1925.

The performance turned out to be not without incident, this time on political grounds. France was at war with Abd-el-Krim in Morocco and the first words in the song "Aoua"—"Aoua, Aoua! Beware of the whites, o dwellers on the riverbanks . . ."—were considered subversive by some members of the elegant audience. They voiced a loud protest and demonstratively left the hall. This, however, did not stop the performers from repeating the song for the enthusiastic audience which remained in the hall, nor did it prevent the Minister of War from applauding when on June 13 of the following year (1926) he attended the "official" first performance of *Chansons madécasses* at the Salle Érard. In addition to "Aoua," Ravel set to music two more of the Madagascan poems:

> "Nadanhove—you leave me, and I shall languish in regret
> and desire,
> I shall languish until evening;
> You will return this evening, Nadanhove,
> o beautiful Nadanhove . . ."

and "It is pleasant to lie down during the hours of the heat . . ."

The cycle of these three songs is considered the best among Ravel's chamber-music works written after World War I. Ravel himself made the following comment: "I think that the three *Chansons madécasses* bring into being a new, dramatic, almost erotic element, resulting from the subject matter of Parny's poems. They form a sort of a quartet with the voice as the chief instrument. Simplicity is all-important. The independence of the voices shown there is more obvious in the Sonata . . ."

Ravel meant the *Sonate* for violin and piano which he had finally completed. Taking as a premise the essential incompatibility of the two instruments, piano and violin, Ravel composed a piece which did not "sink their differences," as he said, "but accentuated this incompatibility to an even greater degree." Despite the obvious influence of jazz in the second movement, and a virtuoso *perpetuum mobile* in the last movement, it remains a cerebral *tour de force*, perhaps another proof of his technical skill rather than a spontaneous product of his inner self.

Ravel was tired and needed a rest. He blamed his weariness on the insomnia which never left him. At one of the concerts at L'École Normale, Hélène Jourdan-Morhange became suddenly aware of Ravel's "lost" appearance as he sat at the piano playing his sonata. She persuaded him to visit a friend of hers, Dr. Vallery-Radot, right after the concert. After several tests and examinations Dr. Vallery-Radot told Morhange that it was not a temporary fatigue due to insomnia, but that Ravel's state of health was far more serious than his friends thought. He advised complete rest and for a long period. Fortunately, Ravel's friends thought, there was an occasion for such a rest without Ravel's actually realizing it. Ravel had been invited for a concert tour in the United States and three months away from his desk would certainly be beneficial, they hoped.

But for a man who had spent almost all his life in his native country, the decision to go on a concert tour to the

United States was an event of real magnitude. In 1925 when Ravel's friends, the pianist Robert Schmitz and his wife asked him to come to America, Ravel said that he was not a concert pianist and would not want to play his own works. Then, in 1926, the couple called on him at Montfort-l'Amaury and this time they had a more concrete proposition. They offered Ravel a minimum of ten thousand dollars for a three-month tour in the United States, five thousand dollars to be guaranteed by "Pro Musica," an organization for promoting the works of contemporary musicians. Robert Schmitz was the president of "Pro Musica," which had branches in all the major cities in the United States. As for the other five thousand, they were sure they could raise it once it was announced that Ravel was coming. And indeed, it was arranged immediately upon the Schmitz' return to this country. Mason & Hamlin, the piano-manufacturing firm, was willing to pay five thousand dollars for the privilege of having Ravel play their piano exclusively.

Ten thousand dollars was a large sum for a man who, when asked about his financial affairs, usually said that he could do with an extra thousand francs. Ravel agreed to come in the season of 1927-28. But the arrangement with Mason & Hamlin meant that he would have to perform as a pianist—the least attractive clause in his contract. Never a good pianist, Ravel had stopped practicing a long time ago. His best piano pieces were technically beyond his reach. Now he toyed with the idea of writing a concerto for piano and orchestra, "but a rather short one, a concertino in length, but not in style, a concerto which would not be too difficult, so that I could play it myself . . . ," he said.

But Ravel was not well enough to undertake a major work. Instead he passed his time composing a song, *Rêves*, after Léon-Paul Fargue's poem and a short piece, "Fanfare," to precede a ballet, *L'Éventail de Jeanne*, for which seven pieces were contributed by seven composers: Poulenc, Auric, Milhaud, Ferroud, Ibert, Roland-Manuel, and Delannoy.

For once Ravel collaborated with three composers out of The Six—Poulenc, Auric, and Milhaud. This fanfare for the children's ballet consists of a few bars crescendo from a distant, hardly audible murmur to a full blast of the whole orchestra. *Wagneramente*—Ravel indicated in the score, to make sure that no one would misunderstand him.

Besides, Ravel was too preoccupied with his preparations for the forthcoming trip to have enough peace of mind to compose. He felt that it was imperative for him to have an ample supply of clothes to meet every emergency of climate and local temperature as well as for every kind of social function, on his travels through the United States. For weeks he fussed with refurbishing his wardrobe with new summer and winter clothes, shirts by the dozens for every conceivable occasion, the double-breasted waistcoats of which he boasted as his invention, ties, shoes, scarves, and gloves and some twenty pairs of pajamas!

A week before he sailed, Ravel suddenly realized how seriously he was in need of rest. One morning as he walked into his bathroom he seemed to see the washstand turning rapidly from right to left, then the same thing happening to the bath, and then to the whole room.

"You can imagine," Ravel later told a friend, "that I

quickly returned to bed and closed my eyes from fear of
seeing my bed do the 'looping' with such agility as I would
never have believed it capable of at its age. Without thinking of telephoning, my faithful *bonne* ran to fetch a doctor
who arrived at a time when I was going to crack up, to give
me a shot of camphor oil, I think."

The doctor advised an even more strict regime and
Ravel's friends could hardly wait for him to leave for the
United States, to have a change of environment, distraction,
and above all a rest from his work.

On December 28, 1927, Ravel sailed for New York on
the *France*. He was told that she rolled worse than any ship
on the ocean and for weeks he fretted about the voyage.
When he finally sailed he traveled in great style. So that he
could work undisturbed, besides his own cabin with bath,
the French company put at his disposal a luxury suite comprising a sitting room, a dining room, two bedrooms, etc.
Ravel liked that. Nonchalantly he referred to the extra suite
of rooms as his "studio." Despite all predictions he enjoyed
the crossing. The rolling of the boat lulled him to "a delicious sleep" and the fresh air gave him "a lion's appetite."
He spent New Year's Eve at the ship's party, which was
just like being at the *Boeuf sur le Toit* with "dancing, jazz,
Russian cabaret singers, champagne, colored balloons, ser-
pentine, and drunk Americans," he said.

Ravel, with his friends' help, managed to avoid the
ship's reporters and photographers on his arrival in New
York. A few days after, he attended a Boston Symphony
concert in Carnegie Hall, and it was then that he received
the first proof of the American welcome. Koussevitzky and

the audience cheered him until he came up on the stage to take a bow.

Ravel's official first appearance in the United States was scheduled for January 15 at the Gallo Theatre in New York City under the auspices of "Pro Musica." However, Koussevitzky managed to spirit him away to Harvard where on January 12, Ravel conducted the Boston Symphony Orchestra in a concert including *Le Tombeau de Couperin*, *Rapsodie espagnole*, and *La Valse*.

Thus, whether officially or not, his concert tour began—a series of triumphs—and the most strenuous he had ever undertaken.

In New York he played his *Sonatine* and, as encores, *Habanera* and *Pavane pour une Infante défunte* and accompanied Greta Torpadie in *Les Histoires naturelles* and *Chansons madécasses* in a concert which opened with his *String Quartet*. The concert was strictly a chamber music affair: Joseph Szigeti played the *Sonate* for violin and piano with Ravel, and Carlos Salzedo, the harpist, closed the program with a performance of *The Introduction and Allegro* for harp, string quartet, flute, and clarinet.

Olin Downes, the New York *Times* music critic, almost predicted the reaction of the musicians and the audiences who applauded Ravel throughout the country when on January 16 he wrote in his column:

> Mr. Ravel would not profess to be a piano virtuoso. What he did was to distinguish the concert with his presence, and, as a pianist, to present clear expositions of his music. . . .
>
> The precision and the taste of his workmanship, the complete technical mastery of his medium, the care with

which each different musical idea was worked out complete, impeccable in form and style, were striking manifestations of the art of a composer whose works rebuke the pretense and dilettantism so fashionable in many quarters of Paris today. . . .

Nothing could have been more typical of the precision, economy and refinement of this music than the slight, aristocratic, gray-haired and self-contained gentleman who bore himself with a characteristic reticence and modesty; well content as it were, to give an accounting of what he had done, and to leave his listeners to their own conclusions. And, indeed, his achievement speaks for itself.

Never to have composed in undue haste; never to have offered the public a piece of unfinished work; to have experienced life as an observant and keenly interested beholder, and to have fashioned certain of its elements into exquisite shapes of art that embody the essence of certain French traditions, is a goal worth the gaining.

That much was agreed upon about Ravel the musician. At the same time, the question of his origins once again became a subject of discussion. According to Roland-Manuel it was "the name Ravel, which belongs to some Jewish families (in such cases the name is derived from *rabbele*—a young rabbi), that gave rise in America to a belief in Ravel's Semitic origins. Many proofs have been produced in support of this mistaken opinion," continues Roland-Manuel, "especially the interest which Maurice Ravel took in Jewish matters, his harmonizations of Hebrew melodies, and, above all, the close friendship he formed with several Jewish people who were—and are—some of his finest interpreters and best friends."

Actually there was additional evidence for this supposition. Ravel had been in this country only a few days when, a cellist in the Boston Symphony Orchestra, Mr. Gdal Saleski, had an interview with him during a rehearsal intermission. "Since he did not speak English (or rather very little) our first violinist René Polain helped out as interpreter," Mr. Saleski said. "It was during this interview that Ravel told me that his mother was of Jewish origin." The question must have been pursued further and finally, upon his return to France, Ravel answered it in the following letter to his American concert manager:

My dear Laberge—

In reply to your letter of June 1st, I want to confirm to you that my father and mother were Catholics and I am not a Jew. I want to add that if I were, I would in no way hide it, but I would like to re-establish these facts.

Cordially yours,
Maurice Ravel.

June 3, 1928.

Ravel was in a strange country, among people he knew only from the tourists he met in France, and whose language he did not understand. Ravel's idea of Americans was one generally held by the French: of men who have not yet grown up, but good boys at heart, rough and loud and wizards in mechanics and gadgets. As a matter of fact, for the first time in his life, whether he ever realized it or not, Ravel landed in his own world: a land of the fantastic and "supernatural," and had not the country been so vast, the distances which he had to cover in his travels so great, the contrasts in climate so sudden, Ravel would have been even happier during the almost four months in this country.

Ravel saw the United States from the windows of express trains speeding him to his engagements from New York to Chicago, to Boston, all the way across the country to San Francisco, Los Angeles, Denver, Minneapolis, Montreal in Canada, and back to New York. "I am seeing magnificent cities and enchanting country . . . ," Ravel wrote to Mme Jourdan-Morhange, but he shared more of his impressions with the sixteen-year-old Annie, Mlle Gaudin's niece, who in the first years of World War I was luckily "so unbearable." He sent her colored postcards from the Twentieth Century Limited, from the Union Pacific System, from Toronto and St. Paul.

> Cleveland, having nothing of interest, gave me a chance to rest a little [Ravel wrote to Annie]. I did not have time to write more. Left Cleveland yesterday morning. Leaving Chicago at eight this evening. *En route* to San Francisco. Three nights and two days! It will get very cold; I don't dare to go out on the observation platform at the back of the train. Inside the compartment it is so hot that I close the radiator and turn on the fan day and night. Up till now the landscape was flat, from time to time cornfields or villages and forests in the genre of the countryside around Paris. . . .

Ravel found Los Angeles too hot and San Francisco too cold, but after "five nights!" on the train returning to Buffalo he was still thinking of the Grand Canyon. He sent Annie a "pictorial" postcard with an English text which, he said, would save him the trouble of description:

> The finest effects at the Grand Canyon are altogether uncommunicable by brush or pen. They give themselves up only to the personal presence, and no painter or writer can do more than suggest what they are. You can not paint a

silence, an emotion, nor a sob. If you are skillful you can suggest them to the imagination but that is all. Here even silence seems to have dimension and color.

Ravel advised his young correspondent to read the text, with which he apparently agreed. "You would run away from home, you would leave your family, to come to see this," he added.

But Ravel was annoyed with the long train stops. "Twenty minutes in Kansas City! The American trains stop more often than the train from Hendaye to Biarritz. One either freezes in them or is suffocated," he wrote. As for the success of his tour, he said that "the triumphs are fatiguing" and that he was "tired of all these receptions, interviews, photographing and even filming with make-up two fingers thick."

Above all Ravel complained in his letters home that he was "dying of hunger." Numerous stories were told with great amusement for every one—except Ravel—how after sumptuous lunches served by butlers at the homes of local society ladies, Ravel would run to his hotel and order for himself what he called a real meal. "All the same," he wrote home, "I have never felt so well as during this crazy tour. I have finally discovered the reason for it: it is because I have never led a reasonable enough life . . ."

Ravel returned to New York for his fifty-third birthday party, given by the French singer Eva Gauthier, and remained in the city for three weeks before he sailed home. Mme Gauthier introduced George Gershwin, who played his *Rhapsody in Blue* for Ravel. According to the stories told later, Gershwin wanted to study with Ravel, but Ravel saw no sense in it. "You might lose your melodic spontaneity and write bad Ravel," he is quoted as having said.

Eva Gauthier told me that while Ravel was in New York he took every opportunity to visit Harlem, where he spent hours listening to jazz. He could not understand why only a few American composers used this source of inspiration.

Financially, Ravel's tour was a great success. It brought him $27,000. He went back to France a rich man.

"Why, you are still using towels! How backward of you!" Ravel exclaimed almost as soon as he got off the boat. "In the United States they use hot air." He could hardly wait to show his friends all the gadgets he had brought with him to install in his kitchen, bathroom, and garden. Ravel was in the best of spirits. The trip had done him a lot of good. He seemed rested and eager to get to work.

Before he left for the United States Ida Rubinstein, the dancer, and Ravel's old friend, had asked him to write a ballet for her. Perhaps because somehow he had had bad luck with ballets or because he had different plans for a major work, Ravel offered instead to orchestrate some of Albeniz' pieces for her. Upon his return from America Ravel talked it over with her and they decided on certain parts out of Albeniz' *Iberia*. This promised to be mere fun for Ravel and to complete the pleasure he thought of doing it in St. Jean-de-Luz.

A few weeks later, at the end of June, Ravel with his old friends M. and Mme Joaquin Nin[1] started to drive

---

[1] Joaquin Nin, a Spanish composer who lived in St. Jean-de-Luz.

south. As they approached the outskirts of Bordeaux, Ravel, who was entertaining his friends with stories about d'Annunzio and Arcachon, suddenly declared that he would like to see the little seaport in the Bay of Biscay. Thereupon they changed their course and arrived at Arcachon a little too late for sight-seeing, but in time for dinner. During the evening's conversation, Joaquin Nin asked Ravel what his plans were for the summer and when Ravel told them about the orchestration of Albeniz' *Iberia*, Nin warned that the rights for Albeniz works had been reserved for Enrique Arbos, the conductor, already at work on a ballet for the famous Spanish dancer Argentina.

"I don't give a God damn!" Ravel said. "Besides, who the hell is this Arbos anyway?" Nin knew that the name of Arbos was no stranger to Ravel than that of Argentina, but seeing that Ravel was upset by the information he changed the subject and asked Ravel's advice as to whose compositions he should consult for Spanish effects. "Study my scores," Ravel replied simply, but categorically. "Then those of Rimsky and some of Debussy's . . . but not d'Indy's nor Wagner's." After a moment's silence Ravel added, "You might look at some of Meyerbeer . . ."

"Meyerbeer?" asked Nin.

"Yes, Meyerbeer . . ." Ravel repeated. "It's Wagner, only better!"

But Ravel did not forget about Arbos and the copyrights for *Iberia*. On the following day he asked Nin to telephone to Paris to find out how the matter stood. When his worst fears were confirmed Ravel flew into a rage. "My season is shot to hell. . . . These laws are idiotic. . . . I need to work. . . . It would have been mere play for me to orchestrate *Iberia.* . . . Who the hell is this Arbos? . . . And what am I to say to Ida? . . . She will be furious! . . ." Nin said later that he had never seen Ravel so nervous and argumentative as during that whole day. Two days later Ravel told Nin that he was returning to Paris to see Ida Rubinstein and to decide what to do. Besides, Ravel said he "adored to be in Paris on the fourteenth of July." Ravel went back to Paris.

On the other hand, when Arbos heard of Ravel's intentions, he was only too willing to cede the rights to him, but by that time Ravel had already made up his mind. "It is too late to begin—Mme Rubinstein's ballets are scheduled for the beginning of next season. And after all," Ravel said, "I would have orchestrated my own music much faster than anyone else's." And back he went to St. Jean-de-Luz.

A few days later, on a hot ninety-five-degree day, Gustave Samazeuilh, his old friend, came to fetch Ravel for their morning bath in the sea. Ravel, dressed in his yellow-and-black-striped bathrobe and a scarlet bathing cap, played him a tune with one finger. "Don't you find that this tune has something particularly . . . insisting?" Ravel asked. This was the beginning of *Boléro.*

In three months, by October 6, Ravel had completed the work, which in his opinion was a joke, a composition made of a "crescendo on a commonplace melody in the genre of Padilla; *Boléro*—seventeen minutes of orchestra without any music." Later, discussing it with Calvocoressi, he made the following statement:

I am particularly desirous that there should be no misunderstanding about this work. It constitutes an experiment in a very special and limited direction and should not be suspected of aiming at achieving anything other or more than what it actually does. Before its first performance, I issued a warning to the effect that what I had written was a piece lasting seventeen minutes and consisting wholly of "orchestral tissue without music"—of one long, very gradual crescendo. There are no contrasts, and there is practically no invention save the plan and the manner of execution. The themes are altogether impersonal . . . folk tunes of the usual Spanish-Arabian kind, and (whatever may have been said to the contrary) the orchestral writing is simple and straightforward throughout, without the slightest attempt at virtuosity. . . . I have carried out exactly what I intended and it is for the listeners to take it or leave it.

On November 22, 1928, at the Opéra, with Walter Straram conducting, Ida Rubinstein gave a performance of *Boléro* both startling and puzzling the audience. Bronislava Nijinska's choreography was a weird spectacle of a Spanish gypsy wrapped in all the fineries of the traditional dress, shawl, high comb, and broad skirts showing her petticoats, as her feet tapped the rhythms of the monotonously maddening dance on a large table in a tavern filled with smoke. The dancer, solitary in the beginning, was eventually joined by hallucinated figures who appeared from the dark of the night to join the wild crescendo of the orchestra.

Contrary to Ravel's own prediction that this piece would never be played at symphonic concerts, *Boléro*, after a triumphant performance on January 11, 1930, at the Concert Lamoureux, achieved a popularity which has never been surpassed. The principle theme of the composition became a tune that has been sung world over ever since. Grand dukes hummed it and street urchins whistled it.

Ravel is quoted to have said that it was all a matter of vogue, that there was nothing extraordinary about the piece, that any Conservatory student could have done the same once he discovered the idea of the relentless crescendo in the orchestra against the steady beating of the drum. However, Ravel was well aware of the importance of his success. Shortly after the Paris performance of *Boléro*, Paul Paray, the conductor, and Ravel were taking a walk together in Monte Carlo. They found themselves in front of the Casino.

"Let's go in and play," Paray suggested.

"No," Ravel said. "I have played. I have won. I don't play any more."

Chapter Fifteen

Two Piano Concertos

MAURICE RAVEL had reached the heights of popularity, if the word fame should be reserved for a later date. As if *Boléro* mirrored his own artistic life, he rose in one final upsurge against the background of past failures to a glorious climax in his career, such as might be envied by every artist. He had become the most talked-of French composer and he was in demand everywhere. His works were being played abroad and offers of concert tours through almost all the countries of Europe were piling up on his desk, while invitations to dinners, luncheons, parties, and festivals of his music were strewn all over the house.

"You know that I had every intention of dining with you," Ravel would write to his friends, "but I must stick to the grind until the middle of October. After that I am supposed to be in Oxford, where I shall don the toga of the

Doctor honoris causa, in Spain on a concert tour, in Paris at Ida Rubinstein's ballets . . . and all this at the same time. I fear it will all get shuffled."

Ravel postponed the ceremony in Oxford, but he did go on a tour through Spain, appearing both as conductor and as accompanist to Madeleine Grey, the singer, who came along with him to interpret his songs and to whom this tour remained a unique experience in her life. Ravel was always late to rehearsals, concerts, dinner or luncheon engagements and, as if he were obeying an order from above, would arrive with two large bags in his hands at the station platform just as the train was about to leave.

Not all of his concerts were triumphant, except of course for *Boléro*, but taking occasional flops merely amused him, for after all he was now Maurice Ravel, the composer of *Boléro*. The northern part of Spain received him with great enthusiasm, but in the south, in Malaga where they were not used to "modern" music, the audience "discreetly and politely" deserted the Grey-Ravel recital leaving the two artists to take their final bow to empty seats. Ravel called this performance "La Symphonie des adieux" and insisted that he was in full sympathy with the public which had the courage of its own conviction.

But true to his own saying— ". . . I don't play any more"—upon his return to Montfort-l'Amaury, Ravel again locked himself in *Le Belvédère* to complete the work he had begun several times, but had had to lay aside either because of interruptions or because of his health. It was the concerto which he intended to play himself. Gustave Samazeuilh, one of the few of Ravel's friends well acquainted with "Zaspiak-Bat"—the Basque rhapsody which had been abandoned at the outbreak of World War I—told me that Ravel used most of its material in this piano concerto. The unmistakable jazz connotations in the concerto are due, of course, to the influences of a later date. To prepare himself for performing the concerto, Ravel began studiously practicing Chopin and Liszt études, as well as the Fugue from his own *Tombeau de Couperin*, which he said was an excellent exercise for developing "independence in the fingers." He was making real progress when he had to stop work to attend the Ravel Festivals.

". . . Now, please, consider my situation, please be patient with me," Ravel wrote to his friends in St. Jean-de-Luz. "In the midst of my pregnancy with the concerto (I am at the stage of throwing up) I am suddenly called to Biarritz. You must have seen the billboards designed by Fugita[1] announcing 'Le grand festival de Maurice Ravel.' Two hundred francs for a ticket! It's lucky that I can get in 'on the house.'"

Within a fortnight Ravel was back at *Le Belvédère*, back at the piano practicing, back at his work on the concerto, while all the time his head was full of projects for future major works, far more important in their scope than anything he had written so far. He talked to Ida Rubinstein about a new ballet he was going to compose for her, "to turn *L'Histoire d'Ali Baba: Morgiane* (from the *Thousand and One Nights*) into a drama, a rich and terrible drama 'full of blood and fire.'" Then he spoke also of "a grand

[1] A famous Japanese painter who lived in Paris.

opera in the genre of Meyerbeer," but he said that it would take him ten years to do it.

Among all these projects the principal place in Ravel's mind was reserved for *Jeanne d'Arc*. He saw it in the form of an opera-oratorio and for which he was going to write his own libretto. "I would like to show both the simplicity of Jeanne as a country girl and her ruggedness as a warrior," Ravel told Jourdan-Morhange. To show this contrast he planned to have two interpreters for Jeanne. In his *Jeanne-d'Arc* Ravel intended to use large choruses representing the crowds and a Greek chorus that would comment on the action in the play. According to Jacques Zogheb, Ravel's old friend and neighbor at Montfort-l'Amaury, he had already sketched out the plan of the play, even though he had not written any music for it: Jeanne with her sheep—The court—Meeting with the King—The siege of Orléans (with "Tipperary" coming from the English side, and the *Marseillaise* from the French)—The capture of Orléans—The judgment before the French priests and the British bureaucrats ("here the music must be sarcastic," Ravel said) —and finally, the gallows, Jeanne's death, and her ascent to heaven.

According to the friends with whom he discussed the play, Ravel was worried that he could not present God on the stage. "I couldn't after all mortify him with a large beard," Ravel laughed, and he finally decided to have Jeanne take her place at the right of Christ, "who did not recognize the abuses from down below."

Like a gambler who suddenly becomes drunk with power, Ravel was taxing his creative strength with more and more projects, accepting every task as a bet he would make with himself, no matter how high the stakes. While he was still at work on his piano concerto, he was approached by the manager of the Austrian pianist Paul Wittgenstein to write a concerto for his client. Ravel accepted the commission with enthusiasm and the fee of around six thousand dollars was only a *charme de plus*.

Paul Wittgenstein was, and still is, a unique figure in musical history. The Vienna-born pianist was only beginning his concert career when in 1914, at the age of twenty-seven, he was called into the Austrian army as a reserve officer. He was wounded in the first months of the war and his right arm had to be amputated. When the army hospital was captured by the Russians, Paul Wittgenstein became a prisoner-of-war, but in the fall of the following year he was exchanged as an invalid and returned to Vienna. Beginning in the winter season of 1916-17, he continued his musical career and made a name for himself all over the world as a one-armed pianist. Many composers, including Richard Strauss, Franz Schmidt, Erik Korngold, Benjamin Britten, Sergei Prokofiev, and Paul Hindemith have contributed to his programs by writing piano concertos, quartets, and quintets for him.

In writing a concerto for a *mutilé de la guerre* Ravel saw an opportunity to create a painful and tragic picture of useless heroism, for his personal experience of the futility of human sacrifice in World War I had left him without any illusions about the "profound reasons" for which it was fought. He began working on it immediately (that is, during the season of 1929-30 while he was still in midst of his other piano concerto), arming himself with Saint-Saëns' *Les Six Études pour la main gauche* and Leopold Godowsky's *Transcriptions for the Left Hand Alone of the Chopin Études* as models for his new composition.

It was an interesting experience [Ravel later told Calvocoressi], to conceive and realize the two concertos at the same time. The first, which I propose to play myself, is a concerto in the strict sense, written in the spirit of Mozart and Saint-Saëns. I believe that a concerto can be both gay and brilliant without necessarily being profound or aiming at dramatic effect. It has been said that the concertos of some great classical composers, far from being written *for* the piano, have been written *against* it. And I think that this criticism is quite justified.

At the beginning I meant to call my work a *divertissement*, but afterward considered that this was unnecessary, as the name Concerto adequately describes the kind of music it contains. In some ways my Concerto is not unlike my Violin Sonata; it uses certain effects borrowed from jazz, but only in moderation.

The Concerto for left hand alone is quite different, and has only one movement with many jazz effects; the writing is not so simple. In a work of this sort, it is essential to avoid the impression of insufficient weight in the sound-texture, as compared to a solo part for two hands. So I have used a style which is much more in keeping with the consciously imposing style of the traditional concerto.

After an introductory section pervaded by this feeling, there comes an episode like an improvisation which is followed by jazz section. Only afterward is one aware that the jazz episode is actually built up from the themes of the first section.

By working all the time, sleeping either four hours with-

out the help of the drugs or five and a half with, Ravel completed his Concerto for the left hand alone a year later, in
August, 1930, but he still had a lot of work to do on the
other concerto. Just at that time the municipality of Ciboure
decided to honor Ravel by placing a plaque on the old house
where he was born and by renaming the street the Quai
Maurice Ravel. Festivities were arranged to celebrate the
occasion—*Journée Ravel*—starting with a brilliant game of
pelota, national Basque dances in Ciboure, and a concert at
Biarritz in which Madeleine Grey, Jacques Thibaud, and
Casadesus were to participate.

"Those darn Cibourians . . . they are making me lose
another week," Ravel complained, but obviously he was
pleased. He enjoyed the excitement of the festivities and
the game of *pelota*, played by national champions. But when
the simple people of Ciboure, who knew neither his name
nor a single page of his music, crowded the little square
where the dignitaries of the community, in official regalia,
were extolling the illustrious son of their country, Ravel,
blushing with embarrassment, told his friends that he could
not face the ceremony, and begged Casadesus and his wife
to go away with him. They took refuge in the nearest café.
Hidden behind a hedge of small trees, they listened to the
local band playing in Ravel's honor. Ravel was much re-
lieved when, in the evening, he reached Biarritz where
once again he was among his friends, the musicians. At the
concert at the Casino he played a duet with Casadesus, accompanied Madeleine Grey in a selection of his songs, and
played his *Sonate pour Violin et Piano* with Jacques Thibaud. However, Ravel was very proud of the Cibourian

homage, and often said to his friends: "Do you know, I
have a quai of my own."

Two months later, Ravel wrote from *Belvédère* to a
friend:

> The time is flying. . . . I have just finished correcting the
> orchestration for the Concerto for the left hand. Thus I
> have only two months and a half left to finish the other—it's
> terrifying to think about it. I don't sleep more than six hours,
> usually less. My only distraction is *walking* (*sic*) between
> seven and eight before dinner. Now I am going to lose
> another two days on account of a concert at the Conserva-
> tory, where I have to conduct *Boléro* and accompany *Les
> Madécasses*.

Four months after, the *Concerto* still was not finished.
"I am not dead," Ravel wrote on March 19, 1931, "although
in the last four months I wish I were. I had to stop all my
work completely. I had hoped that fifteen days of rest
would be enough. Now I have hardly begun working on
the Concerto again, but this time I have to be careful."

Ravel said that he had had to postpone the performance
of the *Concerto* in Brussels and to cancel the one scheduled
in Monte Carlo. "As a matter of fact," he said, "at one time
I felt so badly that I was given *l'extract de taureau, de
phospore, etc.* and was going to be sent down to the Riviera
to rest, when suddenly I began to sleep without a stop—
days and nights. I am sure this saved me. Now, I am going
to lock myself in, I will not answer any one, and I will take
the telephone off the hook."

Finally, Ravel had to admit that he was not well enough
to play the *Concerto* himself. "Would you like to have my

Concerto, which will end with trills and in *pianissimo?*"
Ravel asked his friend, Marguerite Long. Six months later,
on November 11, 1931, he brought her the *Concerto in G*
which ends with a passage in broken chords and in
fortissimo.

During the summer of 1931, urged by his friends who
wanted him to relax and have some distraction from his
work, Ravel finally managed to find time to go to Oxford.
And indeed the occasion proved to be a happy one for the
composer and an amusing one for the spectators.

On previous visits to England Ravel had startled the
conservative Englishmen by his selection of wearing ap-
parel, sometimes going to such extremes as snakeskin ties
with shoes, cigarette case, and lighter to match the color-
scheme of his socks and breast-pocket handkerchief. This
time he appeared in a morning coat set off by a waistcoat
"of such unconventional design that even the politest dons
blinked a little." According to Oxford tradition, Ravel had
to wear the scarlet and white satin academic gown, but the
smallest one available was ridiculously big for him and had
to be pinned up. Looking even smaller than usual because
of the gigantic "body-guards" on both sides of him, Ravel
mounted the stage in the middle of the Sheldonian Theatre
and made his acceptance speech partly in broken English
and partly in Latin memorized for the occasion. He posed
proudly for the photographers in his resplendent gown and
tasseled cap. Since in France the title "Doctor" is generally
reserved for men of the medical profession, it offered him
no end of amusement to be called "Dr. Ravel."

On January 14, 1932, Mme Long gave the first performance of the *Concerto in G* with Ravel conducting. Bubbling over with his success, Ravel told Calvocoressi about his "projected world tour with the *Concerto,* through Europe, North and South America, Japan, and perhaps Java, if an orchestra could be recruited there." But a much shorter tour actually did take place. Immediately after the Paris performance Marguerite Long and Ravel started on a concert tour through Europe which took them to Warsaw, Vienna, Berlin, Prague, Budapest, Bucharest, and London.

It was in Vienna, at a dinner party given by Wittgenstein at his home in honor of the two triumphant French artists that Ravel first heard of certain liberties taken by Wittgenstein in his performance of the *Concerto for the Left Hand Alone.* To Ravel, who was extremely meticulous about every tempo and dynamic marking in his works, a deliberate alteration in a score was a major calamity. No wonder he hit the ceiling. And it took all of Mme Marguerite Long's tact and diplomacy to avert an open break between the two musicians. The bone of contention, Paul Wittgenstein told me, was a section about two pages long in the middle part where he as a performer believed it would gain in dramatic effect if he played the theme, instead of the orchestra, as Ravel had indicated. "It ruins the concerto," Ravel told him and today Wittgenstein admits that Ravel was right. But the small fracas gave vent to rumors and gossip from which the Austrian pianist suffered unduly.

It has not only been said and repeated but also has appeared in print that Mr. Wittgenstein made changes in the *Concerto* because of his inability to cope with its difficulties. Contrary to what has so often been said, that this work demands a colossal technique on the part of the performer, the *Concerto* is actually so well written for the left hand that it should present no difficulty whatsoever to most concertizing virtuosos. Mr. Wittgenstein has performed much harder compositions: the two Strauss Concertos written for him would suffice as an example. The reasons for the malicious distortion of the facts about his first performances of the *Concerto* both in France and in this country still remain baffling. It was neither Alfred Cortot nor Jacques Février (both French pianists) but Paul Wittgenstein who gave the first performances of the *Concerto* in Paris at the Salle Pleyel on January 17, 1933, in Monte Carlo on April 12, 1933, in Boston on November 10, 1934, and in New York on November 17, 1934.

Except for the "Wittgenstein incident" Ravel returned home with the happiest memories of the triumphant trip. Ravel was famous. He had been fêted by musicians and critics all the way across Europe from north to south and east to west and when he returned to Montfort-l'Amaury more mail, more invitations, more contracts, and more announcements of "Le Grand Festival de Maurice Ravel" were awaiting him. And Ravel wanted to be everywhere. He was like the man who jumped on a horse and rode off in all directions. In August he went down to St. Jean-de-Luz for a fortnight, and then on to San Sebastian, where a "Maurice Ravel Festival" had been arranged despite the fact that France had closed its frontiers to Spain. "Oh well, I am not French . . . and they (Ravel meant the Basques), are not Spanish," he said.

Upon his return to Paris Ravel was going to plunge into

one of the major projects he had been talking about for so long, when on October 10, 1932, an accident upset his plans. Toward midnight he was returning from the theater to his hotel at 21, Rue d'Athènes, where he usually stayed when he was in Paris, when his taxi collided with another one. The violent shock threw him headlong against the broken windows of his cab. Ravel was given first aid at a nearby pharmacy for the cuts and bruises on his head and face and then was transported to the Beaujon hospital. But that night he felt well enough to return to his hotel, and only on the following morning complained of internal pain. Professor Dujardin examined him and Ravel was taken to the hospital on the Rue Blomet.

However, his friends' fears for Ravel were far worse than the bruises on his head. Three weeks later he was well enough to joke about it in his letters: ". . . a few cracks, an arched nose to persuade the Americans of my Hebrew origin, but particularly some bruises on my chest which force me to cough in a crooked way." In fact, he was well enough to finish *Don Quichotte à Dulcinée*, a cycle of three songs—one romantic, one epic, and a drinking song. These were to serve as a sample of his work for a film company which planned to do a picture with Chaliapin in the title role. The three songs are written on Spanish themes and rhythms. When he wrote the last chords to the closing cry of the third, the drinking song, "I drink to the joy of life," Ravel did not know he was closing the happiest year in his life.

∽∾∽∾∽∾∽∾∽∾∽∾∽∾∽∾∽∾∽∾∽∾∽∾∽∾∽∾∽∾

Chapter Sixteen

Illness and Death

RAVEL could not know that the closing chords of "I drink to the joy of living" were to be the last he would ever write and that he was destined to have one more, the last, disappointment in his artistic career.

He was not aware that in writing these three songs for the film company he had entered into a sort of a competition with four other composers, Manuel de Falla, Darius Milhaud, Jacques Ibert, and Marcel Delannoy, who had also been asked by the producer to supply similar samples of their music. Ravel was slow in preparing his score, obviously enjoying the material with which he was working, the Andalusian character of the song and the rhythm, and pleasant recollections of Chaliapin. While returning from the United States Ravel had spent a great deal of time in the company of the singer, also on board. No doubt they had emptied many glasses together "to the joy of living." But in trying to adapt his music to the "moving picture taste," Ravel unnecessarily popularized his style. The songs were beneath Ravel's standards. The film company gave preference to Jacques Ibert's score and gave Ravel two reasons for being rejected. Ravel was late with his score and Chaliapin found them lacking in dramatic effect. This hurt Ravel particularly since for years he had been talking about writing an opera *Don Quichotte*. A peculiar imbroglio ensued, according to his friends, Ravel eventually suing the company for damages. But nothing came of it.

For the first time since he had returned from the army Ravel found himself without a pressing unfinished work in his desk. Free from immediate engagements, he was more than ever seen at concerts, theaters, and night clubs. He paid no attention to his friends' warnings to lead a more regular life, and laughed at their unsuccessful attempts to break him of his nocturnal habit of walking about on the streets of Paris. "I do my work, I plan my compositions on those promenades," he explained.

During the summer of 1933 Ravel went to St. Jean-de-Luz to join his old friends "with a dinner jacket, but without music paper" and it was there while swimming that he suddenly felt that he was losing control of his arms and legs. It frightened him, but he said nothing about it until the frequent recurrence of similar symptoms after his return to Montfort-l'Amaury seriously alarmed him. He saw his own hand lying on a piece of music disobeying his will to write. Zogheb rushed to Jourdan-Morhange who lived not far away from Montfort-l'Amaury to tell her how his son

Philip had asked Ravel to write a few words on a photograph for him and how Ravel had to be assisted by a friend who happened to be with him. Jourdan-Morhange begged Ravel to see Dr. Vallery-Radot, who had warned him before he went to the United States that he needed a complete rest for a year or more. Now he suggested that Ravel should go to the country, preferably to the mountains, and in the middle of March of 1934 Ravel left for Mt. Pèlerin, near Lausanne in Switzerland.

"A Wernicke aphasia of moderate intensity, without any trace of paralysis or hemianopia, but with an ideomotor apractic component" was the technical medical description of Ravel's case. Aphasia refers to the loss of the power of expression by speech, writing, or signs, while apraxia is a condition due to an interruption between the ideation center and the center for the limb in which simple movements can be performed, but not complicated ones.

During the following two-year period, frequent examinations by the eminent neurologist Dr. Th. Alajouanine revealed that Ravel's memory, affectivity, and aesthetic taste were not impaired and that his understanding of language was much better than his ability to speak or write.

Tests which were carried out by the physician in collaboration with a musician friend and another neurologist with a good knowledge of music showed that Ravel had no difficulty, as yet, in recognizing his own works and those he was acquainted with when they were played for him. The slightest deviation in tempo or alteration of rhythm or notes never escaped his notice and he would demand that the piece be repeated until it was accurately performed.

This happened when, for example, *La Pavane* from his suite *Ma Mère l'Oye* was played and one of two exactly similar bars was purposely omitted, or when several parts from his *Tombeau de Couperin* were intentionally played with wrong notes. But when Ravel was asked to identify by name notes played for him or pointed out in a score, his hesitation and numerous mistakes plainly illustrated the difficulties associated with aphasia. The process of reading the notes, i.e., first identifying them visually and then reproducing them on the piano, caused extreme difficulty and only occasionally was accomplished correctly.

In addition to this condition Ravel, affected by permanent apraxia, had difficulty in locating the notes on the keyboard, which made accurate piano playing almost impossible. He repeatedly played C major instead of E minor arpeggios, because of the similarity of the hand's position on the keyboard. He heard the difference in sound and yet he was unable to correct his error until someone helped him by moving his hand into the right place.

Ravel was in despair, for his mind was as lucid as ever and yet he was a helpless witness to the calamity which had befallen him, unparalleled in the history of music. The man who had composed virtuoso pieces of such "transcendent difficulty" as *Scarbo* and the *Concerto for the Left Hand Alone* and who was able to play them, even if not well enough for the concert stage, suddenly faced a gruesome reality: he could play only the beginning of his *Ma Mère l'Oye*, a piece he wrote for six-year-old children, and only with one hand—the right one. He had to practice a long time before he could play it with both hands and after a whole week's work he only succeeded in playing the beginning of the *Pavane* and again only with both hands separately.

Suddenly as if fate was playing a cruel trick on him, he could play almost perfectly nine bars out of the beginning of his *Tombeau de Couperin*, even amusing himself by transposing them a third lower without any error . . . then, the game was over—he could not go on, it became too difficult to continue. The first page of this piece illustrates how delicate was the gradation of his capacity, since only a slight technical change followed the preceding nine bars.

But what was even more horrible was Ravel's realization that whereas in playing bits from his own works or those he knew he was helped by his memory, which was still intact, he was completely incapable of playing more than a few notes out of an easy piece by Scarlatti which he had never before seen. Yet he could still listen to and enjoy concerts and voice intelligent criticism of music he heard, whether it was previously known to him or entirely new. He would recognize immediately whether the piano was out of tune or a singer sang flat, was able to evaluate rhythm and style exactly, and even to sing correctly by heart some parts out of his own works. Ravel told the physician that melodies from his own works or those he knew came back quite easily and that he could "hear them singing in his head."

The history of music has examples like Beethoven and Fauré, of musicians going deaf and still able to go on with their work and compose. In Ravel's case he might have been able to continue his work, even without being able to play or conduct, had not the affliction from which he suffered denied him the power of writing a musical thought or even dictating it, as Bach did when he was blind and dying. The writing of notes required an enormous effort, although it was easier than plain writing.

The doctor's tests showed that copying of musical notation had become almost impossible for Ravel and that only very slowly, with great difficulty and numerous errors could he jot down notes dictated to him. Thus he could not play the piano or conduct, dictate or write his own music— all the avenues of his creative ability suddenly reached an end, the end of Ravel as a composer.

The cause of this catastrophe seems to have evaded the physicians whom Ravel consulted, since the taxi accident was discarded as a possible origin and the condition was rather presumed to belong to a group of cerebral atrophies. Ravel would have done anything for a successful cure. He followed every bit of advice, no matter how fantastic it was. He tried electric treatments, injections, suggestion, and even re-education. But the mysterious sickness progressed without anyone's being able to establish its origin firmly.

Ravel became so depressed and self-conscious about his condition that he preferred to stay at home alone. He would sit in his easy chair on the balcony of *Le Belvédère* and look at the magnificent panorama of fields and forests and the winding country road with a vacant look that suggested absence of mind.

"What are you doing, Ravel?" his friends, who visited him almost daily, would ask.

"I am waiting," he replied.

Ravel's friends did everything to distract him. They took him for rides in the country, walks through the Rambouillet Forest, or to Paris to concerts or theaters. Probably because she knew Ravel's childish fascination with the Orient, Ida Rubinstein financed a trip for him to Morocco and asked Léon Leyritz, the sculptor, to go along.

They left in February, 1934, via Spain, spent a night in Madrid—because Ravel wanted Leyritz to see a small chapel full of Goya paintings, and then went on to Tangier where they explored the Oriental bazaars, mingling with the crowds of exotic fruit merchants in their colorful dresses, and watching the snake charmers. Thence they continued on to Marrakesh. The balconies outside their rooms at the Hotel Mamounia hung as if suspended in the air above the Arab city with its gardens like thick carpets. Ravel was enchanted with it. The two friends spent many weeks there.

Ravel and Leyritz wandered about the little streets, watching the barbers shaving the heads of the youngsters in the open air and administering donkeys' dung as a cure for eye disease. They marveled at the water carriers, magnificent-looking young Moroccans whose beautiful bronze bodies reminded Ravel of biblical characters, to be rudely awakened to reality: one of them began to whistle, of all things, *Boléro*. They saw a procession of newlyweds going through the crowded streets; the bride, covered with a veil, rode on a white donkey followed by a group of her friends, while the bridegroom marched in front carrying a huge plate with candles resembling a birthday cake. According to local tradition, if one of the candles fell, the bride would be considered impure and would be sent back home. Ravel secretly hoped that a candle would fall, to punish them for so dangerous a superstition.

Leyritz and Ravel spent an evening with Si Mammri, the local music lover. He played old airs of the sixteenth century for them, and later on took them to see the Chleuh dances, sacred dances in which the roles of young women were taken by frail young boys, "whose ambiguous beauty came close—perhaps too close—to feminine grace." These dances suggest sacrificial rites and Ravel, chosen that night to represent a god, was rather embarrassed to see these young men place imaginary garlands at his feet and make symbolic gestures—strange suggestions to his imagination.

Another time they visited the *caïd de Telouët*, one of El Glaoui's sons, in his Château Atlas, a fortress palace in the middle of the desert, where they dined according to Moslem custom, eating with their fingers, and saw a fantastic spectacle after the sumptuous repast. Some hundred dancers, dressed in white robes bedecked with purple scarves, their hair trimmed with gold, and groups of musicians playing on strange instruments of black wood, participated in a weird performance. "Just like the Russian ballet," Ravel said, and when they returned to the hotel he was still so excited by what he had just seen that he sat down to write a letter to his brother—the only letter he managed to write during the whole journey.

Ravel's health was not improving, he even had difficulty in reading, but he was happy, for he saw in all these Oriental wonders source of material for his future ballet-opera *Morgiane*, which, so he told Leyritz, he still believed he could write, although he knew it was going to be difficult. Ravel was very ill. Leyritz had to watch over him as though he were a baby. There were times when Ravel would take a spoon or fork and try to use it from the wrong end, or would put a match into his mouth and try to light it with a cigarette. The tragedy of it was that while this was happening, one could see in Ravel's eyes that he knew what he was doing and yet was helpless.

His mind, his intelligence were as acute as ever. Nothing escaped Ravel's eye or his ear and he remembered the fragrance of every flower, the smell of the bazaars, and the oily taste of Oriental dishes. Walking one night with a young Arab, Ravel told him (the boy spoke French) how the beauty of the country impressed him and pointed to the depth of the skies and the brightness of the stars. "Yes, it is beautiful," said the young Arab, "but there is nothing extraordinary tonight; some nights the skies open . . . only not everybody can see it." This was the Orient, this was the Shéhérazade, "the thousand and one nights" which had haunted Ravel's imagination all his life. Ravel felt there was still much left for him to say in his music.

When the time came for them to go home Ravel and Leyritz rented a car so that they could go slowly and not miss any of the countryside. They visited the city of Fez which, after red Marrakesh—the red walls, the houses made of red bricks—looked almost white to them. Boris Masslow, the local director of Fine Arts, while showing them the Château de la Résidence and the gardens said to Ravel, "What a background, dear Master, to inspire you to write an Arabian work."

"If I were to write something Arab, it would be more Arab than all this," Ravel replied.

Once again, on the way back to France, they crossed through Spain, the country for which Ravel had a special place in his heart. Leyritz took great pleasure in showing him Seville. Everything delighted Ravel; the beautiful city submerged under magnificent parks and gardens, the crowds' excitement in anticipation of the bullfight, the little taverns and bars decorated with trophies where Leyritz and Ravel spent most of their nights, enjoying the music and dancing, and talking, as best as they could in their Spanish, to the young intellectuals who timidly came up to Ravel to pay him their respects.

Ravel felt perfectly at home in Spain, where people dine after ten o'clock at night, and where night life dominates their living. At last he found an audience who forgave an artist for being late, not for a few minutes but for as much as two hours, as had happened when the famous Nina de Los Peines arrived for her concert at two in the morning instead of midnight, as announced. He was as sympathetic with the audience's delirious acclaim of the singer's interpretation of *Canto Jondo* as he was with Nina de Los Peines for keeping her audience waiting so long.

To reciprocate, Ravel wanted to show Leyritz the Basque country and insisted on driving home through that part of Spain. There, in the middle of the night, they heard *Malagueña* sung in a little café, and spent the night in Pamplona at the Hotel de la Perla in a room with paneled walls ornamented with lyres—the room once occupied by Sarasate.

Nothing could have made Ravel happier than this trip, a journey into a world of wonders, legends, strange customs, of beautiful stories of princesses and Bedouins. It was as if Ravel's good fairy had given him a magic wand, for the one who was responsible for this trip remained anonymous and invisible, except for occasional telephone calls at night to inquire if the two travelers were in need of anything. Ravel was so happy that even the sudden collapse of their vehicle, somewhere in the mountains as they approached the French frontier, did not upset his sense of humor. He left Leyritz with a supply of cigarettes and candies while he set out to look for someone to help them—a situation all too reminiscent of his adventures with Adélaïde.

Upon his return home Ravel felt elated: there were so many new impressions to relate to his friends. "I have written down a melody, thus I still can write music," he said to a friend, but this was his last attempt, for soon he could not even sign his name.

Ravel's general appearance changed little except that he looked older and thinner and the ironic smile lit up his face less and less often, so that no one who saw him casually at concerts or restaurants realized how grave his condition was. Whenever he came to Paris he stayed with his brother Edouard, but somehow he never felt quite at home in his rooms at the Bonnets' house where Edouard lived. Friends like M. and Mme Maurice Delage, Roland-Manuel, Hélène Jourdan-Morhange, Manuel Rosenthal, and Marguerite Long seldom left his side. Usually his housekeeper, Mme Révelot put him on a bus in Montfort-l'Amaury and his friends met him at the end of the journey in Paris. For Ravel

felt lost by himself in the city, particularly in public places
or at concerts where, once he was recognized by his admirers, he ran a gauntlet of ready fountain pens and pencils
and pieces of paper or programs thrust at him for auto-
graphs. Shrinking into himself, his face expressing an agony
of pain, holding to the arm of his friend, Ravel would hur-
riedly make his way to the street and the nearest taxi.

As time went on Ravel grew indifferent to concerts and
when someone asked him if he still liked to listen to music
he said, "No," and when asked if he liked to hear his own
music he replied, "Even less." But he was seen at concerts
up to the last months of his life. At one of the last, during
the summer of 1937, Ravel heard Inghelbrecht, the old
Apache, conducting the National Orchestra in a performance of *Daphnis et Chloë*. "I could never write this again,"
Ravel muttered to Jourdan-Morhange, as he led her out of
the hall, "it's beautiful . . . it's beautiful, after all . . ."

As if life were a garment, Ravel was slowly taking it off
during the following twenty-three months. "I am going
away piece by piece," he said, for in this tragedy Ravel was
both the actor and the spectator. He realized that the local-
ized effects of the disease were spreading, at times he felt
as if he was "living in a fog." He told Jourdan-Morhange
what he thought was the most tragic fate in a composer's
life, how Chabrier, one of Ravel's idols in his adolescence,
sitting at the performance of *Gwendoline* did not know he
was listening to his own opera. A few months after this
remark Ravel himself did not recognize his *Quartet* when
Maurice Delage played a few bars from it on the piano.

For weeks Ravel remained at Montfort-l'Amaury sitting in his easy chair on the bacony at his *Belvédère*.

"Did Edouard telephone?" he would anxiously ask Mme Révelot. "Do you think he will come to see me today?" And then as though speaking to himself he would murmur, "Poor Edouard . . . what is going to become of you when I go?"

Zogheb came to see Ravel every day between five and eight in the evening.

"How do you feel?" Zogheb always asked the same questions and always received the same answers.

"Badly," Ravel would reply.

"Did you sleep well?"

Ravel would shake his head.

"Do you have a good appetite?"

"Yes."

"Did you try to work?"

Ravel would bend his head and tears would cover his face.

"Why should this have happened to me?" he would ask and, after a silence, add, "I have written things . . . they were not too bad . . . were they?"

Yet Ravel never lost hope of being cured. He would be taken to Dr. Bour's magnificent estate at Malmaison. There a skilled staff of specialists took care of distinguished patients from the worlds of politics and the arts. After the treatments there Ravel always seemed much improved and again few would notice that there was anything really wrong.

"Life is so beautiful that it is still better to be like this and live than . . ." he often said. Ravel was afraid of death.

"Up to that moment when all is finished," he said once to Jourdan-Morhange, "one does not believe that it could be so horrible, and afterward one realizes that it would have been better to remain alive even in this state."

But in Ravel's case this decision was made by the doctors, his brother, and some of his friends.

On December 18 Ravel was taken to the *Centre français de Médecine et de Chirurgie* at 12, Rue de Boileau. Dr. Clovis Vincent, a brain surgeon of international reputation, was to operate on him on the following day. What prompted this decision, what Dr. Vincent expected to find and what he actually did discover once Ravel's skull was cut open, has never been officially disclosed.

Even the French biographers who knew Ravel personally cannot agree. José Bruyr says that "what they [the doctors] diagnosed, it seems, was an operable brain tumor, complicated by the hardening of an artery, which caused softening of the brain." But according to Roland-Manuel, Ravel's lifelong friend, "They [the doctors] eventually discarded the possibility of a tumor and arteriosclerosis and admitted that the patient was suffering from a congenital illness affecting that part of the brain which is connected with the control of language."

Medical ethics and a French law guarding family secrets have dropped a final curtain on this last act of a drama worthy of Ibsen or Balzac, leaving the general public to draw its own conclusions in a mystery unparalleled in music history since the death of Mozart.

"He is alive," Dr. Vincent is quoted to have said as he emerged from the operating room.

But Ravel was lost. He never regained consciousness. For eight days he lay in a coma. In the early hours of December 28, 1937, Maurice Ravel died. He was buried in Levallois next to his mother, who had been waiting for her son for twenty-one years less only eight days.

Appendix

A. LIST OF RAVEL'S COMPOSITIONS

1893 *Sérénade grotesque*
Piano.   Unpublished

1894 *Ballade de la reine morte d'aimer*
Voice and piano. After Roland de Marès' poem.
Unpublished

1894 *Le Rouet*
Voice and piano. After Leconte de Lisle's poem.
Unpublished

1895 *Menuet antique*
Piano. Dedicated to R. Viñes. First performance
R. Viñes, April 18, 1898. Orchestrated by Ravel. First
performance Conc. Lamoureux, Jan. 11, 1930, conducted by Ravel, in Paris.   Enoch

1895 *Un grand sommeil noir*
Voice and piano. After Verlaine's poem.
Unpublished

1895-6 *Sites auriculaires*
Two pianos; first perf. Mlle Dron and R. Viñes,
Société Nationale, Salle Pleyel, Paris.   Unpublished
a. *Habanera*, 1895 (has been used again in the *Rapsodie espagnole*).
b. *Entre Cloches*, 1896.

281

1896   *Sainte*
    Voice and piano. After Mallarmé's poem. Dedicated
    to Mme Ed. Bonniot (born Mallarmé).
                                          Durand, 1907

1898   *Deux Epigrammes*
    Voice and piano. After Cl. Marot. Dedicated to
    Hardy Thé. First perf. Hardy Thé and Ravel, Soc.
    Nat., Jan. 27, 1900.   Demets-Eschig
    a. *D'Anne qui me jecta de la neige.*
    b. *D'Anne jouant de l'espinette.*

1898   *Shéhérazade*
    Ouverture de féerie pour orchestre, Soc. Nat., May
    27, 1899, conducted by Ravel.   Unpublished

1899   *Pavane pour une Infante défunte*
    Piano. Dedicated to Princess Ed. de Polignac. First
    perf. Soc. Nat. Salle Pleyel, Paris, May 5, 1902,
    R. Viñes. Orchestrated in 1910, first perf. Conc.
    Hasselmans, Salle Gaveau, Dec. 25, 1911, in Paris;
    conducted by Casella.   Demets-Eschig

1899   *Si morne . . .*
    Voice and piano. After Ém. Verhaeren. Unpublished

1901   *Myrrha*
    Cantata for the Prix de Rome. Text by Fernand
    Beissier.   Unpublished

1901   *Jeux d'eau*
    Piano. Dedicated to G. Fauré. First perf. Soc. Nat.,
    Salle Pleyel, Paris, April 5, 1902, R. Viñes.
                                 Demets-Eschig

1902   *Alcyone*
    Cantata for the Prix de Rome. Text by Eug. and Ed.
    Adenis.   Unpublished

1902-3 *Quatuor à cordes*
    Dedicated to G. Fauré. First perf. Soc. Nat., Paris,
    March 5, 1904, Heymann Quartet.   Durand

1903 *Alyssa*
Cantata for the Prix de Rome. Text by Marg.
Coiffier.   Unpublished

1903 *Manteau de Fleurs*
Voice and piano. Orchestrated. Words by Gravollet.
Hamelle

1903 *Shéhérazade*
Piano or orchestra and voice. Words by Tristan
Klingsor. First perf., Soc. Nat., Paris, May 17, 1904,
Jane Hatto, conducted by Cortot.
Ed. Astruc (1905), later Durand
a. *Asie* (dedicated to Jane Hatto).
b. *La Flûte enchantée* (dedicated to Renée de Saint-
Marceau).
c. *L'Indifférent* (dedicated to Mme Sigismond Bar-
dac).

1904-6 *Mélodies populaires grecques*
Voice and piano. Harmonized by Ravel. Words by
Calvocoressi.   Durand

1904   a. *Quel Galant!* (orchestrated by M. Rosenthal).
b. *Chanson des cueilleuses de lentisques* (orchestrated by Manuel Rosenthal).
c. *À vous, oiseau des plaines.*
d. *Chanson de pâtre épirote.*
e. *Mon mouchoir, hélas, est perdu.* First perf. École
Hautes Études Sociales, Paris, Feb. 20, 1904,
Louise Thomasset and Roelens.

1906   f. *Le Réveil de la mariée* (orchestrated by Ravel).
g. *Là-bas vers l'église* (orchestrated by Manuel
Rosenthal).
h. *Tour gai* (orchestrated by Ravel). First perf. Uni-
versité pop. du faubourg Saint-Antoine, Paris.
Marg. Babaían, début 1906.

1905 *Le Noël des jouets*
Voice and piano. After M. Ravel's poem. Dedicated

to Mme J. Cruppi. First perf. Salle Fourcroy, Paris, March 24, 1906, J. Bathori. Orchestrated. First perf. Soc. Nat., Paris, April 26, 1906, J. Bathori.

Mathot, later Eschig

1905 *Sonatine*

Piano. Dedicated to Ida and Cipa Godebski. First perf. March 10, 1906, Paule de Lestang, Lyon. Soc. Nat., Paris, March 31, 1906, G. Grovlez.   Durand

1905 *Miroirs*

Piano. First perf. Soc. Nat., Salle Érard, Paris, Jan. 6, 1906, R. Viñes.   Demets (1906), later Eschig

a. *Noctuelles* (dedicated to L.-P. Fargue).

b. *Oiseaux tristes* (dedicated to R. Viñes).

c. *Une Barque sur l'Océan* (dedicated to P. Sordes). Orchestrated by Ravel. First perf. Conc. Colonne, Feb. 3, 1907, conducted by G. Pierné. Unpublished, property of Eschig. The second version, first perf. Conc. Pasdeloup, Oct. 30, 1926, conducted by A. Wolff.

d. *Alborada del Gracioso* (dedicated to Calvocoressi). Orchestrated by Ravel. First perf. Conc. Pasdeloup, May 17, 1919. Published by Eschig.

e. *La Vallée des cloches* (dedicated to M. Delage).

1905-6 *Introduction et Allegro*

For harp with accompaniment of string quartet, flute, and clarinet. Dedicated to Alb. Blondel. First perf. Cercle Musical, Paris, Feb. 22, 1907, Micheline Kahn.

Durand

1906 *Les Grands Vents venus d'outre-mer*

Voice and piano. (H. de Régnier). Dedicated to Jacques Durand.   Ed. Durand, 1907

1906 *Les Histoires naturelles*

Voice and piano. After Jules Renard. Orchestrated by Manuel Rosenthal. First perf. Soc. Nat., Salle

Érard, Paris, Jan. 12, 1907, Jane Bathori.   Durand

   a. *Le Paon* (dedicated to J. Bathori).

   b. *Le Grillon* (dedicated to Mme Picard).

   c. *Le Cygne* (dedicated to Mme Edwards).

   d. *Le Martin-pêcheur* (dedicated to Emile Engel).

   e. *La Pintade* (dedicated to Roger Ducasse).

1907 *Sur l'Herbe*

   Voice and piano. After Verlaine. First perf. Zurich, Oct. 28, 1907, Hélène Luquiens. Cercle Musical Salle Gaveau, Paris, May 15, 1911, Gaétane Vicq-Challet, accompanied by Ravel.   Durand

1907 *Vocalise-Étude en forme d'Habanera*

   Voice and piano. First perf. Soc. Nat., Paris, Feb. 22, 1909.   Leduc(1909)

1907 *Rapsodie espagnole*

   Orchestra. First perf. Conc. Colonne, Paris, March 19, 1908, conducted by Colonne.   Durand

   a. *Prélude à la nuit.*

   b. *Malagueña.*

   c. *Habanera.*

   d. *Feria.*

1907 *L'Heure espagnole*

   Musical comedy in one act. After Franc-Nohain. Dedicated to Mme J. Cruppi. First perf. Opéra-Comique, Paris, May 19, 1911, conducted by Ruhlmann.   Durand

1908 *Ma Mère l'Oye*

   Five children's pieces for piano, four hands. After Perrault, Comtesse de'Aulnoy, and Mme Leprince de Beaumont. Dedicated to Mimi and Jean Godebski. First perf. Société Musicale Indépendante, Paris, April 20, 1910, J. Leleu and G. Durony.   Durand

   a. *Pavane pour la Belle au Bois dormant.*

   b. *Le Petit Poucet.*

   c. *Laideronnette, Impératrice des Pagodes.*

    d. *La Belle et la Bête.*

    e. *Le Jardin féerique.* Orchestrated by Ravel (with *Prélude* and *Danse du Rouet*, and interludes). First perf. Théâtre des Arts, Paris, Jan. 28, 1912, conducted by J. Rouché.

1908   *Gaspard de la Nuit*
Three poems for piano. After Aloysius Bertrand. First perf. Soc. Nat., Paris, Jan. 9, 1909, R. Viñes.

                                  Durand

    a. *Ondine* (dedicated to Harold Bauer).

    b. *Le Gibet* (dedicated to Jean Marnold).

    c. *Scarbo* (dedicated to Rudolf Ganz).

1909   *Les Nocturnes de Debussy*
Transcription for two pianos. First perf. S. M. I., Salle Gaveau, Paris, April 24, 1911, M. Ravel and L. Aubert.   Ed. Fromont, later Jobert

1909   *Menuet sur le nom d'Haydn*
Piano. First perf. Soc. Nat., Paris, March 1911.

         Ed. *Revue musicale*, Jan. 15, 1910, later Durand

1909   *Tripatos*
Piano and voice (Greek dance). First perf. Marg. Babaian.   Ed. *Revue musicale*, Dec., 1938

1910   *Chants populaires*
Voice and piano (folk songs). First perf. Salle Agriculteurs, Paris, Dec. 19, 1910, M. Olenin d'Alheim.
    Ed. *Jurgenson* (Moscow, 1911), later Durand, 1925

    a. *Chanson française.*

    b. *Chanson espagnole.*

    c. *Chanson italienne.*

    d. *Chanson hébraïque* (orchestrated).

    e. *Chanson écossaise* (unpublished).

    f. *Chanson flamande* (unpublished).

    g. *Chanson russe* (unpublished).

1910   *Le Prélude à l'Après-midi d'un faune, de Debussy*
Transcription for two pianos.

                      Ed. Fromont, later Jobert

1911   *Valses nobles et sentimentales*
    Piano. Dedicated to L. Aubert. First perf. S. M. I.,
    Paris, May 9, 1911, L. Aubert. Orchestrated: *Adé-*
    laïde, ou le langage des fleurs (ballet). First perf.
    Th. Châtelet, Paris, April 22, 1912, Troukhanova.
                                                   Durand

1909-12 *Daphnis et Chloë*
    Choreographic symphony in three movements. Dedi-
    cated to Sergei Diaghilev. Based on Fokine's adapta-
    tion of a Longus fable. First perf. Ballets Russes Th.
    Châtelet, Paris, June 8, 1912, Nijinsky, Karsavina;
    Bakst, Monteux. First orchestral suite. *Nocturne.*
    Interlude. Danse guerrière. Conc. Colonne, April 2,
    1911, conducted by G. Pierné.   Durand

1913   *Trois Poèmes de Mallarmé*
    Voice and piano, quartet, two flutes and two clari-
    nets. First perf. S. M. I., Paris, Jan. 14, 1914, Jane
    Bathori.   Durand
    a. *Soupir* (dedicated to Igor Stravinsky).
    b. *Placet futile* (dedicated to Florent Schmitt).
    c. *Surgi de la croupe et du bond* (dedicated to Erik
       Satie).

1913   *Prélude*
    Piano. Composed for the piano competition of the
    Paris Conservatory (1913). Dedicated to Jane Leleu.
                                                   Durand

1913   *A La Manière de . . .*
    Piano. First perf. S. M. I., Salle Pleyel, Paris, Dec. 10,
    1913, Casella.   Ed. Mathot, later Eschig
    a. *. . . Borodin.*
    b. *. . . Chabrier.*

1913   *Le Prélude du Fils des Étoiles, de Satie*
    Orchestrated.   Unpublished

1913   *La Khovanshchina, de Mussorgsky*
    Orchestrated. First perf. Th. Champs-Élysées, Paris,
    Diaghilev, June 5, 1913.

1914 *Deux Mélodies hébraïques*
Voice and piano. Dedicated to Mme Alvina-Alvi.
First perf. S. M. I., Salle Malakoff, Paris, June 3, 1914,
Mme Alvina-Alvi, Ravel. Orchestrated. First perf.
Conc. Pasdeloup, April 17, 1920, Mlle Grey. Durand
a. *Kaddisch.*
b. *L'Énigme éternelle.*

1914 *Trio*
Piano, violin, cello. Dedicated to André Gédalge.
First perf. S. M. I., Salle Gaveau, Paris, Jan. 28, 1915,
Casella, Enesco, Feuillard.   Durand

1914 *Carnaval, de Schumann*
Orchestrated.   Unpublished

1915 *Trois Chansons*
Unaccompanied mixed chorus. After Ravel's poem.
First perf. Vieux Colombier Copeau, Paris, Oct. 11,
1917, Chorale Bathori and Engel, conducted by
L. Aubert.   Durand
a. *Nicolette* (dedicated to Tristan Klingsor).
b. *Trois Beaux Oiseaux du Paradis* (dedicated to
Paul Painlevé).
c. *Ronde* (dedicated to Mme Paul Clemenceau).

1915 *L'Oeuvre de Mendelssohn*
Revised.   Durand

1917 *Le Tombeau de Couperin*
Suite for piano. First perf. S. M. I., Salle Gaveau,
Paris, April 11, 1919, Marg. Long. Orchestrated. First
perf. Conc. Pasdeloup, Paris, Feb. 28, 1920, conducted by Rhené Baton. Ballet. First perf. Ballets
Suédois, Nov. 8, 1920, conducted by Inghelbrecht.
                                                        Durand
a. *Prélude* (dedicated to the memory of J. Charlot).
b. *Fugue* (dedicated to the memory of J. Cruppi).
c. *Forlane* (dedicated to the memory of G. Deluc).

d. *Rigaudon* (dedicated to the memory of Pierre and Pascal Gaudin).

e. *Menuet* (dedicated to the memory of J. Dreyfus).

f. *Toccata* (dedicated to Joseph de Marliave). Orchestrated with the exception of *Fugue* and *Toccata.*

1918   *Menuet pompeux, d'E. Chabrier*

Orchestration. First perf. Conc. Pasdeloup, March, 1936, conducted by A. Wolff.   Enoch

1919   *Frontispiece*

Piano, four hands. Written for Canudo's *Poème du Vardar S.P. 503.*   Ed. *Feuillets d'Art,* No. 2

1919–20 *La Valse*

Choreographic poem for orchestra. First perf. Conc. Lamoureux, Paris, Dec. 12, 1920, conducted by Chevillard. Transcribed for two pianos. Dedicated to Misia Sert. First perf. Opéra, Paris, Nov. 20, 1928, Ida Rubinstein, Fokine, and Straram.   Durand

1920-2 *Sonate*

Sonata in four movements for violin and cello. First perf. S.M.I., Salle Pleyel, Paris, April 6, 1922, H. Jourdan-Morhange and M. Maréchal. First movement: *Duo à la memoire de Claude Debussy.*

                            Durand

1920   *Sarabande, de Debussy*

Orchestration. First perf. Conc. Lamoureux, Salle Gaveau, Paris, March 18, 1923.

1922   *Berceuse sur le nom de G. Fauré*

Violin and piano. Dedicated to Claude Roland-Manuel. Written for the supplement of one of the numbers of the *Revue musicale* devoted to Fauré. First perf. *Revue musicale,* H. Jourdan-Morhange.

      Ed. *Revue musicale,* Oct. 1, 1922, later Durand

1922   *Les Tableaux d'une Exposition, de Mussorgsky*

Orchestration. First perf. Conc. Koussevitzky, Opéra,

Paris, Oct. 19, 1922, conducted by Koussevitzky.
Ed. russe de Musique

1923 *Danse (Tarentelle styrienne), de Debussy*
Orchestration. First perf. Conc. Lamoureux, Salle
Gaveau, Paris, March 18, 1923, conducted by Paray.
Ballet. First perf. Opéra-Comique, Jan., 1946, Louis
Lebercher. Jobert

1923 *Nocturne, Étude et Valse, de Chopin*
Orchestration. Unpublished

1924 *Ronsard à son âme*
Voice and piano. After Ronsard's poem. Supplement of one of the numbers of the *Revue musicale:
Le Tombeau de Ronsard*. Dedicated to Marcelle
Gerard. First perf. April 26, 1924. Orchestrated. First
perf. Festival Ravel, Feb., 1935, conducted by Coppola. Ed. *Revue musicale*, May, 1924, later Durand

1924 *Tzigane*
Rhapsody for violin and piano. The accompaniment
has been orchestrated. First perf. London, Jelly
d'Aranyi and Gil Marchex, April 26, 1924. S.M.I.,
Salle Gaveau, Paris, Oct. 15, 1924, S. Dushkin and
B. Webster. Dedicated to Jelly d'Aranyi.
Durand

1920-5 *L'Enfant et les sortilèges*
Lyrical fantasy in two parts. Text by Colette. First
perf. Th. de Monte Carlo, March 21, 1925; Opéra-
Comique, Feb. 1, 1926; Opéra May 17, 1939.
Durand

1925-6 *Chansons madécasses*
Voice, flute, cello, piano. Words by Evariste Parny.
Dedicated to Mme Elisabeth Coolidge. First perf. of
the second piece Hôtel Majestic, Paris, 1925. The
complete work Salle Érard, Paris, June 13, 1926, Jane
Bathori. Durand
a. *Nahandove.*

b. *Aoua!*

c. *Il est doux.*

1927 *Rêves*

Voice and piano. Words by L.-P. Fargue. Dedicated to L.-P. Fargue. First perf. Vieux Colombier, 1928, Bathori and Ravel.

Ed. *Feuilles libres*, Nos. 45-46, June, 1927, later Durand

1923-7 *Sonate*

In three movements. Violin and piano. Dedicated to H. Jourdan-Morhange. First perf. Salle Érard, Paris, May 30, 1927, Enesco and Ravel. Durand

1927 *L'Éventail de Jeanne*

Fanfare preceding the ballet of the same name (written by ten composers). First perf. at Mme René Dubost, June 16, 1927; Opéra March 4, 1929.

Heugel

1928 *Boléro*

For orchestra. First perf. Ballets Rubinstein, Opéra, Paris, Nov. 22, 1928, conducted by Straram. Conc. Lamoureux, Jan. 11, 1930. Durand

1931 *Concerto*

For the left hand alone. Piano and orchestra. First perf. Vienna Nov. 27, 1931, Paul Wittgenstein. Paris, Jan. 17, 1933, conducted by Désormières. Durand

1931 *Concerto in G*

In three movements. Piano. First perf. Salle Pleyel, Paris, Jan. 14, 1932, Marg. Long, Ravel. Durand

1932 *Don Quichotte à Dulcinée*

Voice and piano. Words by Paul Morand. First perf. Conc. Colonne, Dec. 1, 1934, Singher. Orchestrated.

Durand

a. *Chanson romantique* (dedicated to R. Casinou).

b. *Chanson Épique* (dedicated to M. Singher).

c. *Chanson à boire* (dedicated to R. Bourdin).

B. LIST OF LONG-PLAYING (33 1/3) RECORDINGS OF MUSIC BY MAURICE RAVEL

Alborada del Gracioso
Ansermet, Orch. de la Suisse
Romande   10″ London LS-503
Boléro
Ferrero, Sym.   12″ Tempo 2042
Kostelanetz, Robin Hood
Dell Orch.   10″ Columbia ML-2009
Koussevitzky, Boston Sym.
& *Ma Mère l'Oye*   12″ Victor LM-1012
André, Brussels Radio Sym.   10″ Capitol L-8096
List, Berlin Sym.   12″ Royale 1313
Munch, Paris Conservatoire
Orch. & *La Valse*   12″ London LL-22
Munch, Paris Conservatoire
Orch.   12″ London LL-466
Chansons madécasses
Singher, Ulanowsky &
Chants, Histoires   12″ Concert Hall CHS-1124
Tourel, Reeves, Wummer,
Vargo   10″ Columbia ML-2184
Chants populaires
Singher, Ulanowsky &
Chansons, Histoires   12″ Concert Hall CHS-1124
Cinq Mélodies populaires grecques
Kolassi   10″ London LS-568
Concerto for the Left Hand Alone
Blancard, Ansermet, Orch.
de la Suisse Romande &
Concerto   12″ London LL-76
Casadesus, Ormandy, Phil.
Orch.   12″ Columbia ML-4075

Concerto in G
  Haas, Schmidt-Isserstedt,
    NWDR Sym.   12" Decca DL-9515
  Henriot, Munch, Paris
    Conservatoire Orch.   12" London LL-76
Daphnis et Chloë, Suite No. 1
  Ormandy, Philadelphia
    Orch. and *Suite 2*   12" Columbia ML-4316
Daphnis et Chloë, Suite No. 2
  André, INR Sym. & *La Valse* 10" Capitol L-8145
  Ormandy, Philadelphia
    . Orch. & *Suite 1*   12" Columbia ML-4316
  Rodzinski, Cleveland Orch.
    & *Rapsodie*   12" Columbia ML-4039
  Toscanini, NBC Sym.   12" Victor LM-1043
L'Enfant et les sortilèges
  Bour, soloists, orch.   12" Columbia ML-4153
Gaspard de la Nuit
  Glazer   12" Polymusic 1005
  Pennario & *Miroirs*   12" Capitol P-8152
  Weiser, piano & *Tombeau* 12" REB-8
L'Heure espagnole
  Soloists, Chorus, Orch.   12" Vox 7880
Histoires naturelles
  Bernac, Poulenc   12" Columbia ML-4333
  Singher, Ulanowsky &
    Chants, Chansons   12" Concert Hall CHS-1124
  Souzay, Bonneau   10" London LS-536
Introduction et Allegro
  Berghout, van Beinum,
    Amsterdam Ch. Mus. Soc. 10" London LS-621
  La Scala Milan Quartet,
    soloists & *Sonatine*   10" Mercury MG-15006
  Stockton, Gleghorn, Lurie,
    Hollywood Quartet   10" Capitol L-8154
  Vito (Harp), sextet   12" Stradivari 1007

Ma Mère l'Oye
　Ansermet, Orch. de la
　　Suisse Romande　　　　　12″ London LL-388
　Erede, Italian Radio Sym.　12″ Tempo TT-2034
　Gorini, Lorenzi　　　　　　12″ Colosseum 1026
　Kostelanetz　　　　　　　　12″ Columbia ML-4355
　Koussevitsky, Boston Sym. &
　　Boléro　　　　　　　　　12″ Victor LM-1012
　Previtali, London Sym.　　12″ Victor LBC-1009
Miroirs
　Pennario & *Gaspard*　　　12″ Capitol P-8152
Piano Music, Complete
　Casadesus　　　　　　　3-12″ Columbia ML-4518, 19,
　　　　　　　　　　　　　　　　　20

Quartet
　Budapest Quartet　　　　　12″ Columbia ML-4091
　Fine Arts Quartet　　　　　12″ Mercury 10105
　Julliard Quartet　　　　　10″ Columbia ML-2202
　Paganini Quartet　　　　　10″ Victor LM-146
　Pascal Quartet & *Sonate*　12″ Concert Hall CHS-1123
　Stuyvesant Quartet　　　　12″ Philharmonia 104
Rapsodie espagnole
　André, Belgian National
　　Radio Orch.　　　　　　12″ Capitol P-8082
　Ansermet, Orch. de la
　　Suisse Romande　　　　　12″ London LL-530
　Munch, Boston Sym. &
　　La Valse　　　　　　　12″ Victor LM-1700
　Ormandy, Philadelphia
　　Orch.　　　　　　　　　12″ Columbia ML-4306
　Rodzinski, Cleveland Orch.
　　& *Daphnis*　　　　　　12″ Columbia ML-4039
Shéhérazade (songs for voice and orch.)
　Tourel, Bernstein, Columbia
　　Sym.　　　　　　　　　12″ Columbia ML-4289

Sonata for Violin & Cello
  Pascal Quartet members &
    Quartet   12" Concert Hall CHS-1123
  Urban, Hubert   12" Classic 1005
Sonata for Violin & Piano
  Eidus, Smith & *Trio*   12" Stradivari 1005
  B. & V. Urban   12" Classic 1002
Sonatine
  Lerous & *Introduction*   10" Mercury MG-15006
Songs
  Singher, Abravanel, and
    Orch.   12" Columbia ML-4152
Tombeau de Couperin, Le
  Long   12" London LL-452
  Mitropoulos, Minnesota
    Orch.   10" Columbia ML-2032
  Valenzi, piano   10" Remington 149-17
  Weiser, piano & *Gaspard*   12" REB-8
Trio in A Minor
  Albeneri Trio   12" Mercury MG-10089
  Alma Trio   10" Allegro AL-77
  Rubinstein, Heifetz,
    Piatigorsky   12" Victor LM-1119
  Smith, Eidus, Ricci & *Sonata*   12" Stradivari 1005
Trois Chants hébraïques
  Bernac, Poulenc &
    Histoires   12" Columbia ML-4333
Tzigane
  Ricci (violin), Lamoureux
    Orch.   12" Vox PL-6240
Valse, La
  André, INR Sym. &
    Daphnis   10" Capitol L-8145
  Ansermet, Paris Conserva-
    toire Orch. & *Boléro*   12" London LL-22

Munch, Boston Sym. &
  Rapsodie   12″ Victor LM-1700
Reiner, Pittsburgh Sym.
  Orch.   12″ Columbia ML-4021
Valses nobles et sentimentales
  André, INR Sym.   12″ Capitol P-8132
  Schwalb   10″ Academy 307

Bibliography

~~~~~~

ARTICLES

Alvar-Harding, Charles
"Maurice Ravel Away from His Music," *Musical Courier*, May 20, 1933.

Aubry, George Jean
"*Histoires naturelles*," *Le Censeur*, July, 1907.
"*Profils perdus' (Maurice Ravel)*," *Le Censeur*, July 20, 1907.
"A Visit to Ravel," *Christian Science Monitor*, September 17, 1927.

Auric, Georges
"*L'Enfant et les sortilèges*," *Nouvelles Littéraires*, April, 1925.
"Maurice Ravel," *Paris-Soir*, December 29, 1937.

Baruzi, J.
"*Récital J. Duhem*," *Le Ménestrel*, March 2, 1923.

Bloch, Jean Richard
"*Maurice Ravel ou les monstres domptés*," *Revue musicale*, Paris, 1939.

Bréville, P. de
"*Shéhérazade*," *Mercure de France*, July, 1899.

Brian, Harengal
"Maurice Ravel," *Musical Opinion*, London, November, 1939.

Brillant, M.
  "*L'Enfant et les sortilèges*," *Le Correspondant*, February, 1926.
  Bulletin of the Basque Delegation in the U.S.A., August, 1944.
Brussel, Robert
  "*Daphnis et Chloë*," *Le Figaro*, July 9, 1912.
  "*La mort de Maurice Ravel*," *Le Figaro*, December 29, 1937.
Burlingame Hill, E.
  Mercure Musical, November 15, 1906.
  "Maurice Ravel," *Mercure Musical*, November 15, 1906.
Calvocoressi, M.-D.
  "*Le Quatuor de M. Ravel*," *Revue musicale*, April 15, 1904.
  "*Les Histoires naturelles et l'imitation debussyste*," *Grande Revue*, May 10, 1907.
  "M. Maurice Ravel," *Bulletin de S.I.M.*, April, 1909.
  "Maurice Ravel," *I.M.G. Zeitschrift*, Leipzig, 1909.
  "Maurice Ravel," *Musical Times*, London, 1913.
  "When Ravel Composed to Order," *Music and Letters*, Sussex, 1941.
  "Ravel's Letters to Calvocoressi," *Musical Quarterly*, New York, 1941.
Carraud, Gaston
  "*Les Histoires naturelles*," *La Liberté*, January 15, 1907.
  "*Une Barque sur l'Océan*," *La Liberté*, February 5, 1907.
  "*La Rapsodie espagnole*," *La Liberté*, March 17, 1908.
  "*Gaspard de la Nuit*," *La Liberté*, January 12, 1909.
  "*L'Heure espagnole*," *La Liberté*, May 21, 1911.
  "*Daphnis et Chloë*," *La Liberté*, June 11, 1912.
Casella, A.
  "Maurice Ravel," *Musica d'Oggi*, Milan, March, 1938.
Chalupt, René
  "*Ma Mère l'Oye*," *La Phalange*, May, 1911.
  "*L'Heure espagnole*," *La Phalange*, June, 1911.
  "*Adélaïde*," *La Phalange*, June, 1912.
  "*Daphnis et Chloë*," *La Phalange*, July, 1912.

BIBLIOGRAPHY 299

"*Shéhérazade*," *La Phalange*, February, 1913.

Chantavoine, Jean
"*L'Heure espagnole*," *Revue hebdomadaire*, June 24, 1911.
"*Daphnis et Chloë*," *Excelsior*, June 9, 1912.
"*La Saison de Paris*," *Revue hebdomadaire*, July 13, 1912.

Coeuroy, A.
"*L'Enfant et les sortilèges*," *Paris-Midi*, February 2, 1926.
"*La Coix du compositeur Maurice Ravel*," *Le Temps*, April 8, 1920. Not signed.
"*Un Compositeur français refuse d'être décoré!*" *Gazette de Hollande*, April 13, 1920. Not signed.
"*La Confession de Ravel*," *Presse de Bayonne*, July 9, 1933.

Covielle
"*M. Ravel et le Prix de Rome*," *Le Matin*, May 22, 1905.

Cushing, Charles C.
"Maurice Ravel," *Modern Music*, New York, 1938.

Dezarnaux, R.
"*L'Enfant et les sortilèges*," *La Liberté*, February 3, 1926.

Donostia, P.
"*Hommage à Maurice Ravel*," *Gure Herria*, Ustaritz, October-December, 1937.

Dotaz, E.
"*Maurice Ravel tel que je l'ai connu*," *Courier thermal*, Bagnères de Bigorn, August, 1938.

Downes, Olin
New York *Times*, January 16, 1928.

Dumesnil, Maurice
"Ravel," *Passe-Temps*, Montreal, September, 1945.

Dumesnil, R.
"Maurice Ravel," *Mercure de France*, February 1, 1938.

Fargue, Léon-Paul
"Maurice Ravel," *Plaisir de France*, Paris, August, 1936.

Gautier-Villars, Henry
"*Pierre Lalo contre Ravel, Louis Laloy pro Ravel*," *Mercure de France*, April 1, 1907.
"*Daphnis et Chloë*," *Comoedia illustré*, June 15, 1912.

Ghéon, H.
"*L'Heure espagnole*," N.R.F., July 1, 1911.
George, A.
"*L'Enfant et les sortilèges*," *Nouvelles Littéraires*, February,
1926.
Goddard, Scott
"French composers," *Musical Times*, Vol. 66, London, 1925.
Hammond, Richard
"Maurice Ravel, 1927," *Modern Music*, Vol. 5, New York,
1928.
Honegger, Arthur
"*L'Enfant et les sortilèges*," *Musique et Théâtre*, April 15,
1925.
Inghelbrecht, D.-E.
"*Les Arts et la vie (Ravel)*," *Revue de France*, March 1,
1938.
Joaquin, Nin
"*De como nacio el Boléro de Ravel*," *Conservatorio*, La
Habana, April-June, 1948.
Lalo, Pierre
"M. Ravel," *Le Temps*, June 13, 1899.
"*Le Quatuor*," *Le Temps*, April 19, 1904.
"*Le Concours de Rome*," *Le Temps*, July 11, 1915.
"*Les Miroirs*," *Le Temps*, January 10, 1906.
"*M. Ravel et le Debussysme*," *Le Temps*, March 19, 1907.
"*Une Lettre de M. Ravel*," *Le Temps*, April 9, 1907.
"*La Rapsodie espagnole*," *Le Temps*, March 17, 24, 1908.
"*L'Heure espagnole*," *Le Temps*, May 28, 1911.
"*Daphnis et Chloë*," *Le Temps*, June 11, 1912.
"*Le Tombeau de Couperin*," *Le Temps*, November 16, 1922.
Laloy, Louis
"*Au Conservatoire*," *Mercure musical*, June 1, 1905.
"Maurice Ravel," *Mercure musical*, February, March, 1907.
"*Les Partis musicaux*," *Grande Revue*, December 25, 1907.
"*La Rapsodie*," *Grande Revue*, March 25, 1908.

"*Gaspard de la Nuit*," *Grande Revue*, January 25, 1910.
Landormy, Paul
"Maurice Ravel," *Le Ménestrel, Année, 100*, Paris, 1938.
Also in *Musical Quarterly*, Vol. 25, New York, 1939.
Lindenlaub, T.
"*La Valse*," *Le Temps*, December 28, 1920.
Malherbe, H.
"*L'Enfant et les sortilèges*," *Le Temps*, February 3, 1926.
Mantelli, A.
"Maurice Ravel," *La Rassegna Musicale*, Turin, No. 2, 1938.
Marnold, Jean
"*Le Quatuor de M. Ravel*," *Mercure de France*, April, 1904.
"*Shéhérazade*," *Mercure de France*, July, 1904.
"*Le Scandale du prix de Rome*," *Mercure de France*, June 1,
1905.
"*Miroirs*," *Mercure musical*, February 1, 1906. *Mercure de
France*, March 1, 1906.
"*L'Affaire Ravel*," *Revue musicale de Lyon*, May 1, 1907.
Mercure de France, January 16, 1908.
"*Daphnis et Chloë*," *Mercure de France*, August 16, 1917.
"*L'Enfant et les sortilèges*," *Mercure de France*, March 16,
1926.
Mason, Daniel Gregory
"Maurice Ravel and Mother Goose," *New Music Review*,
Vol. 12, New York, 1913.
Mauclair, Camille
"*À Propos des Ballets russes*," *Courier musical*, June 15,
1912.
Messager, André
"*L'Enfant et les sortilèges*," *Le Figaro*, February, 1926.
Milhaud, Darius
"Maurice Ravel," *Ce Soir*, December 29, 1937.
Excelsior, April 10, 1920.
Morris, Reginald Owen
"Maurice Ravel," *Music and Letters*, London, 1921.

"On Peut toujours refuser d'accepter une décoration," Excelsior, April 10, 1920. Not signed.

Photiades, Constantine
  "Maurice Ravel," *Revue de Paris, année 45*, Vol. 2, Paris, 1938.

Prunières, H.
  "L'Enfant et les sortilèges," Revue musicale, April 1, 1926.

Revue musicale, numéro special. *Maurice Ravel*. 1925. Not signed.

Revue musicale, numéro special. *Hommage à Maurice Ravel*. 1938. Not signed.

Rivière, Jacques
  "La Rapsodie espagnole," N.R.F., February, 1910.

"Le Roi des Belges décore Maurice Ravel," Excelsior, March 6, 1926. Not signed.

Roland-Manuel
  "Adélaïde," Revue indépendante, May 7, 1912.
  "Daphnis et Chloë," Revue indépendante, June 18, 1912.
  "Maurice Ravel," *L'Echo musical*, February, 1913.
  "La Valse," L'Eclair, December, 1926.
  "L'Enfant et les sortilèges," Le Ménestrel, February 5, 1906.
  "Maurice Ravel et la jeune École française," Nouvelles Littéraires, June, 1927.
  "Le génie de Maurice Ravel," Temps présents, January 7, 1938.
  "Réflexions sur Ravel," Grande Revue, April, 1938.

Sabaneev, Leonid
  "Maurice Ravel," *Musical Opinion*, London, August, 1938.

Samazeuilh, Gustave
  "Les Ballets russes," Courier musical, June 15, 1912.
  "Quelques souvenirs sur Maurice Ravel," Le Temps, December 29, 1937.

Sauguet, Henri
  "Mes Rencontres avec Maurice Ravel," Revue musicale, Paris, January-February, 1939.

La Tribune de Genève (Suisse), January 8, 1938. Not signed.

Vallas, Léon
"Le Nouveau Style pianistique," Revue musicale de Lyon, January 6, 1907.
"Encore l'affaire Ravel," Revue musicale de Lyon, April 14, 1907.
Vuillemin, Louis
"L'Heure espagnole," Comoedia, May 20, 1911.
"Daphnis et Chloë," Comoedia, June 10, 1912.
Vuillermoz, Émile
"L'Heure espagnole," S.I.M., February 15, 1912.
"Daphnis et Chloë," S.I.M., June 15, 1912.
"Ma Mère l'Oye," S.I.M., February 15, 1912.
"Portrait de Maurice Ravel," Cahiers d'aujourd'hui, No. 10, 1922.
"L'Enfant et les sortilèges," Excelsior, February 3, 1926.
"Maurice Ravel est mort," Excelsior, December 29, 1937.
"Défendons Ravel!" Candide, January 13, 1938.
"Une Grande Figure de la musique française," L'Illustration, January 8, 1938.

BOOKS

Alexandre, Tansman
Igor Stravinsky. The Man and His Music. Putnam's, New York, 1949.
Aubry, George Jean
La Musique française d'aujourd'hui. Perrin et C-ie, Paris, 1916.
Brook, Donald
Five Great French Composers—Berlioz, César Franck, Saint-Saëns, Debussy, Ravel; Their Lives and Works. Rockliff, London, 1946.
Bruyr, José
Maurice Ravel ou Le Lyrisme et les Sortilèges. Ed. Le Bon Plaisir, Librairie Plon, Paris, 1950.

Calvocoressi, M.-D.
   Music and Ballet Recollections of M.-D. Calvocoressi. Faber
   and Faber, Ltd., London, 1933-34.
Cortot, Alfred
   La Musique française de piano. Les Editions Rieder, Paris,
   1931.
Gavoty, Bernard
   Les Français sont-ils musiciens? Ed. du Conquistador, Paris,
   1950.
Goss, Madeleine
   Boléro. Henry Holt and Company, New York, 1940.
Gray, Cecil
   A Survey of Temporary Music. Oxford University, 1924.
Haskell, Arnold L.
   Balletomania. Simon and Schuster, New York, 1934.
   Diaghilev. (In collaboration with Walter Nouvel.) Simon
   and Schuster, New York, 1935.
Jourdan-Morhange, Hélène
   Ravel et nous. Ed. du Milieu du Monde, Genève, 1945.
Karsavina, Tamara
   Theatre Street. William Heineman, Ltd., London, 1930.
Landowski, W.-L.
   Maurice Ravel, sa vie—son oeuvre. Les Ed. Ouvrières, Paris,
   1950.
Lifar, Serge
   Serge Diaghilev, His Life, His Work, His Legend. Putnam's,
   New York, 1940.
Machabey, Armand
   Maurice Ravel. Collection Triptyque, Paris, 1947.
Maurice Ravel par quelques-uns de se familiers (Colette,
   Maurice Delage, Léon-Paul Fargue, Hélène Jourdan-Mor-
   hange, Tristan Klingsor, Roland-Manuel, Dominique Sordet,
   Émile Vuillermoz, Jacques de Zogheb). Ed. du Tambourin-
   aire, Paris, 1939.
Myers, Rollo H.
   Erik Satie. Dennis Dobson, Ltd., London, 1948.

Nijinsky, Romola
  Nijinsky. Simon and Schuster, New York, 1934.
Roland-Manuel
  Maurice Ravel et son oeuvre. Durand et fils, Paris, 1914.
  Maurice Ravel et son oeuvre dramatique. Libraire de France,
    Paris, 1928.
  Ravel. Gallimard, Paris, 1948.
  À la gloire de Ravel. Ed. de la Nouvelle Revue Critique,
    Paris, 1938.
Rosenfeld, Paul
  Musical Portraits. Harcourt, Brace and Howe, New York,
    1920.
  Musical Chronicle (1917-1923). Harcourt, Brace and Howe,
    New York, 1923.
Saleski, Gdal
  Famous Musicians of Jewish Origin. Bloch Publishing Com-
    pany, New York, 1949.
Sert, Misia
  Misia. Gallimard, Paris, 1952.
Stravinsky, Igor
  Chronique de ma vie. Denoel, Paris, 1935. Victor Gollancz,
    Ltd., London, 1936.
Templier, P. D.
  Erik Satie. Ed. Rieder, Paris, 1932.
Vuillermoz, Émile
  Histoire de la musique. Libraire Arthême Fayard, Paris,
    1949.
Yankelevich, Vladimir
  Maurice Ravel. Ed. Rieder, Paris, 1939.

Index